# The Hemmings Motor News Book of

# POSTWAR FORDS

ISBN 0-917808-55-X

Library of Congress Card Number: 00-106569

One of a series of Hemmings Motor News Collector-Car Books. Other books in the series include:
The Hemmings Motor News Book of Cadillacs; The Hemmings Motor News Book of Corvettes; The Hemmings Motor News Book of Chrysler Performance Cars; The Hemmings Motor News Book of Mustangs; The Hemmings Motor News Book of Studebakers.

**Hemmings Motor News**
Collector Car Publications and Marketplaces
1-800-CAR-HERE (227-4373)
www.hemmings.com

The Hemmings Motor News Book of

# POSTWAR FORDS

*Editor-In-Chief*
Terry Ehrich

*Editor*
Richard A. Lentinello

*Designer*
Nancy Bianco

*Cover photo by Robert Gross*

This book compiles driveReports which have appeared in Hemmings Motor News's Special Interest Autos magazine (SIA) over the past 30 years. The editors at Hemmings Motor News express their gratitude to the following writers, photographers, and artists who made this book possible through their many fine contributions to Special Interest Autos magazine:

Arch Brown
Tim Howley
Michael Lamm
Bud Juneau

Vince Manocchi
John Matras
Russ von Sauers

We are also grateful to Dave Brownell, Michael Lamm, and Rich Taylor, the editors under whose guidance these driveReports were written and published. We thank Tom Case, Ford Motor Company, Image International, Lincoln-Mercury Division, Motor Trend, National Automotive History Collection, Petersen Publishing Co., and George W. Walker, who have graciously contributed photographs to Special Interest Autos magazine and this book.

# CONTENTS

---

***Special Interest Autos (SIA)*** magazine's back issues are referred to in this book by issue number. If in stock, copies may be purchased directly from Hemmings Motor News at 800-227-4373 or at www.hemmings.com.

# POPULAR POSTWAR WOODIE

# 1947 FORD V-8 SUPER DELUXE

**B**Y the time the New Year's Eve fireworks heralded the arrival of Anno Domini 1947, life in the United States had commenced to settle down to a fairly normal, peacetime pattern. Wartime shortages of sugar, coffee, meat – even shoes – were a thing of the past, and there were no more ration books. Gasoline was plentiful. So were tires, and the 35-mile-an-hour speed limit, which had been imposed "for the duration," was history.

There was still, however, a desperate need for new automobiles, to replace the nation's well-worn fleet of prewar cars. Every dealer in the country had a long waiting list, and there was a thriving "gray market," catering to those who were either unable or unwilling to wait

**by Arch Brown**
**photos by Bud Juneau**

their turn in line. There was even a shortage of sheet steel and certain other materials required for the manufacture of new cars, with the result that production at both General Motors and Chrysler was still well below the levels of 1940-41.

In allocating critical raw materials, the government evidently gave special consideration to Ford, which was struggling with a drastic reorganization at the time, as well as to independents

Studebaker, Nash and Hudson, for during 1947 all of those companies were able to equal and even surpass their prewar output. Meanwhile, newcomer Kaiser-Frazer received such favorable treatment (thanks perhaps to Henry J. Kaiser's political connections) that it was able to out-produce all of the older independents – and Mercury, Chrysler and DeSoto as well. Not until 1949 would GM and Chrysler be able to resume their prewar pace.

Just as the 1946 models had been basically warmed-over 1941-42 cars, so the 1947s were little changed from '46. At Ford, in fact, there was no change at all, at first – except that the cars were titled (and advertised) as 1947 models (see sidebar, page 66). Not until late

# Driving Impressions

Jerry Bishop, of Los Altos Hills, California, a few miles south of San Francisco, had been looking for a woodie to restore when, in December 1987, he ran across a classified ad in *The San Francisco Chronicle,* offering for sale a 1947 Ford station wagon. The car was in nearby San Jose, so Jerry went to take a look. It had been stored out of doors at Lake Tahoe, and was badly weathered. Even so, it was exactly what he wanted, but the price seemed unreasonably high, so he returned home empty-handed.

A few weeks later Jerry found a pair of '48s – basket cases both, though the price was right. Jerry bought the two and hauled them home. As luck would have it, the very next day an ad appeared for the San Jose car – the same one he had hoped to buy in the first place. This time, the owner was agreeable to negotiating a reasonable price, so Jerry Bishop found himself with three Ford station wagons. He cannibalized a few parts from the two '48s: the two rear seats, the gas tank and the rain gutters, for instance; then sold the pair and concentrated on restoring the car you see here.

Fortunately, the wagon lacked only a few parts. Dashboard instruments were missing, however. Jerry was able to purchase a speedometer from another collector, while the other gauges, along with the "Super Deluxe" fender logo and the fog lamps, were located through ads in *Hemmings Motor News.*

The spare wheel, Jerry found, was the wrong size: 15 inches instead of 16. At this point Lady Luck rode to the rescue: Another hobbyist turned up with a Mercury wagon, which was built with 15-inch wheels but had a 16-inch spare. A trade was made, to the advantage of both parties. At last report, Jerry was still looking for an original type bumper jack.

After removing the body, Bishop sent the chassis to Dave Kibler, of Mountain View, California. Kibler found the engine to be in good condition, but he substituted a good used transmission, overhauled the brakes, and restored the chassis to pristine condition. Meanwhile, to replace all the wood, inside and out, he ordered a new kit from the Cincinnati Wood Works.

Assembly of the body was Jerry Bishop's personal project. There's more work involved in this than one might think, for each piece was shipped slightly oversize and had to be cut to fit. Top and upholstery, both from LeBaron Bonney, also had to be fitted. Between the time the wood was delivered to the Bishop home, during August 1988, and the completion of the job 34 months later, Jerry was kept busy trimming, routing, stretching, fitting, sanding – and finally, varnishing the completely reconstructed body.

The station wagon is intended as a driver, not a "show" car, and Bishop has already taken it on a tour to Watsonville, where he attended an antique fly-in. Still, it was at the 1992 Hillsborough Concours d'Elegance that we first saw the car, and it has also been shown at Palo Alto and the San Lorenzo Valley concours, taking second and first place, respectively, in those shows. (The San Lorenzo trophy, Jerry hastens to point out, was hardly fair, since his car was the only woodie in the competition.)

Bud Juneau selected for his photo location the historic barn that had originally belonged to Senator Leland Stanford, the man who endowed Stanford University in memory of his son, and it was on the Stanford campus that our driving impressions were recorded. The station wagon outweighs the Fordor sedan by 250 pounds, yet the V-8 engine is so lively and responsive that this is really a rather fast automobile.

Jerry Bishop reports that it cruises smoothly and easily at 60 miles an hour. (Even so, he would like to add a Columbia axle, if he can find one.)

It's a very easy car to drive. The clutch chatters just a little bit; presumably it wouldn't be a proper Ford of this vintage if it didn't. Shifts are smooth and easy, and the column linkage is somewhat less sloppy than some that we've experienced. Steering, for a non-powered unit, is quite light; even parking is no major chore.

In terms of its ride the Ford is no match for Chevrolet and Plymouth, with their independent front suspension. But the softer springs of the postwar models made a positive difference, and we found this car to be more comfortable than we had anticipated. The brakes are very good, though of course we had no opportunity to determine whether they fade under hard use.

It's a tribute to Jerry Bishop's craftsmanship that there are virtually no squeaks and rattles in the wooden body. No doubt they will develop in time, but Jerry obviously did an outstanding job of putting the kit together. Fit and finish are undoubtedly better than new.

drive report

*Top:* Wagon has a tall, square-rigged but attractively utilitarian appearance. *Above:* Hood ornament carries engine size designation.

# 1947 FORD V-8

April would even a mild facelift take place.

To recap the early postwar story as it affected Ford: War was still raging in the Pacific in May of 1945, when the directive came down from the War Production Board in Washington, releasing a limited amount of material for the manufacture of passenger cars for the civilian market.

The Ford Motor Company wasted no time. On July 3, 1945, two months before Japan's formal surrender, the first 1946 Ford rolled off the assembly line. It was a Super Deluxe Tudor sedan, traditionally the most popular model in the line. This pilot vehicle was finished in Light Moonstone Gray, probably the most requested color on Ford's palette in those days.

Production got under way on a very limited scale. By the end of August 1945, Ford had just 1,740 cars in inventory – considerably less than one day's output, by 1941 standards. And even those few cars couldn't be sold until the government's Office of Price Administration (OPA) was able to establish ceiling prices, as part of the government's effort to curb inflation at a time when demand far outstripped the supply of new cars. Meanwhile, on August 29 that first new car had been personally presented to President Harry S. Truman by Henry Ford II.

By October 26 new cars had been built in sufficient numbers that a nationwide "V-8" Day was scheduled, and

### 1947 Ford
### Table of Prices, Weights* and Production

|  | Price 6 cyl/V-8 | Weight 6 cyl/V-8 | Production (6 + V-8) |
|---|---|---|---|
| **Deluxe Series** | | | |
| Coupe, 3-passenger | $1,154/$1,230 | 3,007/3,040 | 10,872 |
| Sedan, 2-door | $1,212/$1,288 | 3,157/3,190 | 44,523 |
| Sedan, 4-door | $1,270/$1,346 | 3,187/3,220 | 44,563 |
| Chassis | ---------- | ---------- | 23 |
| **Super Deluxe Series** | | | |
| Coupe, 3-passenger | $1,251/$1,330 | 3,007/3,040 | 10,872 |
| Sedan, 2-door | $1,309/$1,382 | 3,157/3,190 | 132,126 |
| Sedan, 4-door | $1,372/$1,440 | 3,207/3,240 | 116,744 |
| Sedan Coupe | $1,330/$1,409 | 3,107/3,140 | 80,830 |
| Convertible Coupe | -----/$1,740 | -----/3,240 | 22,159 |
| Sportsman Convertible | -----/$2,282 | -----/3,340 | 2,774 |
| Station Wagon | $1,893/$1,972 | 3,457/3,490 | 16,104 |
| Chassis | ---------- | ---------- | 23 |

\* Weights shown are for first series (1946 style) cars. Second series (1947 style) units were about 26 pounds heavier.
(Shipping weights shown; all prices f.o.b. factory)

new Fords were displayed in show-rooms across the nation. Apart from a simpler, more attractive grille, they looked almost the same as the 1942 models. (Not that anybody cared, at that point, *how* they looked.) But under the skin there were some significant mechanical changes.

First of all, there was the engine. The 90-horsepower, L-head six, which dated only from 1941, was provided with a higher-lift camshaft for livelier performance, and the exhaust manifold was re-positioned farther from the fuel pump, in order to minimize the possibility of vapor lock. Meanwhile the venerable V-8 – by far the more popular of the two powerplants – was bored an eighth of an inch, raising the displacement from 221.0 to 239.4 cubic inches, same as the Mercury. This, together with an increase in the compression ratio from 6.20:1 to 6.75:1, boosted the horse-power from 90 to 100 and the torque from 157 to 180 pounds-feet. (The latter figure, by the way, exactly matched that of the six-cylinder engine, though it was achieved at higher rpm's.) The flathead V-8 is an easy engine to criticize, particularly in terms of its tendency to vapor lock when driven slowly for extended periods, but it's a tough old bird, and it made the postwar Ford V-8 by far the fastest car in its price field.

One more modification in the new

*1946 front styling was carried over to cars built through March 1947*

## 1947

The nightmare of World War II was over. The GI's were back home again, many in school completing their long-interrupted education with the help of the GI Bill of Rights. Harry Truman was in the White House; the Republicans were in control of Congress for the first time in 14 years; and General George Catlett Marshall, until recently the US Army's Chief of Staff, was Secretary of State.

In a speech at Harvard University in June, General Marshall announced an unprecedented plan for the postwar rehabilitation of Europe, and China as well. Officially called the Economic Cooperation Administration, it would be popularly known as the Marshall Plan. The nation's economy was prospering, and despite Winston Churchill's dire warnings about the Soviets a few months earlier, most of us looked forward optimistically to a happy, peaceful future.

Change was in the wind. The last street-cars in New York City were replaced by diesel buses (which may or may not have represented progress). Congress refused to seat Senator-elect Theodore Bilbo, on the grounds that he had been elected on an overt "white supremacy" platform. A teacher's strike closed the schools of Buffalo, New York, for seven days – an unheard-of event at that time. John L. Lewis's United Mine Workers bailed out of the American Federation of Labor (AFL) for the second time. Christian Dior man-

aged to persuade the ladies to radically lower their hemlines, to the dismay of legions of leg-watching males. And the name of Boulder Dam was changed to Hoover Dam, honoring former President Herbert Hoover.

There were a number of tragedies that year. The crash of a KLM Royal Dutch airliner took 22 lives, including those of Sweden's Prince Gustaf Adolf, and Grace Moore, American star of opera, radio and motion pictures. A cyclone hit the western part of Texas and Oklahoma, killing 134 persons and injuring 1,300. The United Mine Workers closed all of the nation's soft coal mines for six days in memory of 111 miners who lost their lives in a gas-filled chamber as a result of a mine explosion in Centralia, Illinois. And in a poignant moment at Yankee Stadium, more than 58,000 fans came roaring to their feet in tribute to Babe Ruth, making one of his final appearances before cancer claimed his life.

But on the other hand, life had its lighter, brighter side. In the World Series, Joe DiMaggio paced the New York Yankees to a four-to-three win over the Brooklyn Dodgers. Reports of mysterious "flying saucers" came in from various sections of the country, sparking an endless succession of smart remarks, only a few of them suitable for mixed company. Margaret Truman, the president's daughter, made her professional singing debut.

Blessedly for everyone within earshot, she soon changed direction, becoming a writer of mystery novels instead.

On Broadway a musical fantasy called *Brigadoon* opened a run that would extend for 581 performances, leaving us with such memorable Lerner and Loewe songs as "Almost Like Being in Love" and "There but for You Go I." Another Broadway show, *Allegro*, had an equally fine score by the same songwriting team, including "A Fellow Needs a Girl," "So Far," and "The Gentleman Is a Dope." And at the movies we were entertained by *Life With Father*, starring William Powell and Irene Dunne; and *Miracle on 34th Street*, with Maureen O'Hara.

Books that season included James Michener's *Tales of the South Pacific*, John Gunther's *Inside USA*, Sinclair Lewis's *Kingsblood Royal*, John Steinbeck's *The Wayward Bus*, and Laura Hobson's *Gentleman's Agreement*, soon to become the basis for a memorable motion picture.

But to those involved in the automobile industry, unquestionably the major event of 1947 was the death of Henry Ford on April 7. The old pioneer was 83 years of age, and had not been active in company affairs since relinquishing the presidency to his grandson a year and a half earlier, but nevertheless his passing marked the end of an era – for the Ford Motor Company, and in some respects for the world at large.

illustrations by Russell von Sauers, The Graphic Automobile Studio

# specifications

## 1946-48 Ford V-8 Super Deluxe Station Wagon

| | |
|---|---|
| Price, f.o.b. factory | 1946, $1,553; 1947-48, $1,972 |
| Options on dR car | Radio, heater, fog lights, turn indicators, white sidewall tires, exhaust extension |

### ENGINE

| | |
|---|---|
| Type | 90-degree L-head V-8 |
| Bore and stroke | 3.19 inches x 3.75 inches |
| Displacement | 239.4 cubic inches |
| Compression ratio | 6.75:1 |
| Horsepower @ rpm | 100 @ 3,800 |
| Torque @ rpm | 180 @ 2,000 |
| Taxable horsepower | 32.51 |
| Valve lifters | Solid |
| Main bearings | 3 |
| Fuel system | 1.25-inch single downdraft carburetor, camshaft pump |
| Cooling system | Centrifugal pump, belt drive |
| Lubrication system | Pressure |
| Exhaust system | Single |
| Electrical system | 6-volt battery/coil |

### CLUTCH

| | |
|---|---|
| Type | Single dry plate |
| Outside diameter | 10 inches |
| Actuation | Mechanical, foot pedal |

### TRANSMISSION

| | |
|---|---|
| Type | 3-speed selective, synchronized 2nd and 3rd gears, column-mounted lever |
| Ratios: 1st | 3.12:1 |
| 2nd | 1.77:1 |
| 3rd | 1.00:1 |
| Reverse | 4.00:1 |

### DIFFERENTIAL

| | |
|---|---|
| Type | Spiral bevel |
| Ratio | 3.54:1 |
| Drive axles | 3/4 floating |
| Torque medium | Torque tube |

### STEERING

| | |
|---|---|
| Type | Worm and roller |
| Ratio | 18.2:1 |
| Turning diameter | 40 feet (right) |
| Turns lock-to-lock | 4.5 |

### BRAKES

| | |
|---|---|
| Type | 4-wheel hydraulic, drum type |
| Drum diameter | 12 inches |
| Effective area | 168 square inches |

### CONSTRUCTION

| | |
|---|---|
| Type | Body on frame |
| Frame | Channel section steel; central X-member |
| Body construction | Wood |
| Body type | 8-passenger station wagon |

### SUSPENSION

| | |
|---|---|
| Front | I-beam axle, 44-inch x 2-inch transverse leaf spring, torsional stabilizer |
| Rear | Rigid axle, 48-inch x 2.25-inch transverse leaf spring |
| Shock absorbers | Houdaille 2-way lever hydraulic type |
| Wheels | Pressed steel, drop-center rims |
| Tires | 6.00/16 4 ply |

### WEIGHTS AND MEASURES

| | |
|---|---|
| Wheelbase | 114 inches |
| Overall length | 198.19 inches |
| Overall width | 73.5 inches |
| Overall height | 71.5 inches |
| Front track | 58 inches |
| Rear track | 60 inches |
| Min. road clearance | 8.125 inches |
| Shipping weight | 3,490 pounds (first series 1947) |

### CAPACITIES

| | |
|---|---|
| Crankcase | 5 quarts |
| Cooling system | 22 quarts |
| Fuel tank | 17 gallons |
| Transmission | 2.75 pints |
| Differential | 2.5 pints |

### CALCULATED DATA

| | |
|---|---|
| Hp per c.i.d. | .418 |
| Weight per hp | 34.9 pounds |
| Weight per c.i.d. | 14.6 pounds |
| P.S.I. (brakes) | 21.5 |

### PERFORMANCE

| | |
|---|---|
| Top speed | 81.3 mph |
| Acceleration: | |
| 20-40 mph | 13.64 seconds |
| 10-60 mph | 25.44 seconds |
| (From Ford Motor Company) | |
| 0-50 | 13.5 seconds |
| 0-60 | 21.0 seconds |
| (From Road & Track, June 1947) | |

*This page:* Ford script, so the story goes, was created from a set of child's printing blocks. It pre-dates the Model T. *Facing page:* With third seat in place, wagon's carrying capacity is practically nil.

# 1947 FORD V-8

eight-cylinder cars, not shared by the sixes, was the lowering of the axle ratio from 3.78:1 to 3.54:1. This change resulted in quieter operation and a slightly higher top speed, and probably in a tad better gas mileage as well, but it took a little of the edge off the acceleration for which the Ford V-8 was famous, and during 1947 the company switched back to the original ratio.

Other improvements included tri-alloy bearings, calculated to outlast the old cadmium type by two and a half to one; four-ring pistons instead of three; a new, higher-capacity oil pump, and an aluminum camshaft timing gear.

In both six- and eight-cylinder models, new springs with more leaves – 11 in front, 12 at the rear, instead of ten each – contributed to greater riding comfort, although Ford's archaic transverse springs and rigid axles, front and rear, were retained. New brakes, with a self-centering, floating-type shoe, required less pedal pressure than before, and lining area was marginally increased.

Despite the efforts of the OPA, prices for the first postwar Fords averaged about 50 percent higher than their 1941 counterparts. The model presented to President Truman, for instance, had been priced at $820 in 1941. By 1946 it sold for $1,260, and that was only the beginning. By mid-1947 the price was $1,382. Still a bargain by today's standards, of course; and there was no visible buyer resistance at the time, either. But the increase illustrates very clearly the effect of wartime inflation on the cost of a new car.

Two trim levels were offered, the barebones prewar Special models having been eliminated from the line. The Deluxe (meaning Standard) series included a three-passenger business coupe, as well as Tudor and Fordor sedans. Upholstery came in a choice of tan-striped mohair or broadcloth, and seven exterior colors were available.

Model for model, the Super Deluxe cars cost $75 more than the Deluxe, at first, though by 1947 the differential had risen to as much as $102. The upscale cars outnumbered the Deluxe units by about four to one, a substantially greater ratio than in prewar times. Since the public was prepared to snap up whatever became available, it is safe to presume that Ford was simply building a higher proportion of Super Deluxe cars in order to take advantage of their greater profit margin.

For the extra money the Super Deluxe buyer received a better grade of upholstery in gray and gray striped patterns,

### 1947 Low-Priced Woodie Station Wagons Compared

|  | Ford 6; V-8 Super Deluxe | Chevrolet Fleetmaster | Plymouth Special Deluxe |
|---|---|---|---|
| Price | $1,893; $1,972 | $1,893 | $1,765 |
| Shipping weight (lb.) | 3,487*; 3,520* | 3,465 | 3,402 |
| Wheelbase | 114 inches | 116 inches | 117 inches |
| Overall length | 198.2 inches | 207.5 inches | 195.6 inches |
| Front track | 58 inches | 57.625 inches | 57 inches |
| Rear track | 60 inches | 60 inches | 60.125 inches |
| Passenger capacity | 8 | 8 | 8 |
| Engine c.i.d. | 225.8; 239.4 | 216.5 | 217.8 |
| Hp @ rpm | 90/3,300; 100/3,800 | 90/3,300 | 95/3,600 |
| Torque @ rpm | 180/1,200; 180/2,000 | 174/2,000 | 172/1,200 |
| Compression ratio | 6.70:1; 6.75:1 | 6.50:1 | 6.60:1 |
| Valve configuration | L-head | Ohv | L-head |
| Clutch diameter | 10 inches | 9.125 inches | 9.25 inches |
| Trans. ratios: 1, 2 | 3.12/1.77 | 2.94/1.68 | 2.57/1.83 |
| Differential | Spiral bevel | Hypoid | Hypoid |
| Final drive ratio | 3.54:1 | 4.11:1 | 3.90:1 |
| Braking area | 162 sq. in. | 161 sq. in. | 158 sq. in. |
| Drum diameter | 12 inches | 11 inches | 11 inches |
| Tire size | 6.00/16 | 6.00/16 | 6.00/16 |
| Indep. front susp? | No | Yes | Yes |
| Steering ratio | 18.2:1 | 18.2:1 | 18.2:1 |
| Turning diameter | 40 feet | 41 feet | 39 feet |
| Hp/c.i.d. | .399; .418 | .416 | .436 |
| Weight (lb.)/hp | 38.4; 34.9 | 38.5 | 36.8 |
| Weight/c.i.d. | 15.3; 14.6 | 16.0 | 15.6 |
| P.S.I. (brakes) | 21.3; 21.5 | 21.5 | 21.5 |
| Model year production: |  |  |  |
| This body type | 16,104 (6 + V-8) | 4,912 | N/A |
| All types, series | 485,113 | 684,145 | N/A |
| Calendar year prod.: |  |  |  |
| All types, series | 601,665 | 691,846 | 350,327 |

*First series (1946 style)

# 1947 FORD V-8

again in a choice of broadcloth or mohair. There was some additional brightwork including wheel trim rings, a horn ring in lieu of a simple button, a clock, cigar lighter, and a passenger's side armrest and sun visor.

In addition to the three body types offered in Deluxe trim, the Super Deluxe line included a six-passenger sedan coupe, an eight-passenger station wagon and two convertibles. Complementing the conventional ragtop was a beautifully crafted wood-paneled convertible called the Sportsman (see *SIA* #10). Originally intended as a one-off for the personal use of Henry Ford II, the Sportsman was an expensive car, priced about a third higher than its steel-bodied counterpart. Like that of the station wagon, its body was built at Ford's Iron Mountain facility, on the upper Michigan peninsula. Just 3,392 examples were manufactured between July 1946 and November 1947, making this the rarest as well as the most desirable of all the Fords of this period.

With the exception of the two convertibles, both of which were built exclusively as V-8s, any of the 1946-48 Fords could be ordered with either six- or eight-cylinder power, the latter commanding a premium of $75. Thus Ford was, at that time, the only automaker in the low-priced field to offer the buyer a choice of engines.

If differences in the later 1947 models were minor – and as noted elsewhere in this issue, they were – those distinguishing the '48s were minuscule. The most obvious clues, should the reader wish to distinguish one from the other, are found in the ignition switch and the door lock covers. The '47s used Ford's familiar coincidental ignition and steering lock, fitted to the steering column. By the time the '48s were introduced only the Sportsman retained the toggle. And as to the door-lock covers, the ear-

## Hey, Wait a Minute! Isn't That a '46?

If readers think that our driveReport Ford station wagon looks very much like a 1946 model, rather than a '47, they are exactly correct.

The explanation, as recorded by Ford authority Lorin Sorensen in the 1947 section of *The American Ford*, reads like this: "March 2: Buyers of new Ford, Mercury and Lincoln passenger cars are receiving 1947 titles to their vehicles although the cars are still the same models as produced in 1946. Ford is using this procedure to protect buyers on valuations in the future when their cars are either sold or traded on new models. The company is planning face-lifted versions to be introduced possibly in late March."

Which, of course, is exactly what happened. The facelift was a modest one: Round parking lamps, replacing the previous rectangular type, were located below the headlamps rather than between them; bright moldings were wider, and of plain rather than ribbed design; radiator grille bars had a heavier appearance; the running board molding extended farther forward; there was a new, plastic hood ornament; heavier bumper guards were fitted; and on most body styles the two bright strips on the rear deck were replaced by a large bright metal nameplate. Admittedly minor in nature, the changes freshened up the Ford's appearance very attractively.

The unit featured here is evidently one of the very last of what might be called the "first series" 1947 Fords – that is, cars that were built during 1947 and registered as '47 models, though they carry the 1946-style trim. For the window glass is clearly dated, "March, 1947," and there are other clues that it must have been built toward the end of the model run. For example, 1947's swing-out, rather than the earlier crank-out vent wings are used; the running board trim is also that of the "second series" (1947) model. The same is true of the rear fenders, though they carry the 1946-style brightwork, and when owner Jerry Bishop acquired this car, it was fitted with the later type door handles – since replaced by the earlier style.

Why the mix? Henry Ford was no longer actively involved in the management of the company when our featured car was built; his death, in fact, was no more than a month away. But presumably some of the old man's legendary frugality remained. Besides, components of all kinds were still in short supply in early 1947. Might as well use up stock on hand.

Mechanically, of course, Fords remained essentially unchanged from the time the first postwar car was built on July 3, 1945, until the sensational 1949 models were introduced on June 10, 1948.

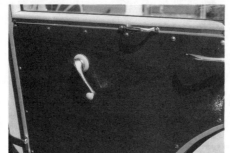

lier cars used an indented design, while the '48s had a cover featuring a sort of teardrop pattern.

For years, Ford dominated the station wagon market. During 1947, for instance, the company built 16,104 woodies, compared to 4,912 produced by Chevrolet and apparently about an equal number from Plymouth. Probably the availability of Ford's Iron Mountain facility had something to do with the matter, but there is no doubt that these old Ford woodies were fine pieces of work. ❑

**Acknowledgements and Bibliography**
Automotive Industries, *March 15, 1946 and March 15, 1947;* Motor, *November 1947;* John A Gunnell, (ed.), Standard Catalog of American Cars, 1946-1975; *Robert Lacey,* Ford: The Men and the Machine; *David L. Lewis, Mike McCarville and Lorin Sorensen,* Ford: 1903 to 1984; Road & Track, *June 1947; Lorin Sorensen,* The American Ford; The V-8 Album *(published by the Early Ford V-8 Club of America).*
*Our thanks to John Cavagnaro, Stockton, California. Special thanks to Jerry Bishop, Los Altos Hills, California.*

Old Henry was in his dotage. This was to be the last model to receive his blessing. For young Henry, the car symbolized a radical break with the past—a test of strength. For the Ford Motor Co., the 1949 Ford became the car that kept Dearborn in business. In every way, 1949 proved a pivotal year—the car was Ford's escape from the Dark Ages.

FORD MOTOR CO. ailed as Henry Ford ailed, and when the elder Ford passed away in 1947, some mourners observed that the company had died even before him. His grandson, Henry Ford II, had become president at age 27 in 1945 and suddenly found himself heir to the fastest-sinking car company in the United States.

Ford Motor Co. had lost money steadily since the machine-smashing labor riots of 1941. By Apr. 1946, losses were running $10 million a *month*. True, Americans clamored for new cars just after the war, but material shortages, inefficiency, work stoppages, and OPA price ceilings kept Ford from posting anything even resembling a profit. In short, the company was falling apart at every seam, and at first there was only one young man trying to shore it up. That was HF II—green but as stubborn and self-possessed as the old man.

He realized he needed help in a hurry—good help. In late 1945, Tex Thornton, now chairman of Litton Industries, sent a long-shot telegram to HF II, asking for jobs for himself and his group of bright young ex-Airforce officers. Ford accepted, and Thornton's "Whiz Kids" came to play key roles, both individually and together, in helping reorganize Ford.

HF II admitted he wanted to pattern his company along GM lines. In May 1946, he succeeded in hiring Ernest R. Breech away from GM's Bendix Div., and in doing so he finally got his key man. Together, working pretty much as equals, Breech and HF II began to bring the Ford Motor Co. back into the world of the living.

Breech immediately threw himself into very aspect of the company's many complex problems—everything from coal mines to morale. One big problem was the fact that all Ford car lines were about 15 years behind the times. Lincolns, Mercurys, and Fords were still riding around on suspension systems designed for the Model T. But Ford Motor Co. had no one who knew anything about independent front suspension; in fact, had no engineering staff to speak of, practically no testing facilities, and no instrumentation. So one of Breech's first acts was to bring in Harold T. Youngren as vice president of engineering.

Youngren had been Oldsmobile's chief engineer for 15 years, but at the time he worked for Borg-Warner. He brought to Ford a broad background in all aspects of modern automotive design, and he'd soon put together a bright staff of 121 enthusiastic engineers (many ex-GM) to work on Dearborn's most immediate project, the 1949 Ford, code named the F-1948 or X-2900.

Breech and HF II recognized the need to come up with an entirely new and different Ford, one *not* based on prewar antecedents. They okayed E. T. (Bob) Gregorie's basic styling designs for the 1949 Mercury and Lincoln (see *Fantastic Ford Finds*, SIA #2, and *Postwar Lincoln-Mercurys*, SIA #3) but con-

## THE SELLING OF THE 1949 FORD

*One of the best articles about the 1949 Ford—perhaps* the *best—appeared in* POPULAR SCIENCE *for July 1948. It spanned 15 pages and constituted a major scoop over that magazine's competition.*

*The man responsible for that scoop was Devon Francis,* POPSCI's *capable, longtime auto editor. SIA contacted Mr. Francis at his home in White Plains, N. Y. and asked him how he managed that scoop. Here is his reply.*

THIS WAS CLOAK-AND-DAGGER work that began with lengthy negotiations at Ford just to get a *look* at pictures of the car. One day in early 1948, Virgil La-Marre, a Ford pressagent, phoned me from his midtown New York hotel. He had photos to show me.

With POPSCI editor Perry Githens in tow, I called on LaMarre in his room. After swapping our usual shares of dirty stories, LaMarre showed us some transparencies. We had to look at them with a magnifying glass just to tell what the car looked like. After a couple of hours of negotiations, Githens had made a deal—a lot of pages in POPSCI plus the front cover in return for early information and photos.

As we emerged from the hotel, I asked Githens, "Did you palm a picture?"

"I couldn't," said Githens. "The s.o.b. counted them as he took them out of his briefcase and he counted them when he put them back. We'll have to play this one straight." Ford was horribly afraid that the daily press would get early pictures of the 1949 Ford and spoil its impact at dealer showrooms.

So our art editor guaranteed security by hiring a suite in a nearby hotel and doing all his work there. The door was kept locked. We had a password and all that. I think this was mostly for show. When we finally got our hands on photos, the art editor personally took them to the engraver in Connecticut and stood over him until he had the plates. When the press run started, the art editor put the engravings in a satchel and boarded the train for Dayton (he was deathly afraid of flying), where we printed. At the 11th hour, he produced the engravings, and as the magazine came off the press, all copies were impounded (by us). I forget how distribution took place, but the shennanigans were worthy of an Orient Express melodrama. **—Devon Francis**

# 1949 FORD

*Nosedive on hard braking comes because engineers put V-8 far forward—this to give more passenger space and so rear riders sit ahead of rear axle.*

First Ford with independent front suspension comes around corners quite well at 30 mph—little lean, good adhesion. But pushed harder, weight up front causes understeer, much tire scrub.

Youngren's i.f.s. put shocks inside coils, cut brake drum diameter for better air circulation.

Ford's trusty flathead V-8 is only item 1949 Ford shares with '48, but it, too, came in for considerable modification and much improvement.

PHOTO: FORD MOTOR CO.

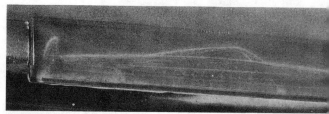

What is it? No one knows whether door inset represents car or plane.

## 1948 vs. 1949 Ford 4-dr. sedans

| | 1948 | 1949 |
|---|---|---|
| Front axle | 1 I-beam | 2 indep. |
| Front springs | 1 transverse | 2 coils |
| Rear springs | 1 transverse | 2 longitudinal |
| Shocks | lever | tubular |
| Frame | X-member | ladder |
| Driveshaft | torque tube | open |
| Differential | spiral bevel, 4 pinions | hypoid, 2 pinions |
| Drive axles | ¾ floating | ½ floating |
| Overdrive (opt.) | 2-spd. axle | behind trans. |
| Brake drums | 12 x 1.75 | 10 x 2.25 |
| Lining area | 162 sq. in. | 177 sq. in. |
| Front hip room | 55.3 in. | 61.5 in. |
| Rear hip room | 51.5 in. | 60.0 in. |
| Max. body width | 73.25 in. | 71.7 in. |
| Loaded height | 66.15 in. | 62.75 in. |
| Curb weight | 3414 lb. | 3175 lb. |
| Wheelbase | 114.0 in. | 114.0 in. |
| Overall length | 196.0 in. | 196.7 in. |
| Engine size/power | same | same |

Assembly line shot shows ladder frame. Exhaust crossover ahead of block means you have to disconnect only one pipe when removing V-8.

Simple, handsome dash groups all gauges in one dial, uses no idiot lights. Fresh air enters through grille, and right duct can be routed into heater.

Acceleration feels stronger than 100 bhp, and '49 Ford can cruise all day at 75 in overdrive.

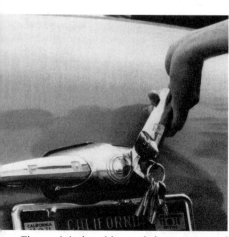

The trunk lock and license light are integrated in handle, with a dust shield over the keyhole.

1949 Ford has less than an inch more overhang than '48, yet by seating passengers farther forward and squaring lines, trunk capacity increased over 50%. Loading sill stands admirably low.

This photo and one below were taken in 1946. Geo. Walker is in foreground, left, with head bowed. Original clay had straight grille bars, spinner came later, perhaps Studebaker-inspired.

PHOTO: GEORGE W. WALKER

Walker, Elwood Engel, and Joe Oros created F-1948's lines, tried to keep body as unadorned as possible. Practicality dictated necessity for side trim, and it's forgotten who turned tail lights 90°.

PHOTO: FORD MOTOR CO.

## 1949 Ford

sidered them too big and bulky for the projected lighter, smaller Ford.

(Actually, initial plans called for building not one but two new Ford cars—a compact version on a 97-inch wheelbase plus a full-sized car on a 114-inch wheelbase. Ford maintained a separate Light Car Div. for the 97 incher until Sept. 1946. This front-wheel-drive compact finally went to France, where it became the Ford Vedette. It was only GM's decision to scrap *its* compact in 1946—GM up til then having planned to go ahead with its own small car—that convinced Ford to do the same.

Youngren worked out a formula for the X-2900, projecting its weight at 2900 pound (thus the code name) and setting parameter for height, width, tread, seating, trunk capacity etc. This became known as The Package. Breech then called in George W. Walker, an ex-pro halfback and freelance auto designer, to style The Package.

Walker at that time held design consultancy contracts with Nash and IHC, but he got those set aside. HF II asked Walker if he could complete drawings for the X-2900 in 90 days. Walker said yes but that Ford would have to come down to his (Walker's) office in Detroit's New Center Building once a week to check progress. This agreed upon, Walker and his two associates set to work on May 6, 1946. Walker was extremely fortunate in having two men of extraordinary talent on his staff—Elwood P. Engel, presently vice president of styling for Chrysler Corp., and Joseph Oros, now vice president of design for Ford of Europe.

Walker, Engel, and Oros worked night and day. In a few weeks, they'd drawn up 10 rough sketches. Ford and Breech chose three and had Walker's group render them as ¼-sized clay models. Bob Gregorie had also worked up a clay, and on Aug. 1, all four unmarked clays were brought out to Dearborn for selection by Ford's executive committee, which included HF II, Breech, John Bugas, Lew Crusoe, Mead Bricker, and J. R. Davis. They narrowed it down to one of Walker's, and work on a full-sized clay began immediately at Ford Engineering Labs in Dearborn. This larger clay, painted yellow and approved by the executive group and even by the senior Henry Ford in Sept. 1946, was put into the works immediately.

About the only dimension common to both the 1948 Ford and the 1949 is wheelbase—114 inches. Youngren's engineering team moved the V-8 forward five inches so the rear passenger weren't sitting over the axle anymore. They switched from the old X-member frame to a lower, lighter ladder type; converted the solid front axle to modern independent wishbones coil springs, and tubular shocks; got rid of torque-tube drive and brought in Hotchkiss completely re-engineered the transmission and differential; same with the brakes; in short, they re-did nearly everything. The one piece of hardware they did save was the V-8, but Youngren improved its cooling, cut oil consumption, completely changed the ignition system, revamped the bearings, same with the intake and exhaust systems, engine mounts, and reduced manufacturing costs.

Although the 1949 Ford turned out to be only 0.7 inch longer than the 1948, its front seat was six inches wider, the car stood four inches lower, and it was 220 pounds lighter (but still 250 pounds short of its 2900-pound projection). Trunk and interior space became much

*continued on page 18*

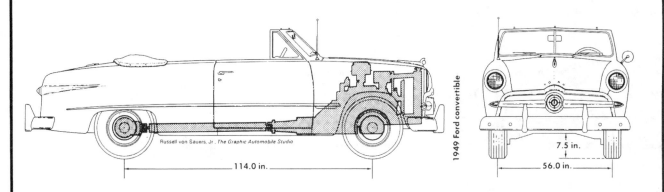

114.0 in.

7.5 in.

56.0 in.

Russell von Sauers, Jr. The Graphic Automobile Studio

1949 Ford convertible

## SPECIFICATIONS

### 1949 Ford 98BA Custom convertible club coupe

**Price when new** . . . . . $1948 f.o.b. Dearborn (1949).

**Current valuation\*** . . . . Xlnt. $1175; gd. $350.

**Options** . . . . . . . . . . . Radio, heater, cigar lighter, turn signals, clock.

**ENGINE**
Type . . . . . . . . . . . . . L-head V-8, water-cooled, cast-iron block, 3 mains, full pressure lubrication.
Bore & stroke . . . . . . 3.1875 x 3.750.
Displacement . . . . . 239.4 cid.
Max. bhp @ rpm . . . . 100 @ 3600.
Max. torque @ rpm . . 181 @ 2000.
Compression ratio . . . 6.8:1.
Induction system . . . 2-bbl. downdraft carb (Ford), mechanical fuel pump.
Exhaust system . . . . . Cast-iron manifolds, crossover pipe, single muffler.
Electrical system . . . . 6-volt battery/coil (Ford).

**CLUTCH**
Type . . . . . . . . . . . . . Single dry plate, woven asbestos lining.
Diameter . . . . . . . . . . 9.5 in.
Actuation . . . . . . . . . Mechanical, foot pedal.

**TRANSMISSION**
Type . . . . . . . . . . . . . 3-speed manual, column lever.
Ratios: 1st . . . . . . . . 2.819:1.
2nd . . . . . . . . 1.604:1.
3rd . . . . . . . 1.000:1.
Reverse . . . . 3.625:1.

**DIFFERENTIAL**
Type . . . . . . . . . . . . . Hypoid.
Ratio . . . . . . . . . . . . . 3.73:1 (3.54 opt.; 4.10 w/o.d.).
Drive axles . . . . . . . . Semi-floating.

**STEERING**
Type . . . . . . . . . . . . . Worm & roller.
Turns lock to lock . . . 4.0.
Ratio . . . . . . . . . . . . . 17.7:1.
Turn circle . . . . . . . . 41.0 ft.

**BRAKES**
Type . . . . . . . . . . . . . Hydraulic, 4-wheel drums, internal expanding.
Drum diameter . . . . . 10.0 in.
Total lining area . . . . 176.0 in.

**CHASSIS & BODY**
Frame . . . . . . . . . . . . Box-section girders, ladder type, 5 cross-members (conv. has X-member).
Body construction . . . All steel.
Body style . . . . . . . . 2-dr., 5-pass. conv. cpe., hydraulic top.

**SUSPENSION**
Front . . . . . . . . . . . . Independent A-arms, coil springs, tubular hydraulic shocks, stabilizer bar.
Rear . . . . . . . . . . . . . Solid axle, longitudinal leaf springs, tubular hydraulic shocks.
Tires . . . . . . . . . . . . . 6.00 x 16, 4-ply.
Wheels . . . . . . . . . . . Pressed steel, drop-center rims, lug-bolted to brake drums.

**WEIGHTS & MEASURES**
Wheelbase . . . . . . . . 114.0 in.
Overall length . . . . . . 196.8 in.
Overall height . . . . . . 62.8 in.
Overall width . . . . . . 71.7 in.
Front tread . . . . . . . . 56.0 in.
Rear tread . . . . . . . . 56.0 in.
Ground clearance . . . 7.5 in.
Curb weight . . . . . . . 3271 lb.

**CAPACITIES**
Crankcase . . . . . . . . 5 qt.
Cooling system . . . . . 22 qt.
Fuel tank . . . . . . . . . 17 gal.

**FUEL CONSUMPTION**
Best . . . . . . . . . . . . . 21 mpg.
Average . . . . . . . . . . 14-17 mpg.

**PERFORMANCE** (from **Popular Science,** July, 1948).

0-30 mph . . . . . . . . 6.2 sec.
0-45 mph . . . . . . . . 8.2 sec.
0-60 mph . . . . . . . . 12.3 sec.
0-70 mph . . . . . . . . 16.6 sec.

\* Courtesy **Antique Automobile Appraisal.**

Our thanks to the following individuals and organizations for technical help and moral support: Chris and Matt Nolan, Hayward, Calif.; George Haviland, Michael W. R. Davis, and John Millis of Ford Motor Co., Dearborn, Mich.; the Ford Archives, Henry Ford Museum, Dearborn; Petersen Publ. Co. Research Library, Los Angeles; BPB Research Library, Newport Beach, Calif.; Wm. E. Burnett, Bloomfield Hills, Mich.; George W. Walker, Delray Beach, Fla.; E. T. Gregorie, Daytona Beach, Fla.; Elwood Engel, Chrysler Corp., Detroit; Devon Francis, White Plains, N. Y.; and the Ford-Mercury Club of America, Box 3551, Hayward, Calif. 94544.

## 1949 Ford driveReport

*continued from page 16*

greater, the car had better balance, a better ride, and better handling.

Bill Burnett, who was one of Youngren's assistants in those days (in charge of development and testing), recalls that Breech and HF II kept pushing Youngren harder and harder, trying to hurry up the production schedule. Early in 1948, HF II and Breech came in and asked Youngren where the X-2900 stood that day. Much testing had been done on public highways with cobbled prototypes (Ford had only 10 miles of test roads in Dearborn).

"What's not done yet?" Ford asked.

"We haven't tackled noise level" said Youngren.

"What else?"

"There's a bit of work to do yet on front-end geometry," answered Youngren in gross understatement. Actually he was having big problems resolving weight distribution, the engine having been shoved so far forward.

HF II said, "Well, get that done quickly and forget about noise for now. We've got to get this thing on the market as soon as possible." Burnett, now retired, maintains that HF II gambled that the public would accept the 1949 Ford even if it was a little noisy. After introduction, Youngren's staff kept right on improving the car, insulating it, changing the fan pitch, the camshaft, body mounts, and exhaust system for less noise. And, says Bill Burnett, "The 1950 model was altogether sweeter."

New tooling and machines for the 1949 Ford cost $72 million and took 10 million man hours to devise and set up. The car made its public debut on June 18, 1948, because HF II had no intention of waiting a day longer than he had to—certainly not until traditional new-car intros in October. The only 1949 models that beat Ford to the showroom were Lincoln and Mercury.

The press had been primed to the hilt, festivities beginning June 8 at the Waldorf Astoria in New York. Several hundred newspaper editors, reporters, and radio men had streamed in by train—in some cases special private trains paid for by Ford. This was the first huge Waldorf press party, and it lasted a total of six days. All the Ford dignitaries showed up, gave speeches, shook hands, drank, and swapped stories. Timing had been perfect, and the newsmen all went home to write glowing reports about the sensational new Ford.

It's claimed that 28,211,048 people flocked to dealer showrooms to see the 1949 Ford during its first three days on display. If so, it was the biggest live audience any Ford model had attracted since the A's debut in 1927. And orders poured in—over 100,000 the first day. Deliveries lagged a bit, but production reached 806,766 for calendar 1949 (plus 186,629 Mercurys and 37,691 Lincolns), and the company showed a profit of $177,265,000. Ford had weathered the hard times of 1945-46 and was now healthy again.

Ford Motor Co. could not have survived had it not brought out the completely re-engineered, restyled 1949 models. Radically different as they were for Ford, they would have been pretty conventional from any other automaker. What sold them wasn't so much their engineering but their styling, particularly the 1949 Ford's. In a cover article published by TIME in 1957, George Walker, then Ford vice president and director of styling, said, "There was a lot more significance in the 1949 Ford

than the fact that it was different. It had to be. But more than that, it provided the basic concept of our styling since then. Practically all cars at that time had bulging side lines, particularly around the front and rear fenders. We smoothed those lines out and began the movement toward the integration of the fenders and body."

The 1949 Ford wasn't first to use a slab-sided body, but it was the first car to really *bring off* the slabsided look. It did this with square lines rather than round ones, and as such it started a trend.

**O**ur driveReport convertible belongs to Chris Nolan, who caught his first glimpse of it one summer evening in 1969 as it was being towed to a wrecking yard. Chris, 22, a senior English major at Cal State in Hayward, followed the tow truck and bought the car the next day for $50. It had no engine, no transmission, needed two new doors, a new hood, top, upholstery, and a good deal of kindness.

Chris' parents had bought one of the first 1949 Fords available when new, had moved across country in it, and Chris still harbors fond memories of that car. But today, 1949 Fords—particularly convertibles—are an endangered species, so Chris considers himself lucky to have found this one. SIA drove his car to get impressions, and here, hastily, they are:

"Still sounds like a Ford. Awkward starting arrangement—key on right, starter button on left. This is to leave the right hand free for manual choking. Really nice dash design; plain but not cheap looking. Very modern. It lacks the 1950 model's chrome arrowheads.

"Seats too low; wheel too high by today's standards. Also, they need some sort of ribbing, pleating, buttons, or something to keep driver's rear end from sliding around.

"Moving out, clutch feels good but trans barks if you rush shifting into low. Once it's in, there's plenty of punch from the 100-bhp V-8. Always *have* felt that Ford underrated horsepower on its flatheads. Very strong though gears, and no more trouble getting into any other gear. No overdrive on this car. Steering heavy at low speeds (very), but not so once moving. No audible rattles or excessive noise with top down, though Chris says it has its normal share with top up.

"In cornering, quite a bit of understeer. Can feel tar strips, etc., distinctly. Brakes on this particular car feel inadequate, but that could be the car. Sure miss overdrive. With o.d., this would be one heck of a highway runner. Size is perfect—not too big, not too small. Again, it's a very modern car in every respect except chronology."

Floyd Clymer owned one of the first 1949 Fords sold in Los Angeles (a club coupe 6). He quickly put 5272 miles on it, then published a book about it. Polling some 3000 1949 Ford owners, Clymer found: 1) average gas mileage for the V-8 was 16.97 mpg in the city and 20.61 on the highway; 2) owners of 6s got about 2 mpg more than owners of V-8s; 3) overdrive upped mpg by 2.5 average; 4) most owners had no complaints about their new cars, and those who did said poor assembly ranked #1; 5) dust and water tended to leak into the trunk, a trait Clymer noted, too, in his car.

Concluding, Clymer wrote this about his '49 coupe, "It is no more like the pre-war Ford than day and night. It does not operate like any previous Ford car and in its roadability, ease of operation and control there is just no comparison between the old and the new models." □

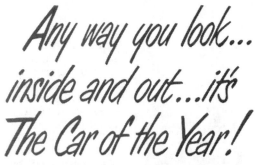

Cutaway views to show "Mid Ship" Ride . . .

. . ."Hydra-Coil" Springs . . .

*Any way you look...
inside and out...it's
The Car of the Year!*

We think you'll agree the '49 Ford has "the look of the year"! Many people say: "It looks like a custom-built automobile!" But the *inside* will thrill you, too! Seats are sofa-wide! Big "Picture Windows" all around! 57% more luggage space. Two new engines...V-8 and Six! Gasoline savings up to 10% . . . with new Overdrive, optional at extra cost up to 25%. 59% more rigid "Lifeguard" Body. New "Hydra-Coil" Springs. New "Mid Ship" Ride. See the new Ford. It's "the car of the year." At your Ford Dealer's now.

. . ."Deep Deck" Luggage Locker

White side wall tires available at extra cost.

There's a New Ford in your future!

*'49 Ford*

*See it today at your Ford Dealers!*

# 1950 FORD CRESTLINER

## "50 WAYS NEW FOR '50"

By Tim Howley
photos by the author

Back in the summer of 1950, when "Goodnight Irene" was number one on *Your Hit Parade* and over in Korea a nasty little war was just beginning, I was a tenderfoot Boy Scout on my way to summer camp in a brand new 1950 Ford Custom Deluxe Tudor sedan. The car belonged to our scoutmaster, Bob Ernt. I can still remember how silently it breezed along the highway west from Minneapolis to Annendale. It was infinitely smoother riding than Gunnar Eck's '49 which looked like a million but bumped over the bricks on Lowry Avenue like a Minnesota farm wagon. Gunnar was the parts department manager for Downtown Ford in St. Paul so his '49 had every conceivable accessory. But Ernt's car had quiet and quality you couldn't buy off the parts shelf at any price.

In those days I was the neighborhood's '49 Ford Whiz Kid. In February 1949, Dad took me on a tour of the Ford assembly plant at Highland Park in St. Paul, and after that trip I collected every scrap of '49 Ford literature I could find. Naturally I was on hand for the introduction of the new '50 model at Minar Ford down on Central Avenue in Minneapolis. Now if my boyhood memory serves me correctly, the Crestliner hardly made a ripple in the '49-'51 Ford stream. I remember seeing a Sportsman's Green one in the window of Boyer-Gilfillan Ford in downtown Minneapolis. A few years later I saw one wrecked, just like it, at a service station in Edina. Perhaps the same car. No, Crestliners did not score a home run in Minneapolis or anyplace else as evidenced by the low survival rate today. My best guess is that no more than 100 survive. Even in their day they were the rarest of the 1950 Fords. One source pegs production at 17,601 out of 1,208,912 shiny new Fords turned out for that model year. Another source says

only 8,703. It is therefore fitting and proper that the Crestliner should be our driveReport car for the 1950 model story.

I'm not going to dwell on the follies of the '49er. Any car that can save Detroit's second largest manufacturer can't be all bad. The '49 had a 17-month production run, shattered all previous Ford sales records and paved the way for Ford's exciting recovery years. Cars built later on in the model year were a lot better assembled and contained some of the features touted in 1950.

The '50 was introduced just before Thanksgiving, '49. There were a lot of new colors, interiors were much better tailored, and for the first time since the

'48 model the doors closed with a solid "klunk."

Starting from the ground-up, the box-type frame rails were made a bit thicker and both the body and frame were strengthened at a dozen points, especially in the door areas. In addition, heavier sealer at 41 points helped shut out rain, wind, dust and road noise, major complaint areas with the '49 Ford. The doors shut much tighter with better rubber sealing, and with push-button handles with rotary locks replacing the old dog bones. The deck lid latch was also redesigned for a tighter fit. The hood was braced and was now spring-loaded so that it no longer closed half cocked or lifted up at the cowl end. Better rubber sealing was put around all of the windows. Unfortunately, the front windows still leaked a little around the outer edges.

In order to achieve the much publicized "Midship Ride," '49 Ford engineers had shoved the engine five inches further forward. Combined with the new (for Ford) independent front suspension with coil springs, this created a lot of front end geometry problems and left the rear end to hop around like a kangaroo. While the problem was never completely solved throughout the three-year run, the '50 had a torsional stabilizer bar redesign. The bar was no longer attached to the frame as well as the A-frame. It was now fastened through bonded rubber to each lower A-frame only. Rear springs were raised a little so that the rear end wouldn't squat under the weight of rear seat passengers and luggage.

Horsepower was the same as the 1949; 100 @ 3,600 rpm, with the same 239.4 flathead cubes and the same 6.8:1 compression ratio. But at least the old problem of piston slap on cold Minnesota mornings was finally addressed. Steel struts were now cast into the skirts of

# Driving Impressions

It's not easy finding a 1950 Ford Crestliner. We estimate that there are no more than half a dozen up and running today in California, where very likely the greatest percentage of them were originally sold. Our driveReport car belongs to Jim Butterfield of Downey. Jim grew up with Fords of this era. Seven years ago he bought this one, a Long Beach car with high mileage and very much in need of restoration. Giving this car its second lease on life was a three-year project which paid off when Jim received the coveted Dearborn Award at an Early Ford V-8 Club Western National Meet at Lake Arrowhead in the summer of 1989.

Jim did just about all of the work himself. He even made the patterns for the upholsterer. In every respect, this little Hawaiian Bronze and Mahogany beauty is everything a Crestliner was when it left the showroom. We couldn't have picked a more worthy candidate for our '50 Ford ride and nostalgic nit-pick.

To slip behind the wheel is to take a trip back in time when steering wheels were big and blocked out the speedometer, when controls were awkward and visibility was limited. Compared with a 1950 Chevrolet or Plymouth, the '51 Ford is a comfortable car to drive with a bit of an edge in the imagination department as far as location of instruments and controls are concerned. The car is a delight to drive at night with its blacklite instruments all within a single, highly readable cluster.

This was the last year of the separate ignition switch and starter. The key is on the right and the starter button is on the left, just where the good Lord and Henry Ford intended them to be. The engine comes to life with the familiar whine of the starter and confident rumble of the faithful flathead.

It is not easy maneuvering your way out of tight parking spots. Happily the short wheelbase and short overall length of the car greatly aid maneuverability in tight spots. Once underway, the steering is effortless although a bit slow. The overdrive cuts in smoothly at any speed above 27 mph and cuts back out under 21. Overdrive is a must for any stick shift Ford of this era. With overdrive the standard 3.73:1 rear axle ratio is changed to 4.10:1. But just for comparison, when the engine is turning 2,306 rpm, a '50 Ford with overdrive will be doing 65, while one without overdrive will be doing 50. This does much for economy and even more for engine life.

At speed, the feel of the steering wheel is very firm and positive. Four turns lock to lock make steering a bit on the slow side, but we can live with it. What we dislike is the way these Fords plow into the turns with way too much understeer. '46-'48 Fords are much better maneuverers. In the final analysis, old Henry was right about his transverse buggy springs. Ford cornering did not begin to smooth out until ball joint independent front suspension came along in '54, but you have to give Henry II a B- or C+ for trying.

Acceleration is not exactly exhilarating, and really slows down above 30. Don't expect a 0-60 time of much better than 15 seconds. Top speed is in the 85 mph range. Above 50 you're going to get a lot of wind noise, and above 65 there's a lot of wind wander. The only thing aerodynamic about this Ford is the way it looks.

The brakes are good at any speed under 50 with a lot less fade than many a Ford that came a few years later. All things considered, for its day and age Ford was as safe as any car built. Gas mileage is a bit of a disappointment for an overdrive-equipped car. In testing a 1950 Ford four door V-8

for *Motor Trend*, Walt Woron got 15.2 mpg under all conditions, but the car was not broken in. Jim's Crestliner will probably deliver 19-20 at best. If it was economy you were after in '50 you would have bought a Ford 6 and the Crestliner came only with a V-8.

Less acceptable than gas mileage was poor traction which Tom McCahill noted in testing a '51 Ford with Fordomatic for *Mechanix Illustrated*. "Oddly enough, I don't know of a car on the road that has less straightaway traction in mud, snow or ice," he grumbled. "A one legged kangaroo on a greased pole has more forward push than a current model Ford bogged down on ice or snow. This is because they shoved the engine so far forward — to get a midship ride for your mother-in-law in the back seat — that a Singer's midget can almost lift the rear wheels off the ground."

McCahill wasn't much on the Crestliner model either, quipping in 1951, "Ford now has a hardtop unconvertible dubbed the Crestliner. When I first viewed this Crestliner, it was painted Worm Green and Crow Black with Banana Yellow trim. I thought this must be some kind of a Halloween gag the boys had worked up, but later I found out they weren't kidding (end of comment, on advice of an underpaid attorney.)"

But nobody could fault the ride. A fine original or well restored '50 Ford will put a passenger to sleep. The smoothness and comfort are just incredible for a low priced car of this era. The back seat in the two door is cavernous and entry and exit even for an NFL linebacker is more than adequate. Frankly, the Crestliner is just a bit too busy looking for my taste. The trim adds not a whit to the performance, handling or ride, but it sure made the carhops take notice when you pulled into Mel's Diner back in the summer of 1950.

*Take a standard Ford Tudor, add some special trim, padded roof, a catchy name, some exclusive colors and you have at least a stopgap answer to Chevy's Bel Air hardtop called Crestliner.*

# CRESTLINER

the aluminum pistons to prevent them from being tight when hot and loose when cold. In addition, an oil squirt hole in the connecting rods lubricated the cylinder walls instantly upon startup. Even though the '49s were not notorious oil burners, rubber seal rings were placed on the intake valve stem guides to help prevent leakage. Better piston fit was another improvement brought about by the newly incorporated strut. Whereas the former pistons had to be fitted loosely to prevent scoring, the new ones were inserted with a clearance as close as .005 inch. The pin was now offset 1/6 inch towards the thrust side to aid in reducing piston noise. The crank-

shaft was reground a hair to provide a slightly longer opening and closing duration. This reduced tappet noise without affecting valve timing. By early 1950, higher mileage '49 Fords were already encountering timing gear failures so the former aluminum camshaft gear was replaced with a new one made of a laminated material. This helped a bit in achieving the overall quieter engine but it didn't do much to alleviate the wear problem which remained the weak link of all '49-'51 models.

A three-bladed fan replaced the four-bladed one on the V-8 and the fan speed was reduced to 9/10 of engine speed to further the quest of quiet. This was accomplished by use of narrow fan belts and a rearrangement of the drive so that each belt drove three pulleys instead of four. Better insulated spark plug wires were used to eliminate low speed miss

and the wires were rearranged slightly to prevent cross-firing.

Some, but not all, of the aforementioned features were incorporated into the much overlooked and underrated 226 c.i.d. L-head 6 engine developing 95 hp.

So much for what I couldn't see (or comprehend) as a lad of 13. The facelift that delighted me in that Minneapolis showroom on a brisk November day was done under the direction of Gil Spear. I can remember quite clearly that the car I inspected on the floor was a Hawthorne Green Custom Deluxe club coupe. Like all the '50s, it had the redesigned "airfoil" grille with the spinner

*Out back, the car looks pure stock Ford except for the roof treatment.*

pushed farther back and new rectangular parking lamps set below the ends of the center bar. Both the bar and the parking lamp housing swept nearly all the way back to the front wheel cutouts. The hood ornament was redesigned and gone was the holy name of "FORD" in chromed block letters on the front of the hood. The name was now part of a regal coat of arms dreamed up by Ford's styling department. It was supposed to have been derived from old Henry's family heritage dating back to jolly old 17th Century England, despite the fact that his immediate family came from Co. Cork, Ireland. But the three grandsons must have been delighted with the three gold lions — Benson, William Clay and Hank "the deuce." The crest on the hood was repeated on the rear deck. The ugly gas filler cap was now put out of sight behind a neat steel flap flush with the body. Not so obvious was the change to stronger bumpers and bumper guards. Actually, this was a mid '49 change.

Inside were some important differences, at least important to any kid intent on being the walking '49-'50 Ford encyclopedia. While that beautiful, simple '49 dash was not tampered with, the round metal knobs were now replaced with less obtrusive plastic ones. Heater controls were completely re-engineered for easier operation of that wonderful "Magic Air" heater that conditioned fresh, outside air. The horn ring was rounded out to keep from snagging your coat sleeves and the glove box was given a stronger hinge and better construction inside.

Seat springs were improved and seat foam was thicker and stronger. Interior colors and fabrics were more attractive, too. In '49 you had just two choices: gray bordering on an army olive drab in the Deluxe models and just plain gray in the Custom Deluxe. Materials were not the most durable in '49 and there was very little vinyl bolstering. 1950 Deluxe sedans and business coupes had their seats upholstered in either striped gray pile fabric or striped tan broadcloth. Complementary colored vinyl was used on the sides and top facings of the seat backs. Door panels and the headliner were done to complement in either tan or gray. The tan, by the way, was almost gray. The instrument panel and garnish moldings were either tan or gray.

Custom Deluxe sedans and club coupes had their seats upholstered in striped gray pile fabric, striped gray broadcloth or striped tan broadcloth. Again, vinyl was used on the sides and top facings of seat backs and door panels, and the headliner was done to complement the seat color. Patterns and details in the Custom Deluxe models were obviously much more attractively done than in the Deluxe models. In all models, the headliner bows were moved up a bit to afford more head room, and the former dome light was replaced with courtesy lights on each side post. All floor mats in the Deluxe were rubber; the back seat floor covering in the Custom Deluxe was pile carpeting. The Custom Deluxe instrument panel and garnish moldings were either gray or tan depending on the upholstery color, and

these metal pieces were a bit richer in color than on the Deluxe.

Here's a bit of trim trivia that few Ford fans know. When a Custom Deluxe car was painted Hawaiian Bronze Metallic, the interior metal trim was the same Hawaiian Bronze. When the model was painted Sportsman's Green (chartreuse), the interior metal trim was painted black and so was the steering wheel. Sportsman's Green was offered on all body styles (except the station wagon), including the convertible. When a convertible was painted Sportsman's Green, the interior metal was also Sportsman's Green with a black steering wheel and the seats were done up in either chartreuse and black cowhide or chartreuse Bedford cord with black cowhide bolsters. Door panels were chartreuse and black vinyl.

All of this colorful trim treatment was no doubt the stepping off point for the Crestliner which evidently arrived in July and was offered in Sportsman's Green and Black, Coronation Red Metallic and Black and later on Hawaiian Bronze Metallic and Mahogany.

To comprehend the muddled marketing strategy behind the Crestliner you must first understand the competitive situation at the time. In mid-1949, General Motors introduced the Cadillac Coupe De Ville, Buick Roadmaster Riviera and Oldsmobile Holiday 98, the first true mass production hardtops without centerposts or window frames; all top end automobiles. Apparently Ford was taken completely by surprise when, for 1950 GM extended the hardtop concept

# specifications

Illustrations by Russell von Sauers, The Graphic Automobile Studio

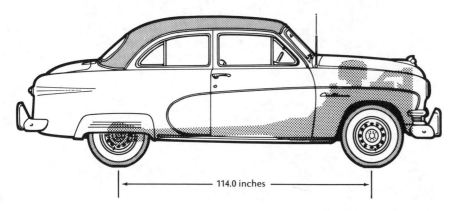

114.0 inches

56.0 inches

## 1950 Ford Crestliner

| | |
|---|---|
| **List price** | $1,711 |
| **Standard equipment** | Vinyl top, fender skirts, Crestliner wheel covers, Crestliner exterior and interior trim package. |
| **Options on dR car** | Radio, heater, wsw, overdrive. |

### ENGINE

| | |
|---|---|
| Type | L-head V-8, water-cooled, cast-iron block, 3 mains, full pressure lubrication |
| Bore x stroke | 3 3/16 inches x 3¼" inches |
| Displacement | 239.4 cubic inches |
| Compression ratio | 6.8:1 |
| Max bhp @ rpm | 100 @ 3,600 |
| Taxable hp | 32.5 |
| Max torque | 118 feet/pounds @ 2,000 rpm |
| Induction system | 2-bbl downdraft Ford carburetor, mechanical fuel pump |
| Exhaust system | Cast-iron manifolds, crossover pipe, single muffler |
| Electrical system | 6-volt battery/coil |

### CLUTCH

| | |
|---|---|
| Type | Semi-centrifugal, dry, single plate |
| Outside diameter | 9.5 inches |
| Total friction area | 85.2 square inches |

### TRANSMISSION

| | |
|---|---|
| Type | 3-speeds forward, one reverse, all helical gears |
| Ratios: 1st | 2.819:1 |
| 2nd | 1.604:1 |
| 3rd | 1.000:1 |
| Reverse | 3.625:1 |

### AUTOMATIC OVERDRIVE (optional)

| | |
|---|---|
| Ratio | 0.70:1 |
| Automatic cut-in speeds above (approx). | 27 mph |
| Automatic return to direct drive when speed drops below (approx.) | 21 mph |

### DIFFERENTIAL

| | |
|---|---|
| Type | Hypoid |
| Drive axles | Semi-floating |
| Ratio | 3.73:1 standard, 4.10:1 with overdrive |

### STEERING

| | |
|---|---|
| Type | Worm & roller |
| Turns, lock to lock | 4.0 |
| Gear ratio | 17.1:1 |
| Overall ratio | 23.2:1 |
| Turning circle | 41 feet |

### BRAKES

| | |
|---|---|
| Type | Hydraulic 4-wheel drums, internal expanding |
| Drum diameter | 10 inches |
| Effective area | 176 inches |

### CONSTRUCTION

| | |
|---|---|
| Frame | Double-drop box section, five cross-members |
| Body construction | All steel |
| Body style | 2-door 6-passenger sedan |

### SUSPENSION

| | |
|---|---|
| Front | Independent A-arms, coil springs, tubular hydraulic shocks, stabilizer bars |
| Rear | Solid axle, longitudinal leaf springs, tubular hydraulic shocks |
| Wheels | Pressed steel, drop-center rims, lug-bolted to brake drums |
| Tires | 6.00x16 4-ply |

### WEIGHTS AND MEASURES

| | |
|---|---|
| Wheelbase | 114 inches |
| Overall length | 196.7 inches |
| Overall width | 72.8 inches |
| Overall height | 63.2 inches |
| Front track | 56 inches |
| Rear track | 56 inches |
| Ground clearance | 7.8 inches |
| Shipping weight | 3,050 pounds (19 pounds more than the Custom Deluxe sedan) |

### CAPACITIES

| | |
|---|---|
| Crankcase | 5 quarts |
| Cooling system | 22 quarts |
| Fuel tank | 16 gallons |

*Airplane style door trim was standard Ford interior item.*

# CRESTLINER

to the Buick Super, Olds 88, Pontiac and even Chevrolet. Given a little more warning and less internal reorganization going on, Ford might have answered with a hardtop in 1950 and, indeed, did in 1951 (see *SIA* #92). But with all their other priorities plus the Korean War shaping up, the decision came down from the top simply to dress up the two-door sedans as best they possibly could.

Hence, a bevy of sporty looking two doors emerged from Ford in the summer of 1950. They were the Lincoln Cosmopolitan Capri, Lincoln Lido, Mercury Monterey and Ford Crestliner. All of them had two things in common. They were the first American postwar production cars with the now-popular vinyl tops. They also had interior sportiness and distinction. Unfortunately, all four had centerposts and window frames which proved to be their ultimate downfall. They were merely trim jobs and were instantly perceived by the public as no more than such.

The trim job on the Fords was done by the late Bob McGuire, assisted by L. David Ash and a few others who worked out some of the interior details. The late Gordon Buehrig, who is mistakenly given credit for the Crestliner and the 1951 Ford Victoria hardtop (see *SIA* #92) had little or nothing to do with either one. It was McGuire who suggested the classic LeBaron sweep of stainless side trim, the Crestliner's trademark. It is hard to say who thought up the vinyl tops. Derham was doing them for some Lincoln Cosmopolitan limousines (including Presidential limousines) at the time.

The Crestliner brochure proudly announced: "A Smart New Ford. All over the country people are talking about the new Ford Crestliner. Asking each other 'Why didn't somebody design a car like this before?' That's because the Crestliner is the perfect answer for those who want to combine the smart styling of a fine sports car with the practical advantages and economy of a conventional Ford two door sedan."

The trouble was, people really weren't asking for it or even talking about it. Despite a base price of $1,711, a mere $200 more than the Custom Deluxe two-door sedan, the Crestliner failed to catch the public's fancy. Ditto for the Mercury Monterey, Lincoln Lido and Lincoln Cosmopolitan Capri. It's also unlikely any dealer ever sold a Crestliner near the base price. These cars were typically sold loaded. Moreover, these were the days before federally mandated

## Crestliner Advertising (or lack of it)

Throughout the 1950 model year, Ford heavily advertised its popular convertible, especially in Sportsman's Green. The station wagon was also heavily advertised until the very end of the year. In fact, Ford's 1950 model advertising was some of the most ambitious and best in the entire industry. Yet the 1950 Ford Crestliner was hardly advertised at all. Then in February/March 1951, a major 1951 Ford Victoria advertising campaign was launched.

This seems to indicate that the Crest-liner was a stopgap model. Once HF II was satisfied with the car, the marketing and advertising boys almost forgot about it. Perhaps there were problems along the way in getting the model into mass production with all the special fabrics and trim items involved. Whatever the politics, the Crestliner seems to be the best kept secret in Ford's early postwar recovery years. The Crestliner had its own separate brochure. Has anybody ever seen one?

window sticker prices. Dealers tended to write their own stickers. In the case of the Crestliners, buyers typically paid around $2,500 plus the usual destination charges, preparation fees, taxes and license fees.

Still the Crestliner buyer got a lot of standard trim, whatever the price. In addition to the stainless steel "airfoil" separating the body colors and the basketweave vinyl top (which was not very durable), there were stainless steel rocker panels, exclusive Crestliner wheel covers, twin outside rearview mirrors and the gold plated Crestliner nameplate on each side of the front fenders. Rear fender skirts, optional on other Fords, were standard on the Crest-liners.

There were three interior color choices to match the exteriors. Sportsman's Green and Black, Red and Black, and

# CRESTLINER

Tan. Seats were identical in colors and patterns to the convertibles. Except in the Crestliners, seat faces were offered in Bedford cord only, not cowhide. Incidentally, the precise Bedford cord colors and patterns today are virtually impossible to find. Crestliner seat bolsters were leather. In some instances the seat backs were leather, too. Door panels differed from the convertibles in that they incorporated some Bedford cord.

Special tone instrument panels matched the outside colors with the predominant of the two tones carried onto the window garnish moldings. The panel colors were separated by a stainless steel band, similar but not identical to the band carried on later 1950 Ford station wagons and all 1951s. (All 1951 Ford station wagons still had 1950 instrument panels.) The Crestliner name was carried on the band just below the radio speaker grille. The inside windshield trim was all chromed. A four-spoke steering wheel, another option on other models, was standard on the Crestliner. It was black on the Sportsman's Green and Coronation Red cars, Mahogany on the Hawaiian Bronze cars with the color impregnated in the plastic composition steering wheels; not painted on. Visors were two-tone. Floor coverings were thick pile carpeting in matching colors. No rubber floor mats here. This author has carefully inspected some original Crestliner interiors. The material and stitching standards were way beyond Ford — definitely up to Lincoln quality.

Radio, heater, overdrive and white sidewall tires were typical options and few Crestliners ever left the dealerships without all of them.

Other than resistance, there were a number of contributing factors to the Crestliner's limited sales. First, it was a mid-year model. As near as can be determined, no 1950 Crestliner was built before July. Second, it was offered only in a two-door sedan, not the popular and sportier club coupe. Third, the color choices were extremely limited. Finally, the poor car received minuscule advertising support. Little wonder that the Crestliner accounted for a pathetic 1½ percent of 1950 Ford production while the 1950 Chevrolet Bel Air hardtop rolled right over it with a healthy 72,662 units produced.

Evidently a few dealers must have offered a Crestliner "airfoil" package with two-tone paint jobs. At least one 1950 convertible so fitted has surfaced, and there may be a few club coupes still around. However, these cars are not true Crestliners, as they lack all of the other trim details.

The Crestliner was continued into 1951 when the colors were Greenbrier Green and Black or all Black with a Greenbrier Green and Black interior and Hawaiian Bronze and Brown with a brown and tan interior. The Red and Black color combination was dropped. The 1951 models still have the airfoil, now a little bit less extreme as it meets the standard 1951 side stainless strip. Crestliners for 1951 are just a little bit nicer in interior detail than 1950 models. For instance, they have stainless steel trim on the foot pedals. But they no longer have the custom steering wheel. While Fordomatic became available for 1951, it was not standard equipment on the Crestliner. A mere 7,506 Crestliners were produced for 1951. The model was phased out shortly after the introduction of the Victoria hardtop in February/March of that year.

The Lincoln Cosmopolitan Capri, Lincoln Lido and Mercury Monterey were all continued throughout the 1951 model year as Lincoln and Mercury did not come out with hardtops until 1952. All three of these makes continued to sell about as well as the proverbial refrigerators to the Eskimos, underscoring the cold, hard fact that for imitation hardtops it was nothing but hard times. □

**Bibliography & Acknowledgements**
Ford Times, *December, 1949 & January, 1950. 1950 Ford Motor Trial*, Motor Trend, *January, 1950. 1951 Ford Motor Trial*, Motor Trend, *January, 1951. 1950 Ford and 1950 Ford Crestliner Factory Brochures. 1951 Ford Salesmen's Manual. Interviews with L. David Ash, retired Ford stylist, West Bloomfield, Michigan.*
*Special thanks to 1950 Ford Crestliner collectors, Jim Butterfield, Downey, California, and Larry Kocks, Jamul, California.*

*Top and above: Combination broadcloth/vinyl seats were used in Crestliner. There's generous room front and back. Below: Stock 100-horse flathead V-8 propels the Crestliner.*

# The New and the Old

# 1952 Ford Six vs. V-8

## Tim Howley
## photos by Bud Juneau

Originally published in Special Interest Autos #143, Sept.-Oct. 1994

THE history of the Ford Motor Company is as much the history of famous engines as famous designs. In fact, for all the collecting of early V-8 Fords (1932-1953), it was the engines that won these cars universal popularity in their day. In 1952 Ford began a move that would soon phase out the legendary flathead V-8. That year they introduced as an alternative a new ohv six from the same engineering school that would soon produce the new Y-block ohv V-8 for 1954, making the old flathead as obsolete as the Andrews Sisters singing Rum and Coca Cola. It didn't just happen overnight. Ford's ohv engine development began in 1946 with engineers developing a whole family of similarly designed engines with big bores, short strokes and deep skirts to support the cranks. It has been rumored that the entire 1952 corporate line would have had new overhead-valve engines were it not for the Korean War. A more likely scenario is that Ford wanted to test an overhead-valve Lincoln V-8 and Ford six before introducing new Ford and Mercury engines in 1954.

How did the new six in 1952 compare with the old V-8? With a displacement of 215.3 cubic inches and a compression ratio of 7:l, it developed its maximum torque at 185 ft./lb. @ 1,500 rpm compared to 196 @ 2,000 rpm for the 239.4 c.i.d. V-8. While the V-8 was rated at a higher horsepower, 110 at 3,800 rpm or .459 horsepower per cubic inch, the new six actually had a higher output at 101 horsepower @ 3,500 rpm or .469 horsepower per cubic inch. Actually, in engineering tests the new six turned out to be so hot that Ford had to improve the performance of the flathead V-8 to keep up with it. In 1952 the horsepower of the V-8 was raised to 110 by raising the compression ratio from 6.8 to 7.2:l, redesigning the camshaft and going to an improved Holley carburetor. Valves for both the six and eight became the rotary type for longer life and to prevent valve sticking.

While the new crankshaft was slightly longer than the old, it compared quite favorably due to the deep skirt crankcase design with the bottom of the block dropping three inches below the crank's center line. Except for this deep skirt block design and some new thinking in terms of oil circulation, there was really nothing new or novel about the new Ford engine in terms of an overhead valve six. Tom McCahill said, "The 1952 Ford and Chevrolet six look as much alike as two hairs on a movie star's toupee." A full-flow oil filter placed low on the crankcase side was standard. Both the oil filter and the fuel pump were placed for maximum cooling from the fan.

One big improvement in the new six was cutting friction. In the old Ford flathead six, which was never a very popu-

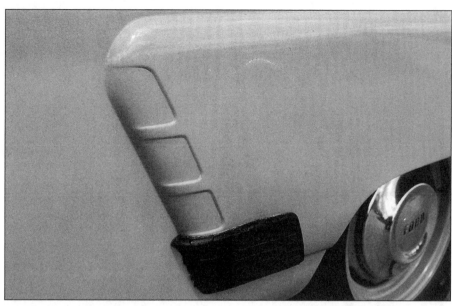

*Above: Mainline was truly a "plain Jane," virtually devoid of any shiny stuff except for bumpers and grille. Piece of molded rubber on rear fender was about as fancy as it got. Below: In contrast, top of the line car gets embossed stainless fender accents and other side trim.*

lar engine, 48 horsepower was lost at 4,000 rpm due to friction. In the new six that loss was down to 31 horsepower. This was accomplished by redesigning the combustion chambers and shortening the stroke. While the pistons were larger, one piston ring was eliminated. Going to overhead valves further cut friction. They also went from a three-port intake manifold to four.

*Speed Age,* in doing an exhaustive analysis and test of the new Ford six, noted that, "The chain driven camshaft carries the hottest timing we've seen in a stock car engine and compares favorably with a semi-race grind. While not as effective as a three-quarter race grind, it still may be considered a hot cam with its long duration and unrestricting design of manifolds. The volumetric efficiency was higher than average and had much to do with its sharp acceleration

and flexibility over the greater portion of its range." Their 0-60 time for a Customline two-door with Fordomatic was 15.57 using low and drive and 16.40 seconds using drive only. Their average top speed was about 89 mph. However *Speed Age* was disappointed at acceleration above 70 mph compared to 0-70 time of less than 20 seconds. Seventy to flat out took another 30 seconds. Much of this they attributed to the car's lack of aerodynamic design.

In testing a 1951 Ford engineering mule with a standard transmission and the new six, *Popular Science's* Wilbur Shaw and Devon Francis were amazed to obtain a 0-60 time of 12.1 seconds, or 0-57 time with the speedometer corrected. Their top corrected speed was 95 mph, and they noted that Ford had not altered its rear-axle ratio to favor acceleration over speed.

*The names say it all. Mainlines were intended for fleet sales and as price leaders for dealers. Crestline was available only as Victoria hardtop or convertible. Customline was mainstay of '52 Ford models.*

*Motor Trend* tested two 1952 Ford Customline sedans with overdrive, a tried and true flathead V-8 and a new ohv six in order to find out which was the better buy. They called the six the engine of the future and the eight the engine of the past, but as the two stood in 1952 the buyer could flip a coin. There was no performance or economy difference, concluded *Motor Trend*.

Wrote *MT*, "The six proved itself to be a slightly faster car on acceleration; it did 0-60 mph in just about one second less than the V-8. Top speed for both cars can be regarded as identical, around 95 mph. The V-8 gets better gasoline mileage at low speeds, but the six is more economical at high speeds. In average fuel consumption, the V-8 actually turns out to be the more economical car but the difference is too slight to be a factor. Both engines are smooth and quiet in operation but the new ohv six should be cheaper to maintain because it's so easy to work on. The six has been set up to match the performance of the V-8 with remarkable accuracy. But the six is the engine to watch — the engine that can and will go places in the years ahead."

*Motor Trend*'s 0-60 time for the six was 19.45 seconds compared to 20.93 for the V-8. Average top speed for the six was 86.28 mph compared to 86.70 for the V-8. The standing quarter mile for both these cars was about 21.5 seconds. (In all of these tests the overdrive was disengaged.) Fuel consumption for the six at a steady 60 was 19.1 compared to 18.7 for the V-8 with both cars in overdrive. Tom McCahill's 0-60 time with a three-speed for *Mechanix Illustrated* was 12.3 seconds, and in one run it was 11.9; with a Fordomatic it was 16.1 seconds. We cannot explain why the *Motor Trend* times were so slow compared to all the others. Nor can we explain why the other tests had such fast times.

Whereas the 1949-51 Fords were famous for their slab sides and sharp edges, the 1952 models took on a more rounded shape. There was a frenched look to the headlights, a pronounced rear fenderline and a more rounded trunk than in previous years.

For 1952 Ford offered three completely new lines of cars, Mainline, Customline and Crestline replacing the former standard and Custom series. The Ford woodie was finally history. Ford replaced it with three all-steel wagons, a two-door Ranch Wagon, four-door Country Sedan and four-door Country Squire with simulated wood decals encased in natural wood frames.

Like the exterior, the interior was completely changed. The instrument panel was well arranged and lighted

## 1952 Ford Advertising

One of the largest advertising collections in the world is that of J. Walter Thompson, produced for Ford from 1944 through 1987. Today it is housed in the Special Collections Library at Duke University, Durham, North Carolina. Within this collection *SIA* was able to find not only most of the 1952 Ford ads catalogued in boxes 17 and 18, but also the strategy behind 1952 Ford advertising. The 1949 Ford had scarcely reached dealer showrooms when Ford engineers and stylists began to create a car that would replace it three years down the road. With the introduction of the 1952 models on February 1, 1952, Ford began an all-out bid for industry leadership, despite Korean War restrictions. "Whereas metals may be frozen by Government decree, the human mind is not," stated J. Walter Thompson's campaign plan. "Our logical goal is to capture public preference in advance of the eventual return to normal competitive selling."

Capitalizing on the agency's and client's belief that "the 1952 Ford took greater strides forward than any car in its field," J. Walter developed a central advertising theme aimed at convincing car buyers that the new Ford was "The Ablest Car on the American road..." because it "meets the widest range of motorists' needs...because it does more things for more people at a lower cost."

The first cooperative dealer and factory sponsored pre-announcement advertising appeared the last week of January 1952. It was headlined "Ford Scores Another Engineering Triumph," and without ever showing the cars the ads zeroed in on the new six and more powerful V-8. Only a silhouette of the automobile was shown with the engines illustrated in full detail. Huge double-page newspaper and magazine ads showing the car hit the newsstands on introduction day. This was supported by a powerful radio and TV effort including ads on many Ford-sponsored TV news shows at local stations across the country. The high point of the introductory campaign was the unveiling of the 1952 Ford on the Ford Festival TV show. A "live" car was displayed at NBC's gigantic Center Theater. Throughout 1952, Ford advertising continued to take a leadership position and invited prospects to "Test drive the big new '52 Ford." This "test drive" strategy, initiated by J. Walter for the 1951 models, was really no different in concept than the highly successful "Have you driven a Ford lately?" campaign of recent years. By the way, J. Walter Thompson, now a part of Saatchi & Saatchi, continues to handle the Ford account after 50 years, which in the fickle advertising business is pretty close to a world record.

with white characters on a black background made doubly effective by brilliant red indicating pointers. While the general layout is the same as in 1953, there are numerous differences in details between the two years. Highlighting on the instrument cluster is black in 1952, silver in 1953. In 1952 each knob has a circular bezel. In 1953 each flank of knobs is housed in a single vertical bezel. There is a full circle horn ring in 1952, a half circle with the fiftieth anniversary medallion in 1953.

The omission of glove and trunk compartment lights in 1952 is somewhat inconvenient, but not nearly as frustrating as failure to provide illumination on the Fordomatic transmission selector. Visibility all around is a lot better than in 1951, especially with the one-piece front windshield and front seat positioning that gives the driver a much better view of the road. Front seating position allows you to sit high and have plenty of head and leg room, yet the position of the wheel in relation to the driver seems a bit high. The Customline interior is better done than in 1951, although there was a noticeable absence of sponge rubber on the rather simply tailored seats. As for the Mainline interior, what can we say? It was the bottom of the line.

1952 bodies were infinitely better engineered and assembled than the 1949-51s. This was really the first post-World War II Ford with good body engineering. Doors and windows are well fitted and gasketed. Door openings, footings and upper pillar joints were rounded to increase strength and provide better sealing. Floor pans were welded to the sills and rear wheelhouses for better sealing and added body strength. The one-piece dash and toeboard was welded to the cowl side panels to become a structural member of the body. Even the package tray was welded into place. Of course, body to frame rubber cushioning was much better than in previous years. 1949-51 Fords tended to be kind of drafty cars at higher speeds. This was corrected in the 1952 body. Moreover, very little road noise is picked up in the body compared to the three earlier years. One new feature for 1952 was the center-fill gas tank hidden behind the license plate allowing drivers to pull up at either side of the pump and eliminating nasty gas spills on the rear quarter. Another new feature was suspended pedals, which helped shut out road noise, drafts and water. The emergency brake now has a pulley to give the driver more leverage with less effort.

Underpinning the new bodies was a new chassis with a one-inch increase in wheelbase to 115 inches and front tread up to 58 inches. The chassis frame, a K-member design, has five crossmembers, is heavier than the 1951 and has greater torsional rigidity. The frame of the con-

**Above and Below:** *More contrasts in cost. Crestline wheel covers approach elegance in their design. Mainline's could have come from a pickup truck instead of a car.* **Bottom:** *Centrally located fuel filler was new for '52 Fords.*

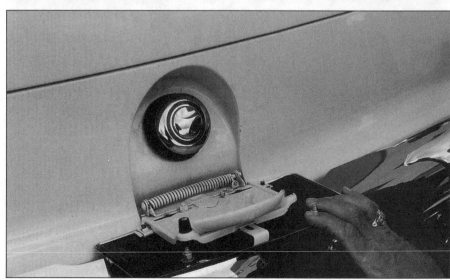

## Specifications: 1952 Ford V-8 vs. 1952 Ford Six

| | 1952 Ford V-8 | 1952 Ford Six |
|---|---|---|
| Base price | $1,925 | $1,389 |
| Price as equipped | $2,400 (approx.) | $1,500 (approx.) |
| Body style | Victoria | Coupe |
| Passenger capacity | Six | Three |
| Options on this car | Deluxe radio, Magic-Aire heater/defroster, overdrive, dual exhausts, windshield washers, turn signals, rear fender skirts, wheel discs, 6.70 x 15 white sidewall tires | Standard heater/defroster, 6.70 x 15 tires |
| Engine | 90-degree L-head V-8, water-cooled, cast-iron block and heads | Ohv in-line six, water-cooled, cast-iron block with removable heads |
| Bore x stroke | 3.19 x 3.75 inches | 3.56 x 3.60 inches |
| Displacement | 239.4 cubic inches | 215.3 cubic inches |
| Compression ratio | 7.2:1 | 7.0:1 |
| Horsepower @ rpm | 110 @ 3,800 rpm | 101 @ 3,500 rpm |
| Max. torque @ rpm | 196 ft./lb. @ 2,000 rpm | 185 ft./lb @ 1,500 rpm |
| Valves | Solid tappets, not mechanically adjustable | Solid tappets, mechanically adjustable |
| Main bearings | 3 | 4 |
| Fuel system | Camshaft driven vacuum pump | Camshaft driven vacuum pump |
| Ignition system | 6-volt | 6-volt |
| Induction system | Holley 2-bbl downdraft carburetor | Holley single downdraft carburetor |
| Exhaust system | Cast-iron manifolds, dual exhausts | Cast-iron manifolds, single exhaust |
| Transmission | 3-speed standard with overdrive | 3-speed standard |
| Ratios | 1st: 2.779; 2nd: 1.614; 3rd: 1.00; Overdrive: 0.700; Reverse: 3.635 | 1st: 2.779; 2nd: 1.614 3rd: 1.00; Reverse: 3.635 |
| Differential | Hypoid, Hotchkiss drive | Hypoid, Hotchkiss drive |
| Ratio | 4.10:1 | 4.10:1 |
| Drive axles | Semi-floating | Semi-floating |
| Steering | Worm and roller | Worm and roller |
| Turns, lock-to-lock | 5 | 5 |
| Ratio | 26.3:1 | 26.3:1 |
| Turning circle | 21 feet, 6 inches | 21 feet, 6 inches |
| Brakes | 4-wheel hydraulic with cast-iron drums | 4-wheel hydraulic with cast-iron drums |
| Drum diameter | 10 inches | 10 inches |
| Total swept area | 173.52 square inches | 173.52 square inches |
| Construction | Ladder type, box section siderails, K-member braces | Ladder type, box section siderails, K-member braces |
| Body construction | All steel | All steel |
| Body style | 2-door, 6-passenger hardtop coupe | 2-door, 6-passenger hardtop coupe |
| Front suspension | Independent, unequal A-arms, coil springs, tubular hydraulic shock absorbers | Independent, unequal A-arms, coil springs, tubular hydraulic shock absorbers |
| Rear suspension | Solid axle, longitudinal semi-elliptic leaf springs, tubular hydraulic shocks | Solid axle, longitudinal semi-elliptic leaf springs, tubular hydraulic shocks |
| Tires | 6.70 x 15, 4-ply tube type originally | 6.70 x 15, 4-ply tube type originally |
| Wheelbase | 115 inches | 115 inches |
| Overall length | 197.8 inches | 197.8 inches |
| Overall width | 74.3 inches | 74.3 inches |
| Overall height | 62.3 inches | 64.3 inches |
| Front track | 58 inches | 58 inches |
| Rear track | 56 inches | 56 inches |
| Weight | 3,274 lb. | 2,984 lb. |
| Cooling system capacity | 22 quarts | 17 quarts |
| Fuel tank | 17 gallons | 17 gallons |
| Engine oil | 5 quarts with filter | 5 quarts with filter |
| Acceleration | 0-30: 6 sec.; 0-50: 12 sec.; 0-60: 17 sec.; standing 1/4 mile: 22 sec., and 72 mph; top speed: 90 mph; | 0-30: 5 sec.; 0-50: 11 sec.; 0-60: 15 sec.; standing 1/4 mile: 21 sec., and 73 mph; top speed: 90 mph |
| Fuel mileage | 20, best; 15, average | 23, best; 18, average |

vertible has an I-beam X-member. The ride was not only improved but tailor fitted with several sets of front coil springs to match the weight variations of the various models. Rear leaf springs were also lengthened.

The '52 Ford option list was short compared to today. You could choose Fordomatic or overdrive for either the V-8 or six. There were two choices of radios, plus a windshield washer, tinted glass and whitewall tires. Two types of heater/defrosters and turn signals were considered options, and a clock was standard on the Customline and Crestline. There were deluxe wheel covers, beauty rings, rear fender skirts, rocker panel trim strips, and assorted vanities. Power steering, power brakes, power windows and power front seat were not added to the option list until later on in 1953.

Production did not begin until February 1, 1952, and introduction of the 1953 models came on December 12. This short model run, plus the Korean War putting limitations on all car production, resulted in only 671,733 1952 Fords produced, and of this number it has been estimated that no more than four to five thousand were sixes which were neither popular nor easy to come by that first ohv six Ford year. When was the last time you saw one? Better yet, when was the last time you read a report on the 1952 Ford V-8 and six compared? Try going back to *Motor Trend*, May 1952.

## Driving Impressions

Our assignment was to come as close as possible to recreating the original 1952 *Motor Trend* comparison between the 1952 Ford flathead V-8 and the new overhead-valve six. Any 1952 Ford is not easy to come by these days, even in California. And 1952 Ford sixes are just about impossible to find. We learned that in a hurry when trying to bring a V-8 and a six together for our test. We had to drive from San Diego to Livermore, southeast of San Francisco, to match the two cars. Even then the pair was about 150 miles apart; so we met at a midway point. This six may be the only running 1952 Ford six in California. The V-8 is probably one of the nicest 1952 Ford restorations in California. With its yellow body and green top it is certainly one of the prettiest.

The 1952 Ford V-8 with overdrive is a Victoria which originally came out of Stockton, California. It is a 90,000-mile car with a rebuilt motor and extensive restoration work including a rebuilt front end. The present owner who restored the vehicle is Louie Wyrsch, a

concrete salesman who lives in Manteca. This car has most of the 1952 accessories including deluxe radio, Magic Aire heater/defroster, skirts, etc., and of course all of the Crestline trim which adds weight. The steering wheel is the Mercury deluxe steering wheel. This car was equipped with dual exhausts which should have added a little to overall performance.

Our initial reaction to the car was that you sit very low relative to the wheel and the hood. The legibility of the instruments is excellent. You look directly through the wheel at them. While unassisted steering requires little effort, it's quite slow (five turns lock-to-lock) and the car throws all its weight into the turns to such a degree that you would not want to take a sharp curve at more than 30 mph. The tires on the car were bias-ply whitewalls very similar to the original 15-inch optional wheels with 6:70 tires. Sixteen-inch wheels were standard. There was some draftiness and wind noise at higher speeds which was characteristic of these Victorias even when they were new. Our average 0-60 time on three tries was 17 seconds, which was better than *Motor Trend* did in 1952 but not as good as *Mechanix Illustrated* or *Popular Science*. Our 0-30 time was six seconds, 0-50 time 12 seconds.

The six was the total stripper. Still, it has the Ford crest front and rear as standard, and the horn ring we believe was also standard. Its hood ornament's the same as the uppity Victoria. This car doesn't have turn signals. This posed a real problem when we found that the window would not crank down easily for hand signaling. But we wonder how many motorists of today's generation would recognize hand signals, and only hoped and prayed that cars behind us

**Top:** *A six beating a V-8 off the line? Yes, it can.* **Above and Below:** *Both cars use virtually identical oil bath air cleaners except for their colors.*

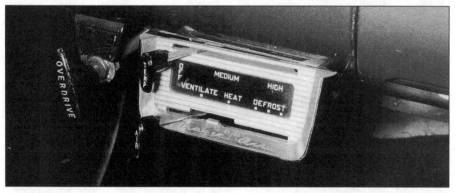

*Top:* Low or high-priced, they're both well styled cars. *Above:* In Mainline, heater hangs down below dash; is operated by little plastic switch. *Below:* Crestline has this all-inclusive panel for built-in heater. *Bottom:* Everything was optional in Mainline including clock and radio.

# SIA comparisonReport

would assume that any car this old might turn in either direction at any moment without warning! The only accessory was the standard Ford heater/defroster without the under-the-hood blower. This car didn't even have bumper guards. But the wheels were the 15-inch options. This is an 81,000-original-mile car owned by Bob Bowers, a water treatment operator who lives in Half Moon Bay, on the foggy coast side of the San Francisco Peninsula. The engine has probably never been rebuilt; the suspension is most likely all original. The gray color suggests that it might have been a Navy or government car stored somewhere for years, but the present owner does not know its complete history.

Slipping behind the wheel of the six was much different from driving the V-8. For one thing, in this car we sat about an inch higher due to its higher front seat. But it moved our line of vision up over the wheel with a much better view of the road than in the V-8. At all speeds this car was much quieter, which we can only attribute to the solid closed-car body as opposed to the breezy Victoria body.

We were surprised to find a marked improvement in the handling of the Spartan six without overdrive over the loaded V-8. Surely the car's very lightness attributed significantly to overall performance and especially handling. This car didn't even have the extra weight of a back seat. It's a business coupe. (It weighs about 400 pounds less than the Victoria.) But that only explains part of it. We tend to think that the flathead V-8 itself created a lot of front-end geometry problems from 1949

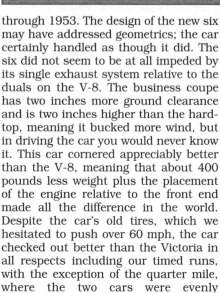

*Above and left: Stripped-down six handles noticeably better than loaded V-8.*
*Below: Ford crest, symbolizing the Crestline series, is mounted in an embossed circle.*

through 1953. The design of the new six may have addressed geometrics; the car certainly handled as though it did. The six did not seem to be at all impeded by its single exhaust system relative to the duals on the V-8. The business coupe has two inches more ground clearance and is two inches higher than the hardtop, meaning it bucked more wind, but in driving the car you would never know it. This car cornered appreciably better than the V-8, meaning that about 400 pounds less weight plus the placement of the engine relative to the front end made all the difference in the world. Despite the car's old tires, which we hesitated to push over 60 mph, the car checked out better than the Victoria in all respects including our timed runs, with the exception of the quarter mile, where the two cars were evenly

matched. Our 0-60 time on three runs was 15 seconds, 15 seconds and 16 seconds. Zero to 30 time was five seconds, and 0-50 time 11 seconds.

We just happened on quarter mile marks and tried both cars. The six did the quarter mile from a standing start in slightly over 21 seconds at 72 mph. The V-8 made it in 22 seconds at 73 mph. These figures are almost identical to what *Motor Trend* achieved 42 years ago. Both cars have plenty of power up to 50 and even up to 65, but are pretty much wound out at higher speeds. Neither one is a car you would want to push up to 80 on today's Interstates. In fact, both of them will peak out in the 90 mph range. Both cars have the 4:10:1 rear end. In making all of our tests we did not factor in speedometer error which could easily have added a second or more of time to

any speed of 50 mph or over.

Radial tires would have worked wonders on both cars. In fact the owner of the six normally drives on radials as he uses the car as a daily driver. But he went back to a set of old blackwall bias plys purposely for our recreation of a 1952 road test.

Looking under the hood, we found easy access to all the accessories on the six. While under-the-hood accessibility of the V-8 was good, it was not quite as good as the six. The V-8 has a much larger radiator, 22 quarts as compared to 17 quarts in the six. The V-8 with two water pumps has two sets of hoses. The cowling around these two radiators is completely different. On the six the radiator is in front of the cowl; on the V-8 it is in back of the cowl. Even the splash

35

pans around the bottom of the radiators are different. Louie Wyrsch praises his car for running cool on Early Ford V-8 Club summer runs where many of the earlier cars get hot when they get held up in traffic and sit there just idling. Bob Bowers reports no trouble with cooling either. Both engines are utterly quiet in operation. The only way you would know which engine was under the hood (other than the V-8 emblems) is by the lighter front-end feel of the six, and that is a really significant difference. While we know how much collectors love their early fifties flatheads, we

*Above: Ford crest also shows up on steering wheel boss. Below: Radiator is mounted further forward on six due to extra length of engine compared to the V-8.*

## Joe Oros on Designing the 1952 Ford

The 1952 Fords, Mercurys and Lincolns were the first Ford-built cars to carry a "corporate look." Joe Oros, who was so instrumental in bringing the 1949 Ford to fruition (see *SIA* #139), recalled his role in the 1952 Ford design for *SIA*. When work was finished on the 1949 design, George Walker lost his contract with Ford for a year. The 1950 Ford facelift was done under George Snyder and Tom Hibbard, then co-heads of Ford corporate styling, with a large infusion of design talent from GM. Before the 1951 facelift there was another styling reshuffle at Ford. Hibbard was out, George Snyder was transferred to Ford of Europe in England, and John Oswald from Oldsmobile was put in charge of Ford corporate styling.

At the same time there were divisional studios with Frank Hershey in charge of Ford and Robert H. (Bob) Maguire directly under him as executive stylist. But now George Walker's outside styling contract was renewed, and it was Joe Oros, still working for Walker, who was first to suggest the "twin spinners" for the 1951 Ford. Then Oros did most of the initial work on the 1952 Ford including overseeing modeling of the first clay. "I was responsible for the aesthetic development of the 1952 Ford car as a consultant," recalls Oros. "The 1952 Ford body was used on the

Mercury as well. I designed the 1952 Ford grille which was a continuation of the 1949-51 spinner theme which I originated. The parking lights were the same theme as the center spinner except they were a lot smaller. I added the frenched-in headlights, and the cowl still had pretty much the same height as the 1949-51, although I believe we managed to knock it down a little bit on the 1952. What I remember about it was that the cowl was up, and I wanted it a little lower. Earle S. MacPherson was the chief engineer at the time, and his engineer and I had a rhubarb because I wanted to knock the cowl down. MacPherson came over and wanted to see why. He understood, and the cowl came down, but not dramatically. I was also responsible for the round 1952 Ford taillights which became sort of a Ford trademark for many years. I added the taillights to look like a jet engine. Louie Crusoe was vice president of the Ford Division at the time. He liked the idea but he just couldn't take the big lights. He said, 'Can't you just reduce them some?' So we reduced them I believe about five eighths or three quarters of an inch in diameter, and that satisfied Louie Crusoe. Anyhow, these taillights just grew and grew through the years.

"Some writers have said that the 1952

Ford was squared up on both ends. It's not true. If you look at the lines on the rear fender you will see they have more thrust, and the side panel goes with the back.

"Some writers at the time credited Ford styling as being more youthful than GM. The GM cars were generally heavier in section and more massive, more weight."

Walker's outside studio continued to contribute on the 1953 and 1954 facelifts, and on the 1955-56 body change. While Joe Oros concentrated on all the Ford Division line of cars and trucks, Elwood Engel concentrated his efforts on the Lincoln-Mercury Division line of cars. This arrangement remained until May 2, 1955, when George Walker was put on the Ford Motor Company payroll as vice president of Design. Oros and Engel were then hired as his staff assistants. On March 19, 1956, Oros was appointed Chief Stylist of the Ford styling Studio, which included all the Ford Division line of cars and trucks. He remained Director of the Ford Styling Studio for the Ford Division line of cars and trucks until he was transferred to Ford of Europe in December 1968 as Director of Ford of Europe, Inc. Design. He retired in 1975. From 1949 through 1968 Oros was involved in one way or another with all of the SIA products including the Falcon, Fairlane, Ford, Mustang and Thunderbird.

**Above:** Mainline doesn't even have ducting for defrosters. Crestline, of course, has that as part of deluxe heater. **Left:** Ford called its new six "Mileage Maker," and it certainly did out-sip the V-8 in fuel stinginess. **Below:** 'Fifty-two marked the penultimate year for Ford's venerable flathead V-8. Despite "old" engineering it outsold the new six by a country mile.

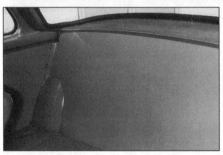

*Top: Semicircular instrument grouping scans clearly and easily. **Above:** Mainline's back area is built for carrying goods; Crestline for coddling passengers. **Right:** Crestline interior even carries "custom coachwork" plate. **Below:** Both cars have clean styling out back, but Mainline still looks so basic.*

## SIA comparisonReport

cannot think of one reason why anyone would want a V-8 over a six other than for nostalgic reasons. With standard transmission there simply is no performance advantage to the V-8, as the motoring press pointed out years ago. Louie Wyrsch, the Victoria owner, said he has heard from old timers that in 1952 the new Ford six was faster and was a better performer in every way than the V-8, but the Ford Motor Company did not want to say it. We know these test results may disturb a lot of early V-8 Ford fans. They disturbed us also because we have always loved Ford V-8s of this era, particularly Victorias and Crestlines. But you just can't ignore the performance figures, especially when they still stand after 42 years! ❏

**Acknowledgements and Bibliography**
"Testing the Ford Six," Speed Age, September 1952; "The 1952 Ford is All New," Popular Science, March 1952; "McCahill Tests The Overhead-Valve Ford Six," Mechanix Illustrated, April 1952; "Two 1952 Fords Tested, Six and V-8," Motor Trend, May 1952; Standard Catalog of Ford, Krause Publications. Special thanks to Joe Oros, Santa Barbara, California, Louie Wyrsch, Manteca, California; Bob Bowers, Half Moon Bay, California, and the Special Collections Library, Duke University.

**They're talking about Ford's modern body construction!** And no wonder! Not only are Ford bodies sealed against dust, draft and weather, they're longer, wider and insulated for quiet! What's more— Ford offers more models and more body, color and upholstery combinations than any other car in the low-price field!

**They're talking about Ford's new "go"**— the "go" of its 110-h.p. Strato-Star V-8— the only V-8 in Ford's price field. You get high-compression power on "regular"— thanks to the Automatic Power Pilot. And it's yours with Fordomatic Drive, Overdrive or Conventional Drive.

# Good news travels fast!

**They're talking about Ford's Automatic Ride Control**—a special teaming of front and rear spring suspension plus diagonally mounted rear shock absorbers. How it gentles the bumps—how it takes the tilt out of turns! It's a honey to handle wherever you go.

### Now more than ever it's
### The One Fine Car in the Low-Price Field!

Ford's long-range planning has now put Ford even further ahead of all other low-priced cars in quality...even further ahead in savings. This progressive thinking has produced a car which can do more things for more people at lower cost . . . the ablest car on the American Road. Your Ford Dealer invites you to "Test Drive" it today!

**He's talking about Full-Circle Visibility!**
In the new Ford Victoria you get a huge, curved one-piece windshield, a car-wide rear window and side windows which leave no center post when lowered. No other car in Ford's class gives you so much vision. It's another "extra" . . . at no extra cost.

## '52 FORD

### You can pay more
### ...but you can't buy better!

### "Test Drive" it today!

Fordomatic Drive, Overdrive and white sidewall tires optional at extra cost. Equipment, accessories and trim subject to change without notice.

# 1953 Ford

*Ford's clean styling for '53 continued the totally new design introduced for '52 model year. Up front, grille bar became solid and center "spinner" became more pronounced.*

# The Final Flathead

**by Tim Howley**

Photos by Vince Manocch

Originally published in Special Interest Autos #56, Mar.-Apr. 1980

THE '53 is a fascinating Ford paradox. It had 20 years of Ford flathead engineering behind it. From a styling standpoint it was the first "product planned" Ford. Its chassis was designed for an ohv V-8 engine and ball-joint independent front suspension, both only one model year away. So the '53 incorporated the body of the present, the chassis of the future and the engine of the past. All of these characteristics made it a very popular car in its day and equally popular as a collector's item now.

In examining the '53 you must first understand the story of the '52, for the 50th anniversary car is essentially, though not completely, a facelifted version of the earlier year. Both models were end products of Ford's dramatic postwar revival.

It all began in 1946, when young Henry Ford II persuaded Ernest R. Breech, a short stick of dynamite, to come over from Bendix and begin rebuilding the Ford Motor Company. At this time Ford didn't even know how much money it was losing on the obsolete automobiles it was selling to a car-hungry America. Breech knew that Ford could be turned around, but not without a complete transfusion of personnel from top to bottom. First he brought in Harold T. Youngren, chief engineer of Olds and general manager of the HydraMatic Division. Youngren was followed by Lewis D. Crusoe, Breech's right-hand man at Bendix, then William Gossett, a New York attorney who had been Bendix general counsel. Finally, Delmar S. Harder came over from Bendix to head up operations. Another important early figure was Earle S. MacPherson, who came over from Chevrolet to serve in engineering under Youngren.

After the managers and engineers came the body engineers and stylists. There was John Oswald, Olds chief body engineer, and ex Olds stylist George Snyder, who would organize Ford's internal design effort.

The idea behind Ford's infiltration of GM was to organize itself after the corporation which owned nearly half the US automobile market. The lures were many: A chance to break away from GM where the policy was to hold past gains, therefore advancement was slow; an opportunity to be a part of a company which was rebuilding with a new youth image. There was talk of overtaking Chevrolet, a radically new 1949 Ford, rising sales and expanding dealerships. But above all the lure was money. Henry Ford II wanted new talent and he was willing to pay for it.

Henry Ford II clearly demonstrated where the company intended to go when George Walker's independent styling firm was brought in late in 1946. Ford directors picked Walker's design for the '49 Ford without even knowing

1.

which one had been done by the outside corporation. Of course, Ford's long-time chief stylist, Bob Gregorie, quickly resigned, a move which clearly pointed out to the industry a "changing of the guard" at Ford.

For a while it looked as though the entire General Motors corporation was migrating over to Ford, the Olds Division in particular. Not that GM was treating its engineers and stylists badly. But once the Ford snowball started, it gained momentum. The word was out that Ford would be the car company of the future.

The migration from GM was accompanied by an 18-month "crash program" to produce an all-new 1949 Ford on the one hand and a complete reorganization of the company on the other. The death of Henry Ford I, April 7, 1947, truly marked the end of one Ford era and the beginning of another. Allan Nevins in *Ford: Decline and Rebirth* wrote, "While Ford plants were rising in half a dozen states, while the design of the 1949 car was growing toward reality, and while the last shadow of the Ford founder flickered and was gone, the new regime was ironing out the last of its major employee problems."

The Fords that America saw in the early fifties were the products of a whole new generation of Ford men—engineers, stylists, production and sales people cradled at General Motors and highly qualified to produce what collectors have now named the Fabulous Fifties Fords.

As soon as the '49 Ford got into production it was apparent that there were body engineering problems which could never be completely solved. But because of the costs of tooling up for the '49, the company simply had to live with the '49 body through the 1951 model. The primary problem of the '49 model was structural weakness which resulted in rattles, dust and water leaks. The improved '49 flathead V-8 engine, new frame and suspension, on the other hand, were well enough engineered to

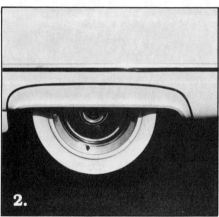

2.

*1. The last flathead offered traditional peppiness, but the ohv six intro'ed the year before could nearly match it in acceleration and top end.* *2. Factory skirts add nice finishing touch to the Vicky.*

be carried beyond the 1951 model year with minimal revisions.

Thus, when it came time in 1949-1950 to develop the 1952 models, there were some very strong "givens" set down by Harold T. Youngren and Earle S. MacPherson. Make no mistake. At that time engineering still called the shots at Ford. Stylists worked within a very tight framework. Length, width, height and weight were all givens. Engineering specifications were quite exact. The styling could not be so revolutionary that it would look more advanced than the then-current offerings of General Motors. Ideally, the 1952 offerings from Ford would have somewhat of a GM look.

In the beginning, ball-joint independent front suspension and an ohv V-8 engine were considered for the 1952 Ford. Both of these advanced engineering features were incorporated in the 1952 Lincoln. However, the Korean War, which broke out in 1950, severely altered Ford's advanced engineering plans. Considering the amount of wartime activities taken on by the Ford Motor Company, it's amazing that the 1952 models were as new as they were. This was a period

# 1953 Ford

when Ford was under rapid expansion, particularly in plants and automation. Yet, despite plans for peacetime postwar expansion, Henry Ford II was ready to sacrifice his most ambitious "dream cars" to put the company's full support behind the war effort. His patriotism was rewarded with government contracts from the one hand of Uncle Sam and a slap in the face from the other. Passenger car allotments after 1950 would be based on 1947-1949 production figures, which put GM at a distinct advantage over Ford. Notwithstanding, from 1950 on, Ford

held a firm second place in the industry.

On the war front, Ford produced Pratt & Whitney R-4360 engines for B-36 bombers. This engine was produced not at the Rouge, but at a government-owned plant in Chicago where Chrysler had built Curtiss-Wright engines and where Preston Tucker had planned to build his ill-fated car of tomorrow. The projected Lincoln-Mercury assembly plant at Wayne, Michigan, was allocated to build J-40 Westinghouse jet engines, a Navy contract that was finally killed. The Ford Division assembly plant begun at Kansas City took on the building of Boeing-designed bomber wings for the B-47. The projected Ford tractor plant at Livonia, Michigan, became a tank factory. The Cincinnati automatic transmission plant was

tooled to make aircraft engine parts and the newly planned Dearborn engine building was partly devoted to the same manufacture. Only a few of the new buildings held to automotive production. Even part of the new Engineering and Research Center and staff office building was temporarily suspended. The Rouge, the Highland Park plant and other Ford centers continued with automotive production but on a limited basis.

By mid-1952, Ford defense production was in full swing. Highland Park was producing the 3.5 inch bazooka rocket and tanks as well as automobiles. The Rouge was producing tanks and automobiles. Aircraft engines, bomber wings, tank engines, a rocket, the M-39, and two types of machine guns all were '52 Fords.

Little wonder that after producing over a million Fords in both 1950 and 1951 model years, 1952 model production was down to 672 thousand compared to 817.3 thousand Chevrolets. Ford was not really losing out heavily to Chevrolet but taking a big slice out of Plymouth. In 1952, Ford introduced four models of all steel-bodied station wagons to compete with the previously successful Plymouth Suburban. The government removed its limitations on automobile production in February 1953, as the war was entering its final phases by this time.

Ford production of the 1953 model soared to 1.25 million units compared to 1.356 million Chevrolets. Ford was closing in fast on number one and

# Fiftieth Anniversary Convertibles

When the final tribute to ragtops is written, few topdowners should rank higher than Ford's immortal '53 Sunliner Crestline convertible. While it wasn't the last convertible, it was the last Ford convertible that was a faithful flathead V-8 at heart. There was a certain intangible something about a '53 Ford convert that endeared it to a whole generation of jukebox and drive-in teenagers in white socks and penny loafers. The ideal '53 Ford collectible today would be a red convertible with overdrive. Though the ones in more sedate cream and green, and coupled with slightly slower Fordomatics, have seemed to outlive their road-burning brothers.

The ultimate, ultimate '53 Ford convertible was the specially painted and trimmed Golden Anniversary job which paced the Indianapolis 500. No, Ford didn't just build one of them. Only one was the actual pace car with its distinctive pace car lettering.

And only one known photograph exists showing it equipped with wire wheels for a special Firestone promotion.

Ford built a number of pace car replicas and made them widely available to Ford dealers. The exterior color was a special mix of white, instead of the popular Sungate Ivory. The interiors had white seats trimmed with gold. The instrument panel and door sills were painted gold. Door panels were gold, black and white, and the carpeting was black. The hubcaps were a special design and utilized the plastic centers from Ford's optional deluxe wheel cover. All had skirts and the Coronado kit, which was then a popular dealer item.

Pace cars do keep turning up all around the country. California vintage Chevrolet dealer Bob Wingate came across one in 1979 with only 7500 miles on it. Reportedly, the car was originally a gift from the Ford Motor Company to racing driver Bill Vukovich.

*1. Rather than stealing Lincoln's thunder, Ford called their spare tire deck kit Coronado instead of Continental. 2. Handling characteristics of the '53 Fords are better than most American cars of the time.*

finally overtook the leader for the 1957 model year. The race never did seriously hurt Chevrolet. It was the independents who took the real beating.

The losing battle of the independents, Ford's rebirth, the Korean War, Ford's new position in the industry and the influx of talent from General Motors were all factors which shaped the 1953 Ford.

We've previously stated that the 1952-53 Ford was engineered and styled within strict limitations. Now let's take a closer look at them. The chassis would have to accommodate both the outdated flathead V-8 and the yet-to-be-completed new ohv V-8. It would also have to accommodate the new ohv six-cylinder engine first offered in 1952. While most transmissions would be stick shifts when the model was to be introduced in 1952, they would very likely be nearly all Fordomatics by 1954, the third and final year of the model run. An improved version of the older suspension would remain for 1952, but the frame would have to accommodate Earle MacPherson's new ball-joint strut front suspension by 1953 or 1954.

The 1952 Lincoln Capri was done first under William B. (Bill) Schmidt, Lincoln-Mercury's chief stylist. Schmidt vividly recalls that it was done not so much to compete with Cadillac as with the Olds 98. The Mercury would compete with the Olds 88, and the Ford with Chevrolet. The Ford would be styled first under Bob MacGuire, then Bob Wieland's team under Bill Schmidt would take the basic Ford plans and give the Mercury its own personality (see 1952 Mercury Monterey, SIA #43). All of these new Ford products would fall pretty much within the same size and weight specifications as their GM counterparts. All would be put into production under the strict supervision

of former GM engineers.

George Snyder, who came over from Olds, was in charge of overall corporate styling. Under him was executive designer Gene Bordinat and then the divisional studios. These 1952 models were the real beginnings of corporate planning and a "corporate look" at Ford. It is no accident that the 1952 Ford, Mercury and Lincoln all look a little like Oldsmobiles of the period as former Oldsmobile men had a strong hand in their development.

George Walker's outside styling firm did not do the 1952 models. These were the first postwar cars done by Ford's new corporate team, although there was some backup from Walker's studio. The 1952 models are loaded with innovations such as hood line lowered to the fender level, suspended pedals (carried over from European Fords) and center filling gas tank concealed behind the license plates.

There was a conscious effort on the part of 1952 Ford stylists to round out the slab sides and sharp edges of the

1949-1951 body. However, a couple of 1949 features were retained. Walker's famous "bustle back" was kept. The "spinner grille" was also continued into the new models. Walker's studio had done a single "spinner" for the 1949 Ford. It was split into two spinners for the 1951 model, then into three for 1952. The larger center spinner was non-functional. But the two side spinners served as parking lamps. Insert headlamps with extended rims enhanced the theme. The taillamps became "tubes." And this was another Ford theme, one which lasted through the 1964 models, interrupted only for 1958 and 1960.

The 1952 Ford chassis was 115 inches, one inch longer than 1951. Overall length was 197.8 inches, up a half inch over 1951. Front tire tread was upped to 58 inches, two inches wider than 1951. The chassis frame, of K-member design, now had five cross members instead of four. It was heavier and had greater torsional rigidity than the previous year. The convertible had

## Ford's Fiftieth

In today's cost-conscious automobile industry, anniversaries are tolerated as necessary evils. Ford's 75th, in 1978, passed with barely a ripple. But Ford's 50th anniversary, in 1953, was one of the most lavish anniversary celebrations ever held in the history of the American automobile industry.

The planning got under way two years earlier under the direction of John R. Davis, senior sales vice president. While there were no 50th anniversary models, per se, Ford did build quite a few limited production models that year. It offered some specially gold-trimmed Lincolns to whet the public appetite at the car shows and displayed some startling advanced designs. But anniversary cars were not the main point of Ford's 50th.

The main idea was to honor the company, its dealers, its employees, and the memory of its late founder. Henry Ford I had only been dead for six years in 1953. He was still an idol of millions of Americans. Norman Rockwell was commissioned to produce a series of six calender illustrations

depicting Henry Ford's accomplishments. Simon and Schuster produced half a million copies of a book titled *Ford at Fifty*, which told the Ford corporate story with elaborate photographs and finely honed company public relations verbiage. Sculptor de Francisi did medallions of Henry Ford I, Edsel Ford and Henry Ford II. Special 50th anniversary buttons were placed on Ford horns and above Mercury glove boxes.

The Ford Archives, founded in 1951, was formally dedicated on May 7, 1953, at Fair Lane, home of the late Henry Ford. It contained more than five million documents and personal papers covering the life of Henry Ford and the company he founded. The archives dedication served as the kickoff to a year of dedications, celebrations and special events. On May 20, President Dwight D. Eisenhower dedicated the new $80 million Research and Engineering Center. When completed in 1958 it covered 750 acres and included an engineering administration building and annex, body engineering building, engineering research building and vehicles

testing building. One of the most exciting features of the center was the $11.5 million styling building with its 12 studios where full-size clay models of cars could be built.

Ford was in a period of rapid expansion at this time. Between 1945 and 1953 Ford had added 14 manufacturing plants, 5 new assembly plants and 19 new parts depots and warehouses, besides expanding or modernizing some 30 other plants and facilities. The cost by June 1953 was more than $900 million. By the close of 1958 Ford had spent another $500 million on expansion.

The 50th anniversary was celebrated on the Ed Sullivan Toast of the Town TV show, Sunday night, June 14, and the following day on an hour-long TV program which went out over both CBS and NBC. On June 16, the actual anniversary date, the rotunda, which had been closed to the public during the Korean War, was reopened, masquerading as a giant birthday cake illuminated for the occasion. On the 17th, the company hosted its dealers and their wives at dinners held all over the country.

# 1953 Ford

an I-beam X member for increased torsional rigidity, and the front stabilizer bar was larger and stiffer.

The ride of the '52 was improved over the '51 with four different sets of front suspensions for the passenger cars and two sets for the station wagons to match the various weights. Shocks were also tailored to the various models and rear shocks were mounted diagonally. Variable-rate rear springs were lengthened. However, Ford's new steering for 1952 was a little too slow to take the best advantage of the improved

suspension. Road shock was reduced, if not eliminated, by the addition of two opposed springs in the steering linkage.

The greatest improvement in the 1952 model over its predecessor was in the all-new body. The 1952 body shell was almost an over-reaction to the defects of the earlier one, and, consequently, was remarkably solid and well engineered for such a low-priced car. Door openings, footings and upper pillar joints were rounded to increase strength as well as promote positive sealing. Doors were hinged to permit adjustment for precise fit. Doors were equipped with cross-arm type window regulators. The dog leg in the rear of the four-door sedans was made smaller to eliminate the possibility of

leaks. Floor pans were welded to the sills and rear wheelhouses to seal against dust and water leaks so common in previous models. Several heavy gauge channel sections were welded across the floor pans to provide extra rigidity. The one piece dash and toe-board was welded to the cowl side panels to form a protective, integral forward section. The package tray between the rear window and the top of the seat was welded between the roof rails. Primary body bolts were rubber insulated between the body and frame to reduce road noise and vibration. Ford was also now using a variety of soundproofing materials to reduce road noise.

Increased visibility was a major feature of this model. Glassmaking technology now permitted the manufacture of distortion-free, curved, one-piece windshields. But some problems remained with wide areas of glass in the rear. The Victoria hardtop still had a three-piece rear window for 1952. This became one-piece for 1953.

Ford's big news for 1952 was a new ohv six-cylinder engine that turned out to be so good that engineers had to improve the performance of the eight to keep up with it. The new six was the result of six years of engineering research which developed both this engine and the 1952 Lincoln ohv V-8. In the six short years prior to the 1952 ohv six introduction, Ford had come a long way in engine development. Postwar Ford engineering under Harold T. Youngren started out in a dirt floored tractor garage, and between 1945 and 1955 grew from 300 to 1800 men (see 1955 Ford Crown Victoria, SIA #37). Ford owned only 11 dynamometers in 1946. Only four were suitable for experimental engines. Between 1948

---

*1. Victoria i.d. is stamped in garnish molding on top of doors. 2. Squared-off styling meant a commodious trunk. 3. Seating position on the '53s was fairly high, offering a good view of the road. There's plenty of knee and upper back support, too.*

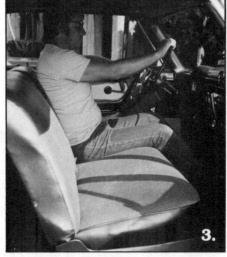

# specifications

Illustrations by Russell von Sauers, The Graphic Automobile Studio

115 in.    58 in.

## 1953 Ford two-door hardtop

| | |
|---|---|
| **Price when new** | $2120.23 fob Detroit. |
| **Options** | Fordomatic, radio, heater, windshield washer, Coronado kit and skirts. |

### ENGINE

| | |
|---|---|
| Type | L-head V-8, water cooled, cast-iron block, three mains, full pressure lubrication. |
| Bore & stroke | 3 3/16 x 3 3/4. |
| Displacement | 239.4 cid. |
| Max. bhp @ rpm | 110 @ 3800. |
| Max. torque @ rpm | 196 @ 2000. |
| Compression ratio | 7.2:1. |
| Induction system | Holley two-bbl. downdraft carburetor, mechanical fuel pump. |
| Exhaust system | Cast iron manifolds, crossover pipe, single exhaust. |
| Electrical system | Six-volt battery/coil. |

### TRANSMISSION

| | |
|---|---|
| Type | Fordomatic three-element torque converter and hydraulically controlled three-speed and reverse planetary gear box. |
| Ratios: 1st | 2.44:1. |
| 2nd | 1.48:1. |
| 3rd | 1:1. |
| Reverse | 2.00:1. |

### DIFFERENTIAL

| | |
|---|---|
| Type | Hypoid, Hotchkiss drive. |
| Ratio | 3.31:1. |
| Drive axles | Semi floating. |

### STEERING

| | |
|---|---|
| Type | Worm and roller. |
| Turns lock to lock | 5. |
| Ratio | 26:1. |
| Turn circle | 40.0 ft. |

### BRAKES

| | |
|---|---|
| Type | Four-wheel hydraulic drums, internal expanding. |
| Total swept area | 172.52 sq. in. |

### CHASSIS & BODY

| | |
|---|---|
| Frame | Ladder type, box section siderails, K-member braces. |
| Body construction | All steel. |
| Body style | Two-door, six-passenger hardtop coupe. |

### SUSPENSION

| | |
|---|---|
| Front | Independent, unequal A-arms, coil springs, tubular hydraulic shock absorbers. |
| Rear | Solid axle longitudinal semi-elliptic leaf springs, tubular hydraulic shock absorbers. |
| Tires | 7:00 x 15, four-ply whitewalls. |
| Wheels | Pressed steel, drop-center rims, lug bolted on brake drums. |

### WEIGHTS & MEASURES

| | |
|---|---|
| Wheelbase | 115 in. |
| Overall length | 197.8 in. |
| Overall height | 62.3 in. |
| Overall width | 74.3 in. |
| Front tread | 58 in. |
| Rear tread | 56 in. |
| Ground clearance | 6.2 in. |
| Curb weight | 3480 (sedan). |

### FUEL CONSUMPTION

| | |
|---|---|
| Steady 30 mph | 21.1 mpg. |
| Steady 45 mph | 19.1 mpg. |
| Steady 60 mph | 15.9 mpg. |

### PERFORMANCE

| | |
|---|---|
| 0-30 mph | 6.5. |
| 0-60 mph | 23.3. |
| Standing ¼ mile | 21.5. |
| Top speed (av.) | 86.5. |
| (From *Motor Trend*) | |
| **Marque Clubs:** | Ford-Mercury Club, Box 3551, Hayward, Calif. 94540; Fabulous Fifties Ford Club of America, Box 33263, Granada Hills, Calif. 91344. |

---

and 1952 Ford engineering built and tested some 400 ohv V-8 engines in batches of 10-20. Their primary purpose was to develop a family of engines from which the 1952 Ford six and Lincoln ohv V-8 were derived. The Mercury and Ford V-8s were not introduced until the 1954 models. Some Ford men who remember the period contend that the new engine's delay was caused by the Korean War. Others say Ford wanted to prove its performance for two full years in the Lincoln before introducing it in the more popular cars. The six proved its reliability and efficiency the very first year. Like the new V-8, it had a wide bore, short stroke design with crank mounted high in the crankcase and a resulting smaller oil pan. In fact, the 1952 six proved to be a much more trouble-free engine than the ohv Ford V-8 introduced two years later.

The 1952-1953 V-8 engine was what

*Motor Trend* described as "the engine of the past" as opposed to the six which they termed "the engine of the future." They found both engines about equal in performance even though the six displaced 24 fewer cubic inches and turned out 9 less horsepower. By 1952-53 the flathead Ford V-8 had reached its practical limit of development.

When Ford introduced its flathead V-8 in 1932 it was not so much an advancement in V-8 technology as it was an achievement at the price. Said Henry Ford I, "We did not invent the eight-cylinder car. What we did was make it possible for the average family to own one." Throughout its 21-year life, the engine was refined and improved, but never basically changed. The biggest improvements came with the 100 hp 1949 model, praised for its better cooling and orthodox distributor. For 1952 Ford raised the horsepower from 100 to 110 by raising the

compression ratio from 6.8:1 to 7.2:1, redesigning the camshaft and going to a new type of Holley carburetor. Another important new feature was the adoption of valve rotation to promote better valve seating and to eliminate sticking. Flathead Ford V-8s of 1952 and 1953 are identical, although the ignition system for 1953 was designed to be more waterproof.

Ford collectors hail the 1952-1953 flathead V-8 as a triumph in quietness and smoothness. From an engineering standpoint, the power plant had reached its practical limits in compression ratio, economy of manufacture, economy of operation and cost of servicing several years earlier. It is no better balanced than any Ford V-8 engine of the late thirties. The smoothness and quietness comes mainly from the rotary valves, improved engine mountings and excellent body insulation. Any 1932-1953 flathead

# 1953 Ford

Ford engine which is properly rebuilt and balanced will probably be equally smooth and quiet in operation.

There is one very noticeable difference between the 1952 and earlier models. That year Ford redesigned the starter to grab the ring gear of the flywheel like a bulldog as it had been doing with the 1951 with Fordomatic. Thus no 1952 or 1953 Ford will have that familiar Ford whine when the starter is engaged and the engine balks.

The differences between the 1952 and 1953 Fords are pretty much the differences you see. The 1953 grille is a clean one-piece design replacing the spinner. The parking lamps are now located below the ends of the centerpiece. For 1954 Ford went back to the triple spinner grille, only now the parking lamps were moved somewhat inboard. Front and rear bumpers in 1952 and 1953 are identical. The front bumpers are bigger than in 1951 and come all the way back to the front wheel wells. The 1953 tail lamp is redesigned from 1952 so that it can be seen from the side when illuminated.

The 1953 frame was slightly beefed up over 1952 and lengthened. Steering still required five full turns to get the wheels from lock to lock, but Ford gave the system more positive control.

Moreover, this year Ford introduced front suspension rubber compression bumpers and new support plates designed to permit greater up-and-down movement of the front wheels. "Good suspension can be spoiled by stability-robbing steering," commented *Motor Trend* of the 1952 Ford. They were much more complimentary toward this same suspension with its 1953 improvements. They found that on rough roads the rubber compression bumpers definitely made a difference. Also, the increased movement of the front wheels on rough roads was not being carried through the frame and into the car. Another reason for this was that for 1953 both front and rear shock absorbers were revalved to give a softer and more shock-free balanced ride.

Magazines who tested both cars felt that the 1953 Fords were better finished and assembled than the 1952 models. This could only have been the result of better assembly line control. Bodies were identical. A 1953 door should fit as well as a 1952. Both doors are fully adjustable and both have push-button handles and rotary latches introduced on the 1950 models. Fords of 1953 have two-stage door openings; 1952 models do not. The 1953 models should have better chrome. Korean War chrome plating quickly gave out on many '52s. It may appear that 1953 Fords run more quietly than 1952 models. This is a deception, however. Ford began putting fiberglass

insulation under the hood in 1953.

The reason why the 1953 Ford appears to be better assembled than the 1952 model is probably because of the interior. While 1952 fabrics and vinyls are good, 1953 materials were somewhat better. Also, for 1953, Ford was offering a wider variety of interior colors and color combinations to match an even wider variety of exterior solids and two-tones. The 1953 Ford has an interesting front seat feature not found on the '52. As the seat slides forward the seat back tilts up and the cushion raises slightly to accommodate the short driver. Both 1952 and 1953 models have foam seat cushions and heavily padded seat backs.

Both 1952 and 1953 Ford instrument panels have the same basic design, but have subtle differences in detail. Highlighting on the speedometer unit is black on the '52, silver on the '53. In 1952 each knob has a circular bezel. In '53 each flank of knobs has its own vertical bezel. The '53 horn has a circular ring and the important 50th anniversary mark placed on the horn button.

The closer you look at the 1952-53 Ford instrument panel the more you will see its striking similarities to that of the 1949-50 Oldsmobile and Chevrolet. Again, the GM styling and engineering influence.

The 1953 Fords, the Victoria two-door hardtops, in particular, are so luxuriously appointed that one might

## Ford's 1953 Show Cars

Some of Ford's first postwar advanced designs were displayed during the 50th anniversary year. The most publicized was the scarlet fiberglass-bodied Lincoln XL-500 which had its debut at the 1953 Chicago Automobile Show. Standing less than 57 inches tall and 216 inches in length, this Ford of the future was distinguished by an all glass roof with a stainless steel basket handle, a feature later incorporated on the 1955-56 Ford Crown Victoria, and teardrop headlamps picked up on the 56 Lincoln. This was one of the earliest of the "waterfall" designs which became the '56 Lincoln. Other features were arched rear fender wells to permit the lower silhouette, air scoop in the hood and integrated two-part bumper grille.

Among the XL-500's interior features were front bucket seats with center console, push-button operated automatic transmission, horn button on the floor-board, engine warning lights on the windshield header bar, throttle type controls, air conditioning, telephone and automatic car jacks. Although the design was intended to incorporate Lincoln's new 1953 205 hp ohv V-8 with all power equipment, evidently this was a non-operating car. Press photos always show the car on display but never on the road.

The XL-500 was on public display throughout the golden anniversary year. Later in the year, they came out with the X-

100, a real running car and, literally, a laboratory on wheels. This was the famous "rain cell" car, so called because the metal top over the driver's compartment would close at the first drop of rain. It was a five-passenger two-door convertible hardtop with a steel and aluminum body painted black. It had 92 switches controlling 24 motors, 53 relays, 50 lights, etc., including hood and trunk lifts. The transmission had an electronic gear selector. Six-way front seats featured nylon web safety belts and electric seat warmers. A special high-compression ohv V-8 engine developed 300 hp and had a four-venturi carburetor. Many of this model's design features were picked up by Lincoln and Thunderbird in the mid-fifties. The rear end treatment was very close to that of the 1961-1963 Thunderbird.

In addition to these two advanced designs, there were two specially trimmed 1953 Lincoln Capris which were displayed at the 1953 Chicago Automobile Show. One was the "Maharjah" sedan with body of gold essence and roof of pearl. The roof lining was white silk against a floor covering of "bengal" red plush. Seats were covered with gold and red brocade. The accent color of frost white was picked up on door panels, seat backs and instrument panel. The "Anniversary" was a gold and white 1953 Lincoln Capri convertible plated with

more than $4000 worth of gold (in 1953 dollars). The body and instrument panel were frost white pearl essence, the seats were white metallic leather with gold leather welts. The car's splendor extended to thick white carpets front and rear.

We have never learned from Ford what was the ultimate disposal of any of these cars. The standard Detroit practice is to cut up the advanced designs so that competitors cannot study them and some private buyer won't sue the company for accidental damage due to mechanical failure. We have heard that the XL-500 was destroyed in the Ford rotunda fire, but have never been able to verify the rumor. We suspect that the specially trimmed Lincolns were eventually sold as they were both regular production automobiles. Do any of our readers know what happened to any of these cars?

be easily led to believe that these cars came loaded with all the power accessories. Actually, Fordomatic, deluxe radio, heater-defroster, electric clock, wheel discs, trim rings, skirts and lower rocker panel trim pretty much marked the limit of the fully loaded 1953 Ford. The Coronado kit was generally offered through Ford dealers. Power steering and power brakes, power seats and power windows, all made their debut with the 1954 model. Cruisomatic did not come along until the 1958 model.

Eleven body styles and 18 models were available in three lines of 1953 Fords—Mainline, Customline and Crestline. Twelve basic single-tone and 14 two-tone colors were complemented by new upholstery fabrics and colors. These colors were picked up on the instrument panel, interior garnish moldings, door trim and headliners to make the 1953 Ford interior appear to be from a lot more expensive car than a Ford.

Owners of 1953 Fords could opt for either an ohv six or flathead V-8 combined with either Fordomatic, standard transmission, or standard transmission with overdrive. Rear axle ratios were 3.90 standard, 4.10 overdrive, and 3.31 for automatic. All axles were the hypoid type introduced with the 1949 model.

Ford collectors today are most enthusiastic about the 1953 V-8, its quietness and power, especially when equipped with overdrive. But test reports of the period do not bear out their enthusiasm. The '52 Ford received fairly good reviews, not simply for its new design but for its innovative ohv six engine, a powerplant which collectors now tend to ignore. The motoring press considered the flathead V-8 obsolete in 1952. The 1953 Ford was so much like the '52 that most motoring magazines didn't bother road testing it at all.

*Motor Trend* proved that the 1952 six was about equal to the V-8 in 0-60 acceleration, top speed and gas mileage. The V-8 got better gas mileage at low speeds and the six at higher speeds. The six, while untried, appeared to *Motor Trend* to be the easier engine to service. Both cars tested by *MT* were equipped with overdrive.

In 1953 *MT* compared a 1952 four-door sedan equipped with overdrive to a 1953 four-door sedan equipped with Fordomatic. Surprisingly, performance figures were very close. Average top speed of the '52 was 86.7 mph while that of the '53 was 86.5 mph. Acceleration from 0-30 was 5.7 seconds for the '52 and 6.5 for the '53. Both cars took 21.4 seconds for the standing quarter-mile. Fuel consumption for the '52 averaged 17.0 with the overdrive locked out and 21.55 with the overdrive in. The '53 with Fordomatic averaged 18.7 mpg. Zero to 60 time was not compared because the

1953 speedometer was off by seven mph. Said *MT*, an overdrive-equipped car, because of its higher axle ratio and lack of wasteful slippage should be expected to give better acceleration at low speeds than a car with a torque converter. With overdrive in operation it should give appreciably better gas mileage and a higher top speed. The performance figures, however, for V-8s of both years with different transmissions were very close.

The 1953's stopping distance, while not as good as the 1952, was still excellent. *MT* was extremely impressed with the 1953 Fordomatic. But remember, for the previous two years Fordomatic development had been severely hampered by both materials and facilities turned over to wartime production.

## Driving Impressions

What is Ford's 50th anniversary car like to drive now? There's no shortage of '53 Fords in California today. They are one of the most popular of all the postwar Fords primarily because they are the last flathead models. We've driven quite a few low mileage original cars and restorations. They all tend to impress us every bit as much as the model did when it was brand new.

Our feature car is a two-tone green Victoria two-door hardtop owned by Pete Bezeck of Covina, California. The car has 119,000 miles, but you'd never know it from the quality of the restoration. Bezeck found the Ford in a shed one and one-half years ago, and has since done everything except remove the body from the frame. His complete engine rebuild included balancing and installing adjustable lifters, two improvements which should not be underestimated in rebuilding flathead Ford engines. While the seat and headliner fabrics are not exactly as per the original, the rest of the restoration is. The car is incredible not simply in overall appearance but in all the little details.

What impresses you most about the car is its utter quietness and smooth ride. This is a 26-year-old hardtop, yet there is hardly a whisper of wind around the windows at 60 mph. There simply are no vibrations in the car, and unless you open the hood and practically use a stethoscope, you will not know that the engine is running. In 1965, Ford advertised that its new model LTD was quieter than a Rolls-Royce. Perhaps Ford could have justly made that claim 12 years earlier with the 1953 model.

By standards of the time, the 1953 Ford handles quite well. There is no appreciable side sway on winding mountain roads or lean on tight curves. While the steering is a little slow, it is quite sure, and not at all heavy. This model probably never needed power

*Coronado kit blends nicely with '53 Ford round taillamp motif. Coronados were dealer-installed option, and a difficult accessory to find at swap meets today.*

steering anyway. The car's only real drawback is its Fordomatic transmission which seems to seriously throttle an engine which otherwise gave the car more than enough power for its weight and size.

The owner has driven the car on a number of club tours, including one recent mountain trek. The car is not prone to overheating, and it will hang right in with other flathead Fords on mountain climbs. Ford's ball-joint front suspension, introduced the following year, was not an immediately noticeable improvement in handling. The 1954 ohv V-8 of the same 239.4 cid was much too small for the same car. In fact, it isn't until you get up to the Fords of the early sixties that you will find better handling than the 1953 offered. Performance, yes, once you get into engines like the 312 and bigger.

The last time we drove a 1953 Ford was in the spring of 1954. We were considering buying a black and white executive-driven Victoria offered by the Ford dealer in Lindstrom, Minnesota. Why we passed on buying that car we'll never know. But we did have the distinct feeling, even then, that it might be a long time before a Ford that smooth and good looking would pass our way again. We were right. It took more than a quarter of a century. And in the end we were right back with the same automobile. □

*Our thanks to Bill Boyer, Ford Motor Company, Dearborn, Mich.; Michael W. R. Davis, Ford Motor Company, Dearborn, Mich.; James J. Bradley, National Automotive History Collection, Detroit Public Library, Detroit, Mich.; members of the Fabulous Fifties Ford Club of America, Granada Hills, Calif.; and members of the Ford-Mercury Club of America, Hayward, Calif. Special thanks to Pete Bezeck, Covina, Calif.*

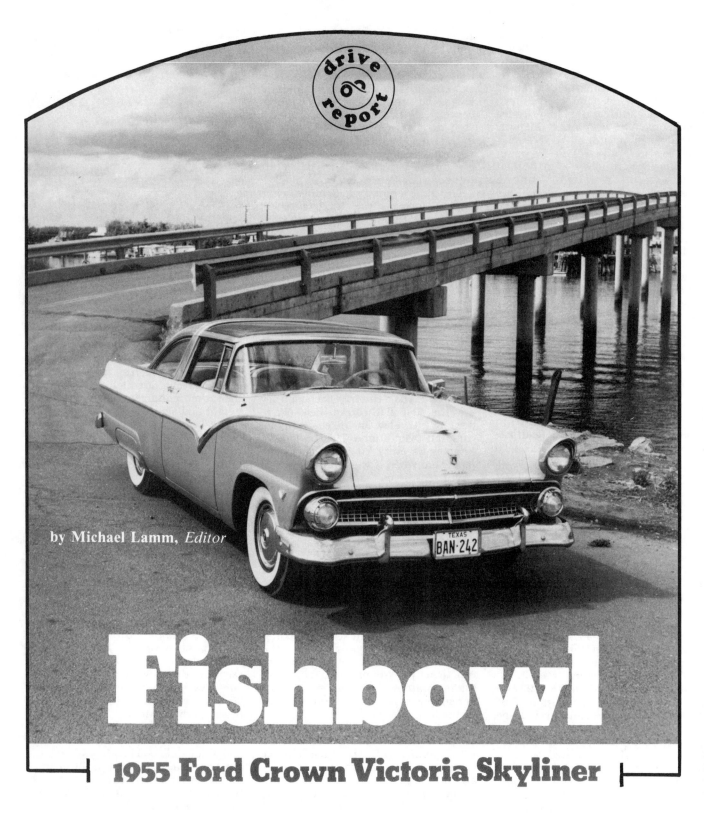

*drive report*

by Michael Lamm, *Editor*

# Fishbowl

## 1955 Ford Crown Victoria Skyliner

THE SAME STUDIOS and the same people who designed the first 2-seater Thunderbird also designed the 1955 Ford. So if you notice a strong family resemblance, it's not coincidental. Ads of the day called these two cars "kissing cousins."

Frank Hershey headed Ford's production studio at the time. He'd come to Ford from GM, where he originated, among other things, Pontiac's famous silver streak. Hershey likewise takes and deserves credit for the first T-Bird.

Assisting Hershey in the Ford design

studios were: Robert H. (Bob) Maguire, studio manager, who'd headed the team that did the 1952 Ford; Damon Woods, previously of Kaiser-Frazer, a man with great styling and development-engineering talents and, as such, very important to Hershey; John Najjar, later in charge of the 1956-57 and 1958-60 Lincolns but for the moment the man who did the 1954-55 see-through speedometer for Ford and T-Bird; and L. David Ash, now Ford's director of interior design and at that time the man who put across the 1954-56 transparent roof.

The bubbletop idea arrived ahead of its time, but it's caught on now in what Ford calls its "moon roof"—same concept, different transparent material (glass instead of Plexiglas), different marketing philosophy, smaller and less conspicuous skylight.

Ford, of course, pioneered the transparent top 23 years ago, and Dave Ash recalls, "We built a showcar around that time called the Mystere. The Mystere had great influence on the 1955 Ford—it wore the swash molding [Fairlane stripe] on the side plus considerable evidence of the

Originally published in Special Interest Autos #37, Nov.-Dec. 1976

*Squared-off trunk holds plenty of luggage; gas filler intrudes little into usable space.*

*Above: Fairlane stripe or swash molding ran two years—1955-56—and at one time was to appear on T-Bird. Below: Thunderbird and Ford shared three exterior items interchangeably: wheelcovers, headlight bezels, and tail lamps.*

*Above: Ford's round tail lamps remained an identification symbol for years; here backup lights are placed into fins. Below: Ford shared T-Bird's headlight bezels but added Fairlane brow.*

*Left: Ford and Mercury received balljoint front suspensions in 1954, following the 1952 Lincoln's lead. All U.S. cars now use balljoint front ends. Below: Balljoints allow good cornering and easy handling under strenuous situations, yet the car rides gently on paved surfaces and takes rough roads in stride.*

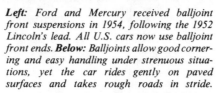

basket handle and the transparent roof. This car had a profound influence on the 1955-56 Crown Victorias."

The transparent top first came out on the 1954 Mercury Sun Valley and the 1954 Ford Crestline Skyliner. Mercury, by virtue of an earlier public introduction, got the lion's share of initial bubbletop publicity. Yet the concept originated in the Ford styling studios, and Ash continues: "I think it was my idea. Oddly enough, the transparent top feature was offered on the 1954 soft-top Sunliner convertible, too — as a tinted vinyl insert on the front part of the convertible roof. Again, that was an option, and I believe we ran it only that one year. It wasn't terribly popular."

Quarter-inch Plexiglas for the victoria transparent roof was supplied to Ford by Rohm & Haas of Philadelphia. The material itself had a neutral blue-green tint that filtered out "60 percent of the sun's heat rays and 72 percent of the glare." The Plexiglas was shaped for Ford and Mercury by two independent companies near Dearborn: Cadillac Plastics and Detroit Macoid, Inc. So far as we can determine, the only other *production* cars of that era to offer a see-through roof were the French Ford Vedette and the Canadian Meteor. However, a number of custom jobs had transparent tops.

To keep out the intense heat, FoMoCo provided an aluminized nylon headliner that snapped and zippered into place just beneath the Plexiglas. Even with that, though, FoMoCo bubbletoppers built up quite a lot of heat inside. Word soon got out that these cars were like saunas on wheels. So, while first-year sales (before the rumor spread) approached a respectable 23,000, Mercury dropped the Sun Valley during 1955 for lack of sales, and Ford sold only 2,602 Skyliners during 1955-56 (see table, page 51).

By the way, the name Skyliner *is* confusing, because Ford used it in 1955-56 for the bubbletopper and then in 1957-59 for the retractable hardtop convertible.

O**N THE ENGINEERING SIDE**, Ford beat both Chevrolet and Plymouth by one year with an ohv V-8. And it *was* a race, because Ford knew that Chevy and Plymouth had ohv V-8s coming down the road.

Ford's 1954 Y-block V-8, along with that year's ball-joint front suspension, marked milestones along the way to erasing all important differences between low- and high-priced American automobiles. And 1954 became Ford's year to add the full complement of power and convenience accessories.

To get some idea of the background of the Y-block's development, you have to understand the tremendous hurry-up program that Ford Motor Co. had to go through in the postwar decade. It's almost incomprehensible now, but between 1945 and 1955, Ford's engineering staff grew from 300 to 18,000 men. Postwar engine research, under engineering v.p. Harold T. Youngren, started out in a dirt-floored tractor garage! And of a total of 11 dynamometers owned by Ford in 1946,

# 1955 Ford driveReport

only four were suitable for experimental engines. (Today Ford runs 90 dyno cells in Research Engineering alone).

Victor G. Raviolo, who eventually became Ford's chief engineer, arrived during WW-II under C.W. VanRanst, who designed the famous Ford 1100-cid, dohc V-8 tank engine. In 1947, Earle S. MacPherson came to Dearborn from Chevrolet (see *Chevy's Cashiered Cadet*, SIA #20) and, in 1952, succeeded Harold Youngren as corporate engineering vice president. Around 1950, Youngren and MacPherson created a new department called Engine Engineering and named Raviolo to head it. Assisting Raviolo was Robert Stevenson, with Allen E. Cleveland in charge of combustion chambers and upper end and Paul Clayton responsible for experimental engine design.

Ford, Mercury, and Lincoln vehicles at that time used two basic flathead V-8s: the warmed-over and ever-faithful continuation of the 1932-48 Ford/Mercury engine plus a new but already archaic L-head Lincoln/truck V-8. Both needed replacement.

Between 1948 and 1952, according to an SAE paper by Bob Stevenson, Raviolo's staff built and tested some 400 experimental engines in batches of 10-20, all of them ohv V-8s. No other configuration was tried, according to Allen Cleveland, because, "...that was definitely the trend from research that we were able to do, and apparently by the research that GM was doing, too. The questions at issue were primarily bore-and-stroke ratio, piston design, combustion-chamber shape and, to a lesser extent, induction system and valves."

V ICTOR RAVIOLO stresses that his department's primary purpose was to design a "family of engines." Prior to the establishment of a centralized engine engineering department, small groups of engineers had worked separately, off in little isolated corners of the company. Those disparate efforts were brought together under Raviolo.

First in the new engine family came the ohv Ford 6 of 1952. This was followed in 1953 by the ohv Lincoln V-8, and the pistons in those two engines interchanged, as did some lesser parts. Then for 1954, the "twins"—Ford and Mercury ohv V-8s— arrived.

I asked Mr. Raviolo how similar the 1954 Ford/Mercury ohv engines were to the 1953 Lincoln ohv V-8. "In concept? All similar," he replied. "Lincoln, the 6, the other V-8s— everything was a family of engines. In other words, what you do when you're doing basic engine development: You develop a cylinder size. Then from that cylinder size you can make a whole group of engines—a 4, a 6, an 8, a 12.... What we made initially was a 6 and a V-8; the Ford ohv 6 and the Lincoln V-8 first. And the other half of the family became the 1954 Ford and Mercury ohv V-8s."

These last two were very similar to the

*Folding armrest and Thunderbird-like Fairlane motif highlight Crown Victoria's rear seat.*

*From left to right, heater controls, radio, and clock group into three round pods across dashboard.*

## Ford's 1956 Safety Campaign
### Quick In, Quick Out

R ARELY does an automaker get credit for trying, but Ford surely deserves credit for its 1956 safety campaign. That year Dearborn gambled on safety and lost.

Ford's 1956 safety package consisted of crashproof door locks, dished steering wheel, breakaway rearview mirror, plus optional padded visors and dash ($16 extra) and factory-installed seatbelts ($9 extra). Supplier problems in getting belts to the company kept factory installation to about 20%.

The moving force behind Ford's safety program was the division's general manager, Robert S. McNamara. Alex L. Haynes, a safety engineer, carried through the actual research and production details. A few top Ford execs were dead set against the safety program even before it got started, while others, including Henry Ford II, were very much for it.

Ford sales for early 1956 got off to a flying start, and *Business Week* quoted dealers as saying that the safety package was helping mightily to sell cars. When sales began to level off later in the year, though, the dealers turned and started blaming the safety push.

All U.S. automakers actually offered optional safety equipment during 1956, including seatbelts, but most buried them in the little-seen recesses of accessory booklets. Ford had, in fact, listed seatbelts for 1955 but didn't really try to sell them until 1956. By that time, the other automakers were stressing horsepower as a safety factor, and the public reacted more positively to horses than to harnesses. Ford ended 1956 190,056 cars behind Chevrolet and has never, to this day, gotten any kudos or congratulations for at least trying to sell safety.  □

*Above: Seat frame body tag harks back to pre-1955 models in which Crestliner marked Ford's top series (before the Fairlane). Below: Bob Page's Skyliner has power windows and seat. Most power options were introduced in 1954, with air conditioning coming along in 1955.*

## Ford Bubbletop Production

| Model year | Plexiglas roofs |
| --- | --- |
| 1954 | 13,344 |
| 1955 | 1999 |
| 1956 | 603 |

**Notes:** Figures courtesy Ford Motor Co. Ford records show 9761 Mercury Sun Valleys being built in 1954, with no figures for 1955-56. However, we know that some 1955 Sun Valleys do exist.

*Above:* Stainless steel inside and out, basket handle lends little roof strength. Skyliners used convertible frame, with extra X-bracing. Wraparound windshield's dogleg tends to bark knees, renders tiny windwings practically useless. *Below:* Nylon headliner stores in hollow basket handle. In non-Crown Victorias, headliner had to be unsnapped and folded for storage elsewhere.

*Owner Bob Page peers through tinted roof of his Crown Victoria to show the softer view riders get than through untinted glass. This photo also reveals speedometer reflected in windshield.*

*Above:* The 182-bhp 272 gives good hillclimbing ability and acceleration. All Fairlane V-8s had twin exhausts, and the Thunderbird 292 became an option late in 1955. **Right:** Bob Page zips in nylon headliner to ward off sun's rays. Despite roof's tint, heat builds up inside this car. The see-through top and see-through speedometer are coincidental, not planned.

51

# 1955 Ford driveReport

FORD MOTOR COMPANY

1953 Lincoln engine and nearly identical to each other, except for bore, valve diameter, and carburetion. The 1954 Ford/Mercury V-8s used precisely the same cast crankshaft, rods, basic cam, valve train, manifolds, and accessories. Many accessories, in fact, such as distributor drive, pumps, gears, etc., interchanged between all FoMoCo V-8s of the mid-1950s.

Were there any major problems in developing this family of engines, I then asked Mr. Raviolo.

"Time. Time because we had to catch up," came the answer. "Instead of having this tremendous organization that had come about in an orderly progression through history, like General Motors, Ford sort of started from scratch, with a clean sheet of paper, and said, 'Bang! We need some engines....' "

It was first under Youngren and then MacPherson that Ford's tremendous engineering surge took place. "We had, for example, an architect's representative, Charles Macchi," continued Raviolo, "who stayed with us for 15-16 years. We started to build *a* building; he never left. Here's a man who spent half of his career working on our job. Now that's how much building we did."

Ford's first ohv V-8 of 1954, like the 1949 Cadillac engine, incorporated several interesting ideas. One was its oversquareness—bore larger than stroke. Although Ford's '54 V-8 arrived with exactly the same 239-cid displacement as the '53 L-head it replaced, bore and stroke were totally different. The oversquareness of the new engine cut friction losses and meant 17% less piston travel plus the space to put in larger valves.

Another feature of Ford's new Y-block V-8 was its deep crankcase skirt. In most V-8s, including GM's, if you draw a line across the bottom of the block, it passes smack through the center of the crankshaft. But in these Lincoln, Ford, and Mercury Y-block engines, the skirt hung down well below the crankshaft axis so that a line drawn from the crank center to the block bottom gave an upside-down vee angle of 120°. Raviolo and others at Ford felt the ohv V-8 benefited mightily by this extra metal, and even at that, the engine had a good weight-to-displacement ratio. The entire V-8 weighed 640 pounds.

Ford's "semi-steel" cast crankshaft came as another innovation. Everyone else in the industry had been forging their cranks. Ford cast them; had been since 1934. Why? Three reasons. First, it was cheaper. Second, Ford had the casting technology down cold—this at a time when no one else in the industry did. Ford's ability went back to the days of Cast-Iron Charlie Sorensen, the master caster and ex-patternmaker. Third, casting allowed eight instead of six counterweights on the crank—the extra two at the center main where forged cranks can't have them for production reasons. Like other modern ohv V-8s, Ford's used five mains, but with the two extra counterweights, stress was

*Above: Ford's experimental Mystere showcar influenced 1955 passenger-car styling with its Fairlane side molding and basket-handle roof. The Mystere also had a glass roof, as did several FoMoCo showsters of that period. Below left: Page's Skyliner registers 115,506 miles. Below right: The 1977 Lincolns offer a moon roof option made of tinted, reflective glass. It's as wide as the 1954-56 Skyliners' and includes an interior, sliding plastic sun screen.*

*Ford's new-for-1954 ohv V-8 began life with 239 cid, grew to 312 by 1956, shared all but dimensions with Mercury. Iron skirts located below crank earned this engine its Y-block epithet.*

reduced, balance improved, and the Y-blocks were smoother throughout the rpm range.

Allen E. Cleveland had responsibility for combustion-chamber shape, heads, valves, and manifolding. The 1954 V-8 arrived with a 7.2:1 compression ratio, but built into it was the capacity to go to 12:1 c.r. or even higher. Kettering's work at GM Research indicated that compression ratios would go that high in the near future—a theory ironically shot down around 1956 by one of Kettering's subordinates, Darl F. Caris.

Cleveland also pioneered the siamesed over-and-under intake manifold, which set passages one above the other instead of side by side. Advantages here included more equal passage lengths and better distribution of wet fuel during warmup.

FORD'S other great engineering coup of that era was its new balljoint suspension, again shared with Mercury for 1954.

Lincoln, of course, pioneered balljoints in 1952.

The man who put them across was Earle S. MacPherson himself, an engineer whose major subject area was front suspensions. "MacPherson—what a guy!" remarked Raviolo. "Do you realize that today half the world's production automobiles are running around on MacPherson-strut suspension systems?" True—everything from Rabbits to Moskvitches use them—it's *the* front end under modern small cars.

As for balljoints, *all* current American passenger cars now have them, and while MacPherson didn't personally nor solely develop the 1952 Lincoln's, he saw the tremendous advantages of balljoints earlier than most. He needed them to make MacPherson-struts work, and it was he who showed the industry the practicality and economy of basic balljoints for larger cars, too.

Not that balljoints came as anything new. Lanchester patented a design in 1900,

52

# specifications

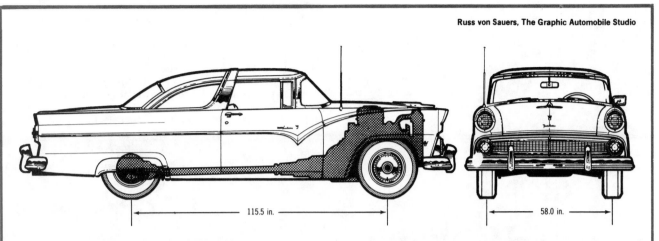

← 115.5 in. →   ← 58.0 in. →

## 1955 Ford Fairlane Crown Victoria Skyliner

Price when new . . . . . . $2372 f.o.b. Dearborn (1955).

Options . . . . . . . . . . . Radio, heater, Fordomatic, power steering and windows, 4-way power seat, high-performance engine package.

**ENGINE**
Type . . . . . . . . . . . . . . Ohv V-8, water cooled, cast-iron block, 5 mains, full pressure lubrication.
Bore & stroke . . . . . . . . 3.625 x 3.300 in.
Displacement . . . . . . . . 272.0 cid.
Max. bhp @ rpm . . . . . . 182 @ 4400.
Max. torque @ rpm . . . . 268 @ 2200.
Compression ratio . . . . . 8.5:1.
Induction system . . . . . . 4-bbl. downdraft carburetor, mechanical fuel pump.
Exhaust system . . . . . . . Cast-iron manifolds, twin mufflers.
Electrical system . . . . . . 6-volt battery/coil.

**CLUTCH**
Type . . . . . . . . . . . . . . None.

**TRANSMISSION**
Type . . . . . . . . . . . . . . Fordomatic 3-speed automatic with 3-element torque converter, planetary gears.
Ratios:  1st . . . . . . . . 2.40:1.
2nd . . . . . . . . 1.47:1.
3rd . . . . . . . . 1.00:1.
Reverse . . . . . 2.00:1.

**DIFFERENTIAL**
Type . . . . . . . . . . . . . . Hypoid, spiral-bevel gears.
Ratio . . . . . . . . . . . . . . 3.31:1.
Drive axles . . . . . . . . . . Semi-floating.

**STEERING**
Type . . . . . . . . . . . . . . Power-assisted worm & roller.
Turns lock to lock . . . . 4.5.
Ratio . . . . . . . . . . . . . . 25.3:1.
Turn circle . . . . . . . . . . 41.1 ft.

**BRAKES**
Type . . . . . . . . . . . . . . 4-wheel hydraulic drums, internal expanding, vacuum assist.
Drum diameter . . . . . . . 11.0 in.
Total lining area . . . . . . 192 sq. in.

**CHASSIS & BODY**
Frame . . . . . . . . . . . . . . Box-section steel, central X-member, 5 crossmembers.
Body construction . . . . . All steel.
Body style . . . . . . . . . . 2-door, 6-passenger coupe with Plexiglas roof section and "tiara" B-pillar.

**SUSPENSION**
Front . . . . . . . . . . . . . . Independent A-arms, balljointed spindles, coil springs, tubular hydraulic shocks, anti-roll bar.
Rear . . . . . . . . . . . . . . . Solid axle, longitudinal leaf springs, tubular hydraulic shocks.
Tires . . . . . . . . . . . . . . 7.10x15 tubeless whitewall.
Wheels . . . . . . . . . . . . . Pressed steel discs, drop-center rims, lug-bolted to brake drums.

**WEIGHTS & MEASURES**
Wheelbase . . . . . . . . . . 115.5 in.
Overall length . . . . . . . . 198.5 in.
Overall height . . . . . . . . 58.2 in.
Overall width . . . . . . . . 75.875 in.
Front tread . . . . . . . . . . 58.0 in.
Rear tread . . . . . . . . . . 56.0 in.
Ground clearance . . . . . . 6.6 in.
Curb weight . . . . . . . . . 3431 lb.

**CAPACITIES**
Crankcase . . . . . . . . . . . 4 qt.
Cooling system . . . . . . . 21 qt.
Fuel tank . . . . . . . . . . . 17 gal.

**FUEL CONSUMPTION**
Best . . . . . . . . . . . . . . . 18.4 mpg.
Average . . . . . . . . . . . . 13.4 mpg.

**PERFORMANCE**
(from Motor Trend trest of 1955 Customline 162-bhp V-8 4-door sedan with Fordomatic):
0-30 mph . . . . . . . . . . . 4.5 sec.
0-40 mph . . . . . . . . . . . 7.6 sec.
0-50 mph . . . . . . . . . . . 11.3 sec.
0-60 mph . . . . . . . . . . . 14.5 sec.
0-70 mph . . . . . . . . . . . 18.2 sec.
0-80 mph . . . . . . . . . . . 26.7 sec.
Standing ¼ mile . . . . . . 19.4 sec. & 74.0 mph.
Top speed (av.) . . . . . . . 95.2 mph.

and Citroen, Daimler-Benz, and Rohr all used variations during the 1930s. But before Ford and an independent supplier, Thompson Products, Inc., began to experiment with balljoints after the war, the European systems remained too expensive and gave too stiff a steering feel for American cars and drivers.

Thompson's first experiments in 1946 used a cobbled Buick and soon advanced to a cobbled Mercury. Neither car showed much promise at first. But with encouragement from Harold Youngren and later from MacPherson, Ford and Thompson Products worked out the manufacturing and performance kinks and, in 1952, introduced this country's first successful balljoint front suspension under the 1952 Lincoln.

Industry skeptics, including some at Ford, predicted that Lincoln would go back to kingpins within the year. Balljoints, they said, might carry light little European cars, but they'd break like

kindling under something as heavy as a Lincoln.

No such thing, of course, and the new system soon proved itself in competition events from Pikes Peak to Mexico. Balljoints, in fact, held out a great number of advantages over kingpins, including lower cost, lighter weight, easier manufacturing and assembly, better ride and handling, anti-dive braking, longer wear, lighter steering, sharper turning, more engine space, fewer lube points (from 16 to four in the case of the 1953 vs. 1954 Fords), and much easier serviceability. Balljoint replacement took half the time of kingpins.

As an aside—*before* 1952, all U.S. cars used kingpin front suspensions. These got to be so much alike that—so goes the story—Murray Fahnestock offered money to 200 engineers if any one of them could identify (from pictures) even half the front suspensions in use in the early 1950s. No one could. Today no U.S. car uses kingpins, and it's doubtful once again

whether engineers could distinguish today between the various balljoint setups.

THE FAIRLANE SERIES, the Crown Victoria, wraparound windshields, factory air conditioning, seatbelts—these were some of the cake icings Ford introduced for 1955.

The 1955s used a slightly modified frame, with the center section 1.7 inches lower than before. The body, too, was considerably revamped, although basically it retained the same shell from 1952 through 1956. A couple of roof treatments were changed for 1955.

The 1955 V-8 was increased from 239 to 272 cid, this jump in size coming as a direct result of the horsepower race. Comments Allen Cleveland: "As I recall, the first redesign of this engine was intended to go from 239 to 254 inches. We had everything sized and set for 254, but then when Chevrolet came out with its 265 V-8 for

## 1955 Ford driveReport

1955, we went to 272. That was a last-minute flurry, and it caused everybody considerable headaches."

Ford very much wanted to stay on top of the horsepower race—to retain V-8 supremacy. So when the Chevy 265 announced 160-bhp in late 1954, Ford announced 162 (Chevrolet later revised its rating to 162). When Chevy made the power pack available at 180 bhp, Ford popped with a 182-bhp power pack. Then when Chevrolet introduced the 283, Ford made the Thunderbird 292 V-8 a Ford passenger car option.

The Y-block V-8, which began life at a modest 239 cid, eventually blossomed out in 1956 to 312 cubes and, by 1957, could be ordered with such factory hop-up options as twin 4-barrel carburetors or the Paxton-McCulloch supercharger.

FOR this driveReport, we were fortunate enough to capture Bob Page's 1955 Skyliner during its short stay near our editorial offices in Stockton, Calif. I say "short" because Bob had bought the car in Texas about a month before he sold it to a fellow in Canada. And I say "fortunate" because we'd been looking for a clean, stock bubbletopper for over four years, tracking many a lead and rejecting several candidates.

For a car with 115,506 miles on its clock, this one is amazingly tight. The first thing that struck me upon slipping behind the wheel was the see-through speedometer. It's one of those undeniable focal points that catches and holds the eye. The thought suddenly struck me: "Aha! Here's a detail follow-through with the Plexiglas roof—see-through speedometer, see-through top." But when I mentioned this observation to several of the 1955 Ford's stylists (thinking myself so clever), they all said no—it's pure coincidence.

The speedometer proved a bit too eye-catching, because it reflects badly in the wraparound windshield. I hear it's even worse in 1954 Fords and 1955 T-Birds. Ford ads called this speedo "Astra-dial."

The Skyliner's Plexiglas roof gives a great feeling of freedom and spaciousness. It's like an open convertible in that respect, but without the wind and noise. Heat does build up inside the car. This was an overcast day, and even then we finally zippered shut the roof curtain. Air conditioning seems a natural with this body style.

The 182-bhp V-8 gives good performance despite some slippage in the Fordomatic. Ride feels smooth, and the car handles with ease and grace, even without power steering. The 1955's brakes were an inch larger in diameter than the '54's, and they give good stopping power.

There's some distortion through the curved windshield sides, and the Crown Victoria basket handle seems to obstruct more view than it actually does (all that chrome makes it look bigger than it is). Those are minor criticisms but the major ones we could find.

It's a fine car in every way—a worthy big brother of the Thunderbird. And with the T-Bird's looks, its own snappy performance, its distinctive roof, and that touch of luxury that comes from having all those power accessories, here's a car that's logically becoming highly prized by collectors. □

*Our thanks to Bob Page, Stockton, Calif.; Michael W.R. Davis, Charlotte Slater, L. David Ash, and Tom Page of the Ford Motor Co., Dearborn, Mich.; Victor G. Raviolo, Grosse Pointe, Mich.; Allen E. Cleveland, Ann Arbor, Mich.; John Reed and Bob Gardner of Rohm & Haas, Philadelphia, Pa.; Franklin Q. Hershey, Manhattan Beach, Calif.; Robert H. Maguire, Milford, Conn.; Hans Matthias, West Bloomfield, Mich.; Alex L. Haynes, Stuart, Fla.; V.J. Jandasek, Dearborn, Mich.; James J. Bradley, National Automotive History Collection, Detroit Public Library, Detroit; Larry Blodget, Fabulous Fifties Ford Club, Box 2012, Winnetka, Calif. 91306; Clarence F. Kramer, Birmingham, Mich.; Robert Stevenson, Ft. Lauderdale, Fla.; and John Payton of the National Crown Victoria Assn., 2807 N. High St., Muncie, Ind. 47302.*

# Little Bird Meets Big Bird

driveReport

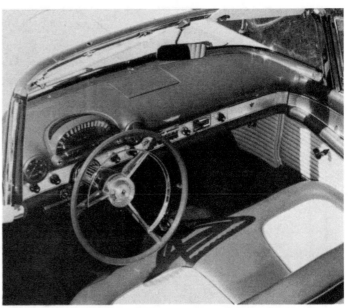

*1958-60 Thunderbird keeps its "personal" touch by compartmentalizing each passenger, was one of the first U.S. cars with buckets and con-* *sole. Little Bird (right) uses passenger-car speedometer housing but 150-mph speedo. Steering column length can be adjusted with sleeve.*

# Ford had half a mind to kill the Thunderbird altogether, but then in mid-1955 word came down to go ahead with a 4-seater

THE LAST 2-SEATER now belongs, ironically, to the son of the man who designed the 1949 Ford. Holden (Bob) Koto styled the '49 Ford, and his son David owns the final 1957 Bird. It came off the Dearborn line on Dec. 13, 1957.

TIME Magazine recorded that transition with these words: "As a black Thunderbird rolled off the Ford plant assembly line, a worker affectionately scrawled in soap on its hood, 'Bye, bye, baby.' It signaled the end of the 2-seater Thunderbird. This week [Jan. 6, 1958], Ford put out the car's 1958 successor, the ballyhooed 4-seater."

Bill Boyer, who'd been one of the 2-seater's stylists and who, in 1955, became head of the newly created Thunderbird design studio, recalls the Big Bird's hatching: "The Little Bird had sold just about on projection—an average of about 16,000 cars a year—and on the basis of that volume, it wasn't really a very profitable car. Whether to continue with the Bird was a big question.

"At that time, the Corvette wasn't going much of anyplace. The general consensus was, 'Gee, the Thunderbird's such a great little car, but I wish I could get the kids in back.' That kind of sentiment was current, and that's really what gave impetus to the 4-seater Bird.

"There was a purist group within the company who wanted to continue the 2-passenger Bird, and there was a faction that said, 'No, this is a business venture and we're not doing cars for you purists.' So we were asked to do the 4-passenger Bird, beginning around the end of 1955."

The original Thunderbird's father, if such a title can be given, has to be Lewis D. Crusoe who, in the early 1950s, was a Ford executive vice president and general manager of Ford Div. It's not fair to say that he alone came up with the Thunderbird idea, but it was Crusoe who pushed it through once he believed it would do the company some good.

Crusoe and George Walker [see 1949 Ford driveReport, *SIA #5*] had been browsing around the Paris salon in Oct. 1951, looking over the latest European sports jobs. Being aware of a wave of sports car and hot rod fe-

## Thunderbird Puzzlements

What makes the Little Bird (1955-57) today's darling and the Big Bird (1958-60) today's wallflower? New, the 4-seater outsold the 2-seater by margins of 3:1 to 5:1. It started the whole trend to luxury/personal cars, a class that now includes Riviera, Toronado, Continental Mark IV, Eldorado, Grand Prix, and Monte Carlo as well as the present Thunderbird.

Today there's great demand for the Little Bird and relatively little for the 1958-60 4-place. Why this switch? Why the mania to seek out and restore every remaining 2-seater while the 4-seater hardly turns a head? Does the reversal in popularity tell us something about initial sales volume not being the true measure of a car's success? And what caused this reversal? Is it the difference in the cars themselves? Or a difference in us? Or a difference in the times? We haven't come up with satisfactory answers. Perhaps you can. □

*Four-place Thunderbird was originally programmed for retractable hardtop. 1960 convert uses mechanism similar to Ford Skyliners. 1958-60 ragtops' trunklids had to be raised manually.*

## Thunderbird Engines & Power Teams

| Year | Displ. | Bhp @ rpm | Torque @ rpm | Carb. | C.R. | Trans. |
|------|--------|-----------|--------------|-------|------|--------|
| 1955 | 292 | 193 @ 4400 | 280 @ 2600 | 4-V | 8.1 | 3-spd. & o.d. |
|      | 292 | 198 @ 4400 | 286 @ 2500 | 4-V | 8.5 | F-O-M |
| 1956 | 292 | 202 @ 2600 | 289 @ 2600 | 4-V | 8.4 | 3-spd. |
|      | 312 | 215 @ 4600 | 317 @ 2600 | 4-V | 8.4 | o.d. |
|      | 312 | 225 @ 4600 | 324 @ 2600 | 4-V | 9.0 | F-O-M |
|      | 312 | 260 @ 4600 | 324 @ 2600 | 2 4-V | 9.0 | F-O-M |
| 1957 | 292 | 212 @ 4500 | 297 @ 2700 | 2-V | 9.1 | 3-spd. |
|      | 312 | 245 @ 4500 | 332 @ 2300 | 4-V | 9.7 | all |
|      | 312 | 270 @ 4800 | 336 @ 3400 | 2 4-V | 9.7 | all |
|      | 312 | 285 @ 5200 | 343 @ 3500 | 2 4-V | 9.7 | all |
|      | 312 | 300 @ 4800 | 345 @ 3600 | 4-V* | 8.3 | all |
| 1958 | 352 | 300 @ 4600 | 395 @ 2800 | 4-V | 10.2 | all |
| 1959 | 352 | 300 @ 4600 | 380 @ 2800 | 4-V | 9.6 | all |
|      | 430 | 350 @ 4800 | 490 @ 3100 | 4-V | 10.1 | C-O-M |
| 1960 | 352 | 300 @ 4600 | 380 @ 2800 | 4-V | 9.6 | all |
|      | 430 | 350 @ 4800 | 490 @ 3100 | 4-V | 10.1 | C-O-M |

* Supercharged.

## Little/Big Bird

ver then sweeping the U.S., Crusoe decided it couldn't hurt Ford to bring out what later came to be called a "personal car"—a cross between a factory sports car, factory hot rod, and factory custom car. It was this observation that eventually put the Thunderbird on wheels.

Unofficially, according to Franklin Quick Hershey, Ford Div. design director at the time, the Bird had been brooding even before Crusoe got behind it. "My guys and I got wind that GM was doing the Corvette," says Hershey, "so I took a fellow named Bill Boyer, and we had a room off the main studio, and we started working on a clay model. It was just Bill and myself, more or less. And I went down without anybody knowing it and talked to one of the chassis engineers. I don't remember his name, but he got so excited about it that *he* decided to work on the chassis without anybody knowing it. He laid out the chassis for us, gave us the dimensions and so on.

MOTOR TREND

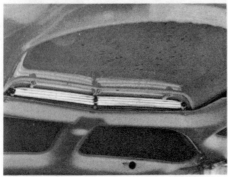

In 1960, T-Bird became one of first U.S. cars with sunroof, sold 2536 sliding tops that year.

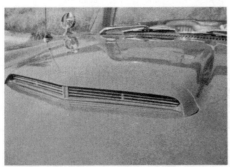

PETERSEN PUBL. CO.

Looking out from inside, we see that Big Bird's hood scoop drew in air, also lent room for carb.

1960's console hides big trans hump, holds ashtrays, speaker, switches, temperature controls.

Tachometer is standard in Early Birds, but dash uses warning telltales for oil and temperature.

For $140 extra, '56 Bird got power windows and seat. Electric seat had been standard in 1955.

TOM CASE

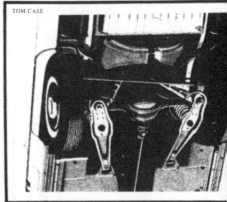

1958 Bird's rear coils caused wheel hop, so for 1959, system was re-engineered back to leaves.

Ford speedometers were originally supposed to be freestanding on dash, later became enclosed.

"Well, in the meantime, my boss, who was E.S. MacPherson of the MacPherson-strut front suspension—he came in and found out, and he was hopping mad, not because we'd started this project but because we hadn't told him anything about it. Things looked bad, and no one thought we were going to do anything more with this car until Chase Morsey [head of Ford corporate product planning] came to bat for us, and he thought it was a great idea. So when George Walker called up from Europe, we had the model already under way long before anybody found out about it. Regardless of what anybody tells you, that's what happened."

Hershey's last sentence is significant, because other versions of the 2-seater's birth abound. Tom Case, Ford's first Thunderbird product planning manager and a man who very carefully noted both the 2- and 4-seater's development, remembers, "Bob Maquire [Ford passenger car studio head under Hershey], in my opinion, was the man who did the greatest amount of styling that stuck on the Little Bird."

Likewise, Tom Page, presently president of Philco-Ford in Philadelphia and at that time

one of about five key product planners at Ford Motor Co. (his title was assistant car planning manager), recalls, "I remember seeing Bob Maquire sketch out the first lines for the 2-seater on a blackboard during the presentation, and those lines were very close to what the car finally became." Damon Wood is another Ford designer who gets much credit for the Little Bird.

Work on the 2-seater started as a Ford Div. side project, beginning officially on Feb. 9, 1953. The first production Thunderbird appeared in the fall of 1954, and then in Oct. 1954, Lew Crusoe asked that an investigation be begun on the feasibility of a 4-seater Bird. This was coded Project 195H, and paperwork on the 195H got under way on Mar. 9, 1955.

Ford couldn't decide at first, though, whether to drop the Thunderbird altogether or whether to go full-steam ahead with the 195H 4-seater. The Little Bird wasn't making money, yet is was outselling the Corvette 6:1, and it had that day's other domestic sportsters (Nash-Healey, Kaiser-Darrin, etc.) beat all hollow. But even the T-Bird's value as an imagemaker was open to question. Finally, in Apr. 1955, Ford decided to set up a separate,

detached Thunderbird department within Ford Div. to work on future planning, design, and T-Bird engineering. The Thunderbird department's first assignment was to revamp and update the 1956 and 1957 models, and this design work was done under Rhys Miller.

Tom Case, who'd been a Ford product planner, became the primary overseer of subsequent Thunderbird development. He acted as liaison between Bill Boyer, the new head of the Thunderbird design studio; John Hollowell, chief Thunderbird engineer; and Ford Motor Co. management. A few months after setting up the separate Thunderbird department, the decision came down to go ahead with a 4-seater—Project 195H.

Tom Case recalls, "The 2-seater program was set up originally by Mr. Crusoe to be a promotion—to improve the prestige of the Ford passenger car lines—performance and sporty image. And if we broke even, that would meet our objectives. So the Little Bird wasn't meant to be a profit car as such. But the 4-seater was.

"When I became Thunderbird planning manager, I got approval from the company to make a separate organization of Thunder-

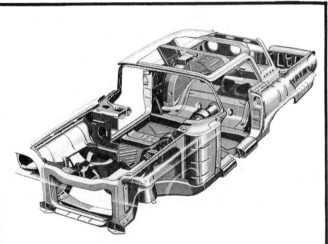

*Budd built bodies for both 2- and 4-seater Birds. The 1958-60's was unitized and was assembled along with Lincolns at Ford's Wixom plant.*

*Big Bird's smooth ride sacrifices cornering. Little Bird puts the windshield in wheelbase center, seats riders just ahead of rear axle.*

TOM CASE

*2-seater's seat slides forward as back is tilted. Top hides behind trim panel. Square ahead of bumper outlet drops water, prevents rusting.*

*4-seater offered continental kit as dealer-installed extra. All 1956s had them. They tipped back for gas/trunk access, almost always dented.*

FORD MOTOR CO.

*Transitional sketches (top) show 1958 2-seater with formal roof and podded tail lights. Roof design stuck (lower left), and if you look*

*closely, you'll see breaks in retrac top. Photo on lower right shows initial styling clay with 1955 wheel covers and on 108-in. wheelbase.*

---

### THE 2-SEATER WAS MISSED

The 2-place Thunderbird was an unusual car in that it hit its purpose right on the head. It was what it was supposed to be. Thus immediately after dropping the Little Bird, Ford Motor Co. began having second thoughts. Dealers kept asking for it back. So did customers.

Ford took a sideways step toward the 2-seater when they put out the makeshift 1962-63 Roadster. This was a 4-place Thunderbird convertible with wire wheels and a removable fiberglass rear-seat cover cum built-in headrests. Ford made 1427 for 1962 and 455 for 1963.

Then, when Ford began planning the Mustang in the early 1960s, Lee Iacocca suggested trying to put the Little Bird's *flavor* into it. Budd Co., who still had (and still has) the old 2-seater body dies, went so far as to make up a running protytype of a 4-place "Mustang" using 2-seater Thunderbird body panels. While this didn't go further than a proto, the Mustang did somehow incorporate much of the Little Bird's indefinable flavor. □

---

### T-BIRD PRODUCTION

| Year | Retail Deliveries | Annual Prod'n. |
|------|-------------------|----------------|
| 1954 | 2,784 | --- |
| 1955 | 14,190 | 16,155 |
| 1956 | 16,763 | 15,631 |
| 1957 | 15,173 | 21,380 |
| 1958 | 48,482 | 37,892 |
| 1959 | 72,859 | 67,456 |
| 1960 | 81,555 | 92,843 |

**Note:** Retail deliveries are for calendar years; production figures are for model years. **Source:** Ford Motor Co.

---

## Little/Big Bird

bird engineering and styling. This was in 1955. With that separate activity, we were able to launch a small group of people with a lot of authority. Mr. Crusoe wanted a car with a backseat. The 4-place Bird was the smallest 4-passenger car we could make at that time and still get adequate seating and performance. Like the 2-seater, it was again Mr. Crusoe's car—he pretty much monitored the initial styling and engineering. We would meet once a week and go through the engineering spex, and then Mr. Crusoe always spent one day a week in Styling."

The original 2-seater, since it had been developed in part of the Ford passenger-car engineering and styling studios, looked a lot like the standard 1955-6-7 big Fords. This wasn't coincidental. Crusoe's idea had been to give the regular Ford lines as much Thunderbird rub-off as possible. Ford Engineering had at one time proposed cutting down a standard Ford 2-door sedan to make the Little Bird, and that idea came up again when someone suggested sectioning and revamping a '57 Ford Sunliner convertible to become the 1958 Bird. While those approaches came to nothing, dicta

from top management said that the Little Bird should use as many standard production components as possible. Part of this came from the knowledge that the 2-seater would never make much money. So the Little Bird used the Mercury V-8, Ford wagon running gear, passenger-car tail lights, headlight bezels, speedometer housing, and so on.

On the 4-seater, though, with Market Research projecting 40,000 to 100,000 sales a year, enough budget could be made available to completely redesign and re-engineer the 195H Thunderbird—make it an entirely new and different car.

Back now to Bill Boyer, T-Bird's styling director. "So we were asked to do the 4-passenger Bird, beginning toward the middle of 1955, but we couldn't get any cooperation from Engineering, because it wasn't what they called a validated program at that time. 'Validated' means fully approved by Management. They were still hanging back. Not being validated, Engineering couldn't devote much time, not that they could even if they'd wanted to; not without validation. So we in Styling more or less proceeded with our own 4-seater package development: the wheelbase, overall seating arrangement, the general concept.

"Lew Crusoe had been the man behind the

2-seater, of course, and it was Crusoe, too, who pretty soon insisted that we start working on a 4-place Bird. But I think it was really Bob McNamara [at that time Ford Div. general manager, later to become U.S. Secretary of Defense and now president of the World Bank]—I would really attribute to him the fact that the 1958 Bird was ever born, because, as I said, there was a lot of controversy about the car, whether to drop the Bird altogether, and McNamara really fought for it. He thought it was a good concept. He went in and fought for it and won.

"Then all of a sudden the program did become validated, and Engineering hadn't done any work on it. They were really caught off guard. They came over and got all our drawings, put their little title block on them, so it ended up pretty much the way we modeled it—a styling office concept. Which explains its rather radical nature, I guess. It was a very advanced-looking car for its day: bucket seats, center console, the whole shot. It didn't get made conservative through the long ordeal of engineering feasibility. And ultimately the car was justified. The Little Bird's production topped out at 21,500 for 1957, and it was that high only because they continued the run an extra three months beyond normal—through December. The first year the Big Bird was introduced,

*Glamor kit dresses up Early Bird engine, which came in many versions with either automatic or overdrive transmissions. During 1959-60,*

*Big Bird shared Lincoln's 430-cid V-8 optionally. Note exposed bell housing. Cross-flow radiator had separate tank to help keep hood low.*

*Even with spare out back, there's precious little room in Little Bird's trunk, partly because*

*floor is high to clear tank. Squarebird convertible has plenty of luggage space when top is up,*

*but with it down there's none. Electric screws latch decklid to body sides as in the retractable.*

they delivered 48,500, so from a sales standpoint it was justified."

Initial designs on the Big Bird were done on a 108-inch wheelbase. This, though, soon proved too short for an adult-sized rear seat, so wheelbase went to 113. The 113-inch base also gave a better silhouette.

Engineering, as mentioned, was under John R. Hollowell, who, just before he took over at Thunderbird, had helped develop Ford's retractable hardtop for the Lincoln Continental Mark II [*see SIA #3, p. 5*]. Hollowell reported to Donald N. Frey, Ford car executive engineer. Under Hollowell, as his assistant, was James L. Martin.

Ford, around this time, had become very interested in unitized body construction. The 1958-60 Lincolns and Thunderbirds both used unibodies (but completely different designs). Too, 1958 became a year of major change in engines and running gear for all FoMoCo divisions. This helped account for the Big Bird's being entirely different from the 2-seater, with about the only carried-over piece being the rear brake drums. The 1957 and 1958 rear drums are identical, but nothing else interchanges.

From an engineering standpoint, the Big Bird remains a much more interesting car than

the Little. Its unit body made possible an overall height of 52.5 inches and yet allowed excellent seating and interior dimensions. MOTOR TREND made it its 1958 Car of the Year for that reason. With no frame to fight, the floor could be set low, and doors weren't hampered with a big step sill. Ground clearance was 5.8 inches as against 7.1 for the Little Bird. The only problem was a huge floor tunnel, and Bill Boyer effectively beat that by covering it with a console, mounting the power window buttons, radio speaker, two ashtrays, and heater/air-conditioner controls in it.

By the time of the 4-seater decision, Ford had given up any thought of making the Thunderbird a true sports car. The Little Bird had hit the "personal car" nail directly on the head. It satisfied the buyer's hot-rodding and custom car appetites as fully as his sports car urges. The 2-seater looked like a beautifully sectioned, lowered, shortened big Ford—something an expert customizer might build if he had the taste and know-how. Its engine was hopped, beefed, and dressed up in the best hot rod tradition: a big V-8 in a little (though heavy) car. It had fine acceleration, good top speed, better-than-average handling, plus the unexpected luxuries and gadgets of a prestige car. And it also had some of the compromises of a sports

car. Chevrolet finally decided to go the purist route with the Corvette, but Ford decided to go "luxury/personal" with the Bird.

Two things became unusual and un-Ford-like about the Big Bird: its unit body and its all-coil springing. More unusual than that, a MacPherson-strut front suspension was initially programmed for both the 1958 Lincoln and the '58 Thunderbird. E.S. MacPherson was, at that time, Ford Motor Co. vice president of engineering. He'd been with GM, where he developed the Mac-Pherson strut in the 1940s, and he later followed ex-Olds engineer Harold T. Youngren to Ford's top engineering spot. Nothing came of the MacPherson strut for these big FoMoCo cars, but it was (and is) used in British and German Fords plus plenty of other small cars. Another item that was considered for the '58 Bird was air suspension, but this, too, was discarded.

At any rate, the 1958 Thunderbird did get rear coils, and that was odd enough. These were the first and last rear coils Ford used until 1965, and the '58 coils gave their share of trouble. Under hard acceleration, especially in reverse with standard transmissions, the rear arm system caused wheel hop. To compensate, Ford

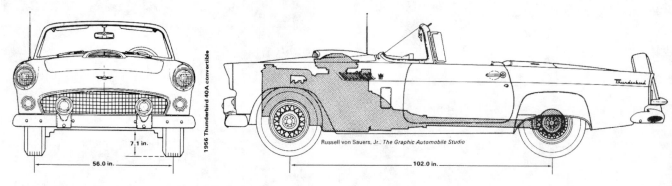

1956 Thunderbird 40A convertible

7.1 in.  56.0 in.

Russell von Sauers, Jr.: The Graphic Automobile Studio  102.0 in.

**Price when new** . . . . . . $3163 f.o.b. Dearborn (1956).

**Current valuation\*** . . . . Xlnt. $4100; gd. $1900; fair $510.

**Options** . . . . . . . . . Radio, heater, power seat, power windows, power steering, automatic transmission.

### ENGINE
Type . . . . . . . . . . . Ohv V-8, cast-iron block, watercooled, 5 mains, full pressure lubrication.
Bore & stroke . . . . . . 3.80 x 3.44 in.
Displacement . . . . . . 312.0 cu. in.
Max. bhp @ rpm . . . 225 @ 4600.
Max. torque @ rpm . . 324 @ 2600.
Compression ratio . . . 9.0:1.
Induction system . . . . 4-barrel downdraft carburetor, mechanical fuel pump.
Exhaust system . . . . . Cast-iron manifolds, crossover pipe, twin exhausts.
Electrical system . . . . 12-volt battery/coil.

### CLUTCH
Type . . . . . . . . . . . None.

### TRANSMISSION
Type . . . . . . . . . . . Fordomatic 3-speed automatic, torque converter, planetary gears.
Ratios: 1st . . . . . . 2.40:1.
2nd . . . . . . 1.46:1.
3rd . . . . . . 1.00:1.
Reverse . . . 2.00:1.

### DIFFERENTIAL
Type . . . . . . . . . . . Hypoid.
Ratio . . . . . . . . . . . 3.31:1.
Drive axles . . . . . . . . Semi-floating.

### STEERING
Type . . . . . . . . . . . Linkage power steering, worm & roller.
Turns lock to lock . . . 3.4.
Ratio . . . . . . . . . . . 23.1:1.
Turn circle . . . . . . . . 36.5 ft.

### BRAKES
Type . . . . . . . . . . . 4-wheel hydraulic drums, internal expanding.
Drum diameter . . . . . 11.0 in.
Total lining area . . . . . 169.66 sq. in.

### CHASSIS & BODY
Frame . . . . . . . . . . . Box-section siderails, central X-member, 4 crossmembers.
Body construction . . . All steel, bolted to frame.
Body style . . . . . . . . 2-dr., 2-pass. conv. cpe., manual top.

### SUSPENSION
Front . . . . . . . . . . . Independent A-arms, coil springs, balljoints, tubular hydraulic shock absorbers, link stabilizer bar.
Rear . . . . . . . . . . . Solid axle, longitudinal leaf springs, hydraulic tubular shock absorbers.
Tires . . . . . . . . . . . 6.70 x 15, 4-ply, tubeless whitewalls.
Wheels . . . . . . . . . Pressed steel discs, drop-center rims, lug-bolted to brake drums.

### WEIGHTS & MEASURES
Wheelbase . . . . . . . . 102.0 in.
Overall length . . . . . . 185.1 in.
Overall height . . . . . . 52.2 in.
Overall width . . . . . . 71.3 in.
Front tread . . . . . . . . 56.0 in.
Rear tread . . . . . . . . 56.0 in.
Ground clearance . . . 7.1 in.
Curb weight . . . . . . . 3570 lb.

### CAPACITIES
Crankcase . . . . . . . . 5.0 qt.
Cooling system . . . . . 21.0 qt.
Fuel tank . . . . . . . . . 17.5 gal.

### FUEL CONSUMPTION
Best . . . . . . . . . . . . . 17.5 mpg.
Average . . . . . . . . . . 14.0 mpg.

### PERFORMANCE (from **Road & Track**):
0-30 mph . . . . . . . . 3.3 sec.
0-45 mph . . . . . . . . 5.0 sec.
0-60 mph . . . . . . . . 9.3 sec.
0-70 mph . . . . . . . . 12.1 sec.
Standing ¼ mile . . . . 17.0 sec. & 85.0 mph.
Top speed . . . . . . . . 112.2 mph.

\* Courtesy **Antique Automobile Appraisal,** Prof. Barry Hertz.

## Little Bird/Big Bird

service engineers added torque reacting links— short arms pivoted at both ends, running forward from the spring pockets to the body. While these links cured wheelhop during acceleration, they *caused* it on washboard roads. John Hollowell comments, "Any friend of mine who bought the 1958 Bird would notice this bounce on washboard roads and say, 'Wow,

is that bad!', and I'd tell him to take off those links, throw them away. They were never needed anyway. Service Engineering insisted on putting them on. But we thought this coil-spring rear suspension was so bad that the 1959-60 models had regular leaf springs, and we got those into production in a big hurry."

Bodies for both the Big and Little Birds were made by the Budd Co. The 2-seater's bodies used to come over from Budd's Charlevoix plant complete except for interiors, trim, and

paint. They were trucked to Ford's main assembly lines in Dearborn, painted along with Ford station wagons, then shunted to a special T-Bird trim and interior line, finally to be assembled on the regular Ford passenger-car line. You'd see perhaps six Ford sedans come off that line, followed by a Bird, then more sedans. Bodies were numbered in sequence with the big cars, which makes body numbers an awful mess for Thunderbird historians.

The Big Bird's unit body, though, used an

# SPECIFICATIONS
## 1960 Thunderbird 76A convertible

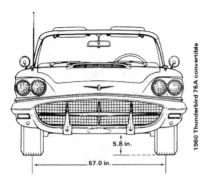

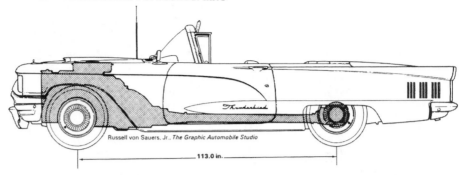

1960 Thunderbird 76A convertible

5.8 in.

57.0 in.

113.0 in.

Russell von Sauers, Jr., *The Graphic Automobile Studio*

**Price when new** . . . . . . $4222 f.o.b. Dearborn (1960).
**Current valuation\*** . . . . Xlnt. $1350; gd. $1020; fair $160.
**Options** . . . . . . . . . . . None.

### ENGINE
Type . . . . . . . . . . . . Ohv V-8, cast-iron block, watercooled, 5 mains, full pressure lubrication.
Bore & stroke . . . . . . 4.30 x 3.70 in.
Displacement . . . . . 430.0 cu. in.
Max. bhp @ rpm . . . . 350 @ 4600.
Max. torque @ rpm . . 490 @ 2800.
Compression ratio . . . 10.0:1.
Induction system . . . . 4-barrel downdraft carburetor, mechanical fuel pump.
Exhaust system . . . . . Cast-iron manifolds, crossover pipe, twin exhausts.
Electrical system . . . . 12-volt battery/coil.

### CLUTCH
Type . . . . . . . . . . . . None.

### TRANSMISSION
Type . . . . . . . . . . . . Cruise-O-Matic 3-speed automatic, torque converter, planetary gears.
Ratios: 1st . . . . . 2.37:1.
2nd . . . . . 1.84:1.
3rd . . . . . 1.00:1.
Reverse . . . 1.84:1.

### DIFFERENTIAL
Type . . . . . . . . . . . Hypoid.
Ratio . . . . . . . . . . . 2.91:1.
Drive axles . . . . . . . . Semi-floating.

### STEERING
Type . . . . . . . . . . . Linkage power steering, recirculating ball & nut.
Turns lock to lock . . . . 4.1.
Ratio . . . . . . . . 25.0:1.
Turn circle . . . . . . . . 42.7 ft.

### BRAKES
Type . . . . . . . . . . . 4-wheel hydraulic drums, internal expanding.
Drum diameter . . . . . 11.0 in.
Total lining area . . . . 175.32 sq. in.

### CHASSIS & BODY
Frame . . . . . . . . . . Fully welded unit body/chassis.
Body construction . . . All steel.
Body style . . . . . . . 2-dr., 4-pass. conv. cpe., hydraulic disappearing top.

### SUSPENSION
Front . . . . . . . . . . . Independent A-arms, balljoints, coil springs, hydraulic tubular shock absorbers, link stabilizer bar.
Rear . . . . . . . . . . . Solid axle, longitudinal leaf springs, tubular hydraulic shock absorbers.
Tires . . . . . . . . . . . 8.00 x 14, 4-ply tubeless whitewalls.
Wheels . . . . . . . . . Pressed steel discs, drop-center rims, lug-bolted to brake drums.

### WEIGHTS & MEASURES
Wheelbase . . . . . . . . 113.0 in.
Overall length . . . . . 205.3 in.
Overall height . . . . . 53.0 in.
Overall width . . . . . . 77.0 in.
Front tread . . . . . . . 60.0 in.
Rear tread . . . . . . . 57.0 in.
Ground clearance . . . . 5.8 in.
Curb weight . . . . . . . 3897 lb.

### CAPACITIES
Crankcase . . . . . . . . 5.0 qt.
Cooling system . . . . . 23.5 qt.
Fuel tank . . . . . . . . . 20.0 gal.

### FUEL CONSUMPTION
Best . . . . . . . . . . . . 14.0 mpg.
Average . . . . . . . . . 10.4 mpg.

### PERFORMANCE (from **Road & Track**):
0-30 mph . . . . . . . . 2.9 sec.
0-45 mph . . . . . . . . 4.7 sec.
0-60 mph . . . . . . . . 8.2 sec.
0-70 mph . . . . . . . . 11.8 sec.
Standing ¼ mile . . . . 16.2 sec. & 84 mph.
Top speed . . . . . . . . 120.0 mph.

\* Courtesy **Antique Automobile Appraisal,** Prof. Barry Hertz.

---

entirely different system of assembly and, in fact, it was the assembly method that partly caused Ford's decision to go unitized. Tom Case explains. "When we went to the 4-passenger Bird, it was designed concurrently, really, with the opening of our Wixom assembly plant. Wixom is where we build the Thunderbird and Mark IV Continentals today. But at that time, the Big Bird was keyed into the fact that we were also building unit-bodied Lincolns there. Budd made the 4-seater main section plus hoods, fenders, and so forth, and shipped these to Wixom by railcar. So the 4-passenger Bird became part of the Wixom assembly plant complex in the sense that the same people were buying and scheduling the Big Bird as the Lincoln. This became another reason why it was easier to put the 4-seater in the new plant and build around it—also why they stuck the Lincoln's 430-cid V-8 into the 4-seater. Unit-bodied Lincolns and Thunderbirds were all assembled on the same lines at Wixom."

Not that it was easy to get the 4-seater's unit body ready for production. John Hollowell recalls taking early mechanical prototypes (prototypes whose dimensions and structural components tried to duplicate production cars but whose bodies didn't look anything like the final design) down to Ford's desert proving grounds near Kingman, Ariz. This was in 1956 and 1957. The idea was to try to see how well the unit-body mechanical prototypes would

## Little Bird/Big Bird

hold up, and to do that, they tried to destroy them in the shortest possible time.

The Kingman desert test course was 4.6 miles long, with 2.8 miles of chuckholes and ruts plus 1.8 miles of washboard. The washboard consisted of furrows plowed both straight across and diagonally into the road—a cement-hard unpaved surface. Minimum acceptable test standard was set at 1500 miles at 30 mph over the chuckholes, 23 mph over the washboard, with 3.1 miles of running (per circuit) on a smooth airstrip to give the shocks a chance to cool. Even at that, shocks were changed every 120 miles.

The first mechanical prototype broke down after only 82 miles. It pulled loose three spot welds on the front siderail near the front cross-member. Rewelded, the tests and repairs continued. A number of other welds let go between 300 and 1000 miles.

Meanwhile, the body engineers were also

measuring sag. The prototype was driven onto a level plate, and marks along each side of the body were measured. After a few hundred miles, the first mechanical prototype sagged a little over two inches in the rear, according to Hollowell, indicating some buckling of sheetmetal over the rear axle.

As reference cars to check against, Ford also ran a 1957 Thunderbird and a 1956 Hudson (Nash) over the course. The Little Bird ran the full 1500 miles with no body-panel buckling and no structural failure. Rear-end sag amounted to only 0.6 inches. The 1956 Hudson, chosen simply because it was an acceptable unibody design under normal conditions, ran only 1100 miles. At that point, the Ford engineers felt it was too badly beaten up to continue.

Ford and Budd body engineers added extra welds and gussets to the 4-seater prototypes as failures occurred. The front spring pockets and outer side metal gauge were beefed and arc welded. A 0.125-inch-thick plate was added to the underside of the rear trailing arm bracket, and the inner and outer parts of the track bar brackets were redesigned. A tie plate was added from the inner siderail to the upper suspension arm bracket, etc., etc. All these changes were made long before Ford released the body for tooling and before Budd built a true prototype with 1958 styling.

The final true prototype ran the prescribed 1500 miles with no mechanical failures, no buckling, and only 0.3 inches of sag at the rear. An SAE paper describing these tests concluded, "The torsional rigidity of the 1958 Thunderbird over the wheelbase is 56% higher than the 1956 Thunderbird, and torsional front wheel center-line-to-dash is 31% greater. In maximum bending, the 1958 Thunderbird is 11% stiffer than its predecessor."

As mentioned, Ford V-8s for 1958 were entirely new. They came in two basic engine series, each with three different displacements.

The small series (332, 352, 361) was used in 1958 Fords, some Edsels, Thunderbirds, and Ford trucks. The larger series (383, 410, 430) went into the Mercury Monterey and Montclair, Edsel Corsair and Citation; and Mercury Park Lane and Lincolns respectively. For 1959 and 1960, the 430 became available in Thunderbirds with automatic transmissions.

**W**e drove a 1956 Bird belonging to James V. Gray, M.D., of Sacramento, Calif. And a 1960 convertible belonging to Ed Brown, a real estate broker from Loomis, Calif. Both cars had been restored, the '56 to showroom condition by Andrews Antique and Classic Restoration Center of Sacramento, and the '60 by Jack Whittle, a private restorer

and T-Bird enthusiast also from Sacramento.

Dr. Gray's 2-seater had belonged to Bob Estes, who'd stored it for five years, meaning to restore it. Dr. Gray bought the car in Dec. 1969 and drove it as-was until June 1971, when he decided to put "little things" to rights. Once started, little things led to bigger things, and next thing he knew, he had Phil Andrews restoring it from the ground up. "We took it all apart to every bolt and nut," says Phil, "replaced all rubber, tore down the engine, trans, rear end, and replaced everything that showed any wear at all. We now have about 1200 hours in this restoration."

Ed Brown bought his Squarebird, ". . . because I've always wanted a red convertible." Jack Whittle, who restored it, found the car abandoned near McClellan Air Force Base in Sacramento. This was in Jan. 1971. Nothing worked, especially the power accessories. Jack spent one full year putting it all together, rebuilding the engine, trans, and almost all power servos, including the complicated electronics of the trunk and top mechanism.

Since the Little Bird and the Big Bird are such completely different animals, it came as no surprise that they behaved and felt different. The 2-seater handles very well, even with the heavy spare on back. Gassed and with two aboard, weight distribution is 47/53. It's stable, a bit stiff, and while we didn't corner it too hard, it goes just where it's pointed. Ride, though, tends to be jouncy. This particular car didn't rattle, but most Little Birds we've driven do—it's the rattling kind of car.

The Big Bird also didn't rattle. Its unit body still feels very tight. And its ride is extremely smooth. This comes at the expense of handling, which tends to be wallowy and imprecise. The big 430-inch V-8 gives impressive acceleration and contributes to gross understeer. Yet considering that the 4-seater has over 100 more cubic inches and only 850 more pounds, its acceleration edge isn't all that great.

Both Birds show compromises. The 2-seater's trunk is tiny even with the spare out back, and to get at the gas filler you *have* to scratch or dent the tire cover by tilting it rearward. (Ford, by the way, offered an optional and very similar continental kit for the 4-seater.) The 1960 4-place convertible has no trunk at all with the top down and, like the retractable Ford, there's too much to go wrong. The 1958-59 convertible had a less complicated top lift.

Which would we rather have? Yes—the Little Bird. But that's not to say we wouldn't like the Big Bird, too. It's a misunderstood and maligned car that we feel certainly has its own distinctive charm. For one thing, it's now becoming rarer than the Classic Thunderbird, especially a convertible in good condition. And if you've got a family, as we do, the 4-place remains the way to go. The cult of the Big Bird is growing, and we can see why. □

*Our thanks to James V. Gray, M.D., Phil Andrews, and Jack Whittle, all of Sacramento, Calif.; Ed Brown, Loomis, Calif.; Tom Case, Bill Harris, Bill Boyer, Lou Lataif, Woody Haines, and Mike Davis of Ford Motor Co., Dearborn; John R. Hollowell, Dearborn, Mich.; Tom Page, Philco-Ford, Philadelphia; Frank Hershey, Manhattan Beach, Calif.; Roger Neiss, Jim Petrik, Rick Reichardt, and other members of the Classic Thunderbird Club International (1955-57), 48 Second St., San Francisco, CA 94105; and Larry Seyfarth, Vintage Thunderbird Club of America (1958-60), 26056 Deerfield, Dearborn Hgts, MI 48127.*

# SIA comparisonReport

**by Arch Brown**
**photos by Vince Manocchi**

A FTER a record-shattering season like 1955, it was predictable, even inevitable, that the automobile industry would experience something of a slump the following year. And so it did. Only Lincoln showed a gain in sales, on the strength of a dramatically restyled new model (see *SIA #60*). A downward curve appeared on the production charts of every other manufacturer.

Especially hard hit were the medium-priced marques. Chrysler, for instance, was off by 45.8 percent, Mercury by 43.3 percent. Even high-flying Buick, the industry's number three seller in those days, experienced a drop of 31.5 percent.

It's easy enough to see what had happened. In almost every respect — size, power, styling, comfort — the gap between cars of the low-priced field and their more expensive corporate siblings had narrowed. It simply wasn't easy any longer to justify laying out the extra money for a Buick over a Chevrolet or a Mercury over a Ford. The result was that, while the less expensive cars took some lumps, they fared a good deal better than the more costly models. Ford sales, for instance, were down by a comparatively modest 22.2 percent, while Chevrolet's dropped by only 11.4 percent. What we were seeing — though even most industry analysts apparently failed to understand it at the time — was a major, long-term shift in the market!

And yet, for all of their merits and despite their historic significance, the 1956 models from Chevrolet and Ford

## The Leaders,

are sometimes overlooked, or at least underrated, by today's collectors. Both, of course, represent face-lifted versions of the previous year's cars. But both merit more attention than they've ever received; and that's what this comparisonReport is all about.

It seems appropriate that Ford, which in 1932 had introduced V-8 power to the low-priced field (see *SIA #21*), should have been the first to bring to its price range a truly modern V-8 engine, that is, a powerplant of short-stroke, overhead-valve design. This was the "Y-block," first featured in 1954. A heavy, sturdily constructed piece of machinery, it displaced — initially — 239 cubic inches, same as the long-stroke flathead whose place it took. Horsepower, however, was advertised at 130, up from 110 in the 1953 L-head version.

And of course there was more to come. Both bore and stroke were increased for 1955, stretching the displacement to 272 cubic inches and standard horsepower to 162. An optional V-8, bored to 292 cubes, was available, rated at 193 horsepower — 198 as coupled to the Ford-O-Matic transmission.

Bear in mind that the "horsepower race," fueled by the rivalry between Chrysler and Cadillac, was in full cry at the time. 1955, for instance, saw the introduction of the first of Chrysler's great "Letter" cars, developing a record 300 horsepower (see *SIA #51*). And in 1956 the Chrysler 300-B became the first American production car to develop one horsepower for every cubic inch of displacement!

Ford had also, by the way, introduced the first of the short-stroke, overhead-valve sixes. Originally offered for the 1952 season, it was rated then at 101 horsepower — which was probably a deliberate understatement on the company's part, in the interest of maintaining, at least on paper, the V-8's advantage. By 1956, bored to 223 cubic inches (up from 215, originally), the six-cylinder engine produced 137 horsepower at 4,200 rpm.

Originally published in Special Interest Autos #98, Mar.-Apr. 1987

# 1956 Chevrolet vs. Ford

# Head-to-Head

The big seller, however, was the V-8. For 1956 the 272-c.i.d. version was rated at 173 horsepower, 176 with Ford-O-Matic. And the top-of-the-line Fairlane series carried the "Thunderbird 292," essentially the 1955 Mercury Montclair engine, as its standard V-8 powerplant. Horsepower in this instance was posted at 200 with the standard transmission, 202 with automatic. And for those who wanted something even quicker, four-barrel versions rated at 215 and 225 horsepower were available at extra cost.

Chevrolet was a year behind Ford in introducing a modern V-8 (or any V-8 at all, come to that, if one disregards the short-lived, slow-selling 1918 version). But with Ed Cole and Harry Barr, late of Cadillac, as its engineering team, it was to be expected that in due season Chevy would come up with something very special.

Drawing upon their experience in developing the great 1949 Cadillac engine, Cole and Barr — employing precision casting techniques, lightweight valve trains and an even greater bore/stroke ratio than the Ford (1.25:1 vs. 1.14:1) — did just that. The 265-c.i.d. V-8, introduced for the 1955 season, was actually lighter by 41 pounds than the Chevrolet six. And if its displacement was somewhat smaller than that of the Ford, one would never know it by the way the cars performed. Starting out in 1955 at 162 horsepower, same as the Ford, the

Chevy was advanced, for 1956, to 170 horsepower in cars fitted with the Powerglide transmission. Equipped with a four-barrel carburetor, the Chevy V-8 developed 205 horsepower, or with two four-barrel pots and dual exhausts its output came to 225 bhp — identical to the top-rated Ford engine, though its displacement was ten percent smaller.

The venerable Chevy "stove-bolt six," which dated from 1929 (with a major revision eight years later — see *SIA* #39), was continued in production, rated by 1956 at 140 horsepower. (That's 94 percent more than the original version, by

the way.) Dated though it unquestionably was, the in-line six still enjoyed a substantial following, thanks to its long-standing reputation for durability.

If Ford was the first in its field with an overhead-valve V-8, it was Chevrolet that led the way, in 1950, with the first automatic transmission to be offered in a low-priced car. The first-generation Powerglide, which like the early Buick Dynaflow depended entirely upon the torque converter for added thrust, was notably sluggish. A planetary low gear was provided, but it had to be engaged manually — something a good many Chevy owners soon learned to do.

The Ford-O-Matic transmission came along in 1951. Though it had three planetary gears, it started in "second" unless the driver manually engaged the "low" range — an odd arrangement, looking back upon it. But even the second-gear start gave this transmission a substantial advantage over the Chevrolet unit. Not until 1953 did Chevrolet introduce the second-generation Powerglide, a much-improved unit which automatically engaged the low gear for quicker starts.

Optionally available on both Ford and Chevrolet was the Borg-Warner overdrive. First adopted by Chevy in 1955, it had been a Ford feature since the advent of the 1949 model. Some of the independent manufacturers, notably Studebaker and Nash, had used the overdrive since the mid-1930s, thus enhancing their reputation for fuel economy. Used in conjunction with the standard three-speed transmission, the o.d. cut engine revolutions by 30 percent. Thus a numerically higher axle ratio became feasible, enhancing the car's off-the-line acceleration as well as

*Right and below:* Four-door hardtop was new body style in '56 for Ford and for Chevrolet. Ford offered it only in Fairlane series; Chevy had both Bel Air and 210 models. Chevy comparison car weighs over 200 pounds less than Ford. **Center:** Chevy's hood ornament has a slight resemblance to its Eagle mascot, which dates back to 1932. What Ford's ornament is supposed to suggest is open to broad interpretation. **Bottom left:** Ford's parking lamp/turn signal went from round shape in '55 to this oval in '56. **Bottom right:** While Chevrolet went from '55's oval to '56's rectangle.

## SIA comparisonReport

its hill-climbing prowess. Priced at $108 on the Chevrolet, $110 on the Ford, the overdrive may or may not have paid for itself in fuel savings. But unquestionably it cut engine wear and reduced the noise level, in addition to enhancing overall performance.

Ford styling for 1955 was an evolutionary development of the 1952-54 theme. Lines were sharper and straighter; brightwork was more lavishly applied. The cars looked longer (which they weren't) and heavier (which they were, though the margin was slight). A wraparound windshield, *de rigueur* in the mid-fifties, was added and a concave mesh grille was fitted.

Unquestionably the fashion leader of the Ford line was the Fairlane Crown Victoria, a premium edition of the two-door hardtop. Standing a full inch lower than the garden-variety Victoria, it featured a wide chrome band wrapping across the top. The "crown" rather resembled a roll bar, but its function was purely decorative. And for an additional $70 Ford would add an extra fillip: a transparent Plexiglass roof section forward of the headband. It was an interesting gimmick, inherited from the 1954 Mercury, and no doubt it would add to the pleasure, for instance, of a drive along the Redwood Highway. But it resulted in so much interior heat that it sold poorly. Only 1,999 "sky roof" Crown Vickies were delivered in 1955, 603 the following (and final) year.

If Ford's styling was evolutionary, Chevy's would have to be called *revolutionary!* Nothing about the 1955 (see *SIA #27*) and '56 (see *SIA #76*) Chevrolets resembled what had gone before. Rather, their inspiration appears to have been drawn from various GM "show" cars — and especially from the Cadillac Eldorado of 1953. Curves were emphasized, the beltline dipped in a manner that was almost sexy, the windshield wrapped around to vertical pil-

lars and — on the 1955 version — the grille was evidently lifted from the Ferrari. The latter feature, so popular today, drew mixed reviews at the time and was replaced for 1956 by a wider, more conventional unit.

Three trim lines were offered by both marques. (Ford advertised four series, but the fourth consisted of a collection of station wagons in various stages of dress.) The base car from Dearborn was known, as it had been for several years, as the Mainline — a word that had not yet, in those days of innocence, taken on a negative connotation. Its counterpart from Chevrolet was unimaginatively titled the "One-Fifty." Both were plain to the point of severity, with the result that they were consistently outsold by the upscale versions.

For an extra $90 or so, a much nicer grade of trim — inside and out — was offered by Chevrolet's Two-Ten series and Ford's Customline. And at the top of the line, at a premium of about $100 — a little more in the case of the Chevy — were the Chevrolet Bel Air and the Ford Fairlane, the latter bearing the name of

the Ford family's estate at Dearborn. These cars were finished off so nicely that they literally could hold their own with anything from the medium-priced field. Of course, all of these automobiles could be purchased with the buyer's choice of six-cylinder or V-8 power.

Some interesting comparisons may be found in the production tables (see sidebars, below). For instance, Chevrolet's four-door models, both sedans and hardtops, consistently outsold those from Ford. On the other hand, Ford's station wagons, two-door hardtops and convertibles were far more

popular than their Chevrolet counterparts. And while Chevrolet's two-door sedans were best-sellers in the middle trim line, Ford enjoyed a long lead in both the base series and the fanciest model. The real contrast, however, as we were to discover, lay in the realm of performance. Briefly stated, the Ford is a "lugger," the Chevy a "revver." With standard V-8 power the 1956 Ford had a 30-horsepower edge, which gave it a slight advantage in acceleration and just a little something extra at the top end. A revised camshaft in the '56 Chevy, however, cut somewhat into the

## 1956 Chevrolet
### Table of Prices and Production

|  | Price, 6-cyl | Price, V-8 | Production |
|---|---|---|---|
| **Series One-Fifty** |  |  |  |
| Utility Sedan | $1,700 | $1,799 | 9,879 |
| Sedan, 2-door | $1,792 | $1,891 | 82,384 |
| Sedan, 4-door | $1,835 | $1,934 | 51,544 |
| Station wagon, 2-door | $2,137 | $2,236 | 13,487 |
| **Series Two-Ten** |  |  |  |
| Sedan, 2-door | $1,878 | $1,977 | 205,545 |
| Sedan, 4-door | $1,921 | $2,020 | 283,125 |
| Delray coupe | $1,937 | $2,036 | 56,382 |
| Sport coupe | $2,029 | $2,128 | 18,616 |
| Sport sedan | $2,083 | $2,182 | 20,021 |
| Station wagon, 2-door | $2,181 | $2,280 | 22,038 |
| Station wagon, 4-door | $2,229 | $2,328 | 113,656 |
| Station wagon, 9-pass. | $2,314 | $2,413 | 17,988 |
| **Bel Air Series** |  |  |  |
| Sedan, 2-door | $1,991 | $2,090 | 104,849 |
| Sedan, 4-door | $2,034 | $2,133 | 269,798 |
| Sport coupe | $2,142 | $2,241 | 128,382 |
| Sport sedan | $2,196 | $2,295 | 103,602 |
| Convertible | $2,310 | $2,409 | 41,268 |
| Station wagon, 4-door | $2,448 | $2,547 | 13,279 |
| Nomad station wagon | $2,574 | $2,673 | 7,886 |

Notes: 1. All prices are f.o.b. factory, for cars with standard equipment, federal excise tax included.
2. Production figures cover both six- and eight-cylinder cars.

## 1956 Ford
### Table of Prices and Production

|  | Price, 6-cyl | Price, V-8 | Production |
|---|---|---|---|
| **Mainline Series** |  |  |  |
| Sedan, 4-door | $1,895 | $1,995 | 49,448 |
| Sedan, 2-door | $1,850 | $1,950 | 106,974 |
| Business sedan | $1,748 | $1,848 | 8,020 |
| **Customline Series** |  |  |  |
| Sedan, 4-door | $1,985 | $2,086 | 170,695 |
| Sedan, 2-door | $1,939 | $2,040 | 164,828 |
| Victoria, 2-door | $2,093 | $2,193 | 33,130 |
| **Fairlane Series** |  |  |  |
| Town sedan, 4-door | $2,093 | $2,194 | 224,872 |
| Club sedan, 2-door | $2,047 | $2,147 | 142,629 |
| Town Victoria, 4-door | $2,249 | $2,349 | 32,111 |
| Club Victoria, 2-door | $2,194 | $2,294 | 177,735 |
| Crown Victoria | $2,337 | $2,438 | 9,029 |
| Crown Victoria Skyliner | $2,407 | $2,507 | 603 |
| Sunliner (convertible) | $2,359 | $2,459 | 58,147 |
| **Station Wagon Series** |  |  |  |
| Ranch wagon, 2-door | $2,185 | $2,285 | 48,348 |
| Custom ranch wgn. 2/dr | $2,249 | $2,350 | 42,317 |
| Parklane wagon, 2-door | $2,428 | $2,528 | 15,186 |
| Country sedan, 6-pass. | $2,297 | $2,397 | 85,374 |
| Country sedan, 8-pass. | $2,428 | $2,528 |  |
| Country Squire | $2,533 | $2,633 | 23,221 |

Notes: 1. All prices are f.o.b. factory, for cars with standrd equipment, federal excise tax included.
2. Production figures cover both six- and eight-cylinder cars.

*Right and below: Both makes played the popular fifties game of hide-the-gas-cap; Chevy stuck it under the left taillamp, Ford behind its rear license plate holder.*
***Bottom:*** *Ford taillamps were typically round, as all of them had been since 1952. Chevy changed to this smaller round lamp in flashy housing from '55's simple triangular wraparound design.*

# SIA comparisonReport

Ford's lead — especially at passing speeds.

And with the 205-horsepower "Power-Pak" engine it was another story entirely. Though it retained the 265-cubic-inch displacement (not until 1957 would the legendary 283 appear), it developed three more horsepower than the 292-c.i.d. Fairlane. This translated into an eight-mile-an-hour advantage at the top end; and so-equipped the Chevy was two and a half seconds faster in the zero-to-sixty run. More important, it was something like 25 percent quicker in passing times.

But of course that's hardly a fair comparison; the PowerPak came at extra cost.

Both cars drew highly favorable reviews from contemporary road-testers. Tom McCahill, whose leaning toward Ford was no secret, wrote, "These are truly great cars, the finest Fords ever built in Ford's long history. I heartily recommend them to anybody." But then, after driving a Chevy fitted with the PowerPak V-8 (which he described as "the greatest performing engine ever built in America, bar none") "Uncle Tom" went on to say, with his customary hyperbole, "This bargain-price Mercedes is the greatest performance buy ever offered at any time in America. It would whiz by a Duesenberg like Halley's Comet and the vacuum as it went by would suck the stork off an His-pano-Suiza."

Other reviewers were similarly impressed. *Motor Trend*, while expressing some disappointment in the Fairlane's acceleration, gave the car generally high marks, calling special attention to its safety features. And of the Chevrolet that journal said, "Taking away the glitter (which you can do in varying degrees by selecting any number of models), you come up with a car highly impressive in performance, a genuine pleasure to drive, and a car with mechanical features that point up low-cost, long-term ownership."

For our photo session, Vince Manocchi selected a Bel Air hardtop belonging to Don St. Ours, Jr., of Covina, California, and a Town Victoria (Ford's term for a four-door hardtop) owned by Jim Marsden, of nearby Glendora. Since the Town Victoria is fitted with a Ford-O-Matic transmission while the Bel Air uses the stick-and-overdrive combina-

tion, we borrowed a second, overdrive-equipped Ford from Gary Richards, president of the Fabulous Fifties Ford Club, in order to record our driving impressions from a more comparable vehicle.

The difference in feel and handling, as between Chevrolet and Ford, is greater than one might expect. After all, the two cars are closely comparable with respect to size, though the Ford is a couple of hundred pounds heavier than its rival. But the Chevy — despite its smaller displacement and lower horsepower — somehow feels livelier than the Ford. Its engine fairly begs to be wound up to high rpm's, and conversely, it does not take kindly to low-speed lugging. The Ford, on the other hand, has tremendous low-end torque, which eliminates some down-shifting and would obviously be useful in mountain travel.

Both cars provide comfortable, supportive and reasonably roomy seating. Tom McCahill commented, "If cars must be bigger than this, then the family should reduce, either by the calorie or

*Above: Some of Ford's biggest news for '56 was inside, where its new "deep dish" steering wheel and optional "safety" dash turned off customers. Chevy, meanwhile, looked virtually the same as '55 on the inside.*

shotgun method." Of course, both Ford and Chevrolet *did* grow larger in succeeding years, but that may have been to their detriment. We fault the Chevrolet in one respect, in this connection: The steering wheel comes too close to the tall driver's lap. A little more front seat travel would help that, and provide a bit more leg room as well.

Suspension is firm enough in both cars to provide flatter-than-average cornering — at least by 1956 standards — and a good feeling of control. The ride isn't cushy in either instance; it's relatively firm, and we like it that way. Both power steering units give the driver a reasonable degree of "road-feel," unlike the "full-time" power steering employed at that time by rival Plymouth. Overall we give the edge to the Chevrolet with respect to handling precision, but we suspect that it could be further improved by the use of a front roll bar.

In our limited test drives the brakes on both cars behaved well, stopping the machines in a nice, straight line. We detected little difference between the two in this respect. *Motor Trend* noted that neither one was subject to any appreciable brake fade until after the eighth stop. But that magazine also recorded a significantly shorter stopping distance for the Chevrolet — 146 feet from 60 miles an hour, compared to 174 for the Ford. Surprising, that, given the fact that the Ford brakes have a 14 percent advantage in lining area.

Both cars feel tight and solid, with perhaps a slight advantage to the Chevy. Both display an excellent level of fit and finish, particularly for cars priced so low. And both have obviously held up

## Comparative Specifications

| | Chevrolet Bel Air hardtop | Ford Fairlane Town Victoria |
|---|---|---|
| Price, f.o.b. factory w/standard equipment, federal excise tax included | $2,241 | $2,349 |
| Options on photo subject car | Overdrive, power steering, deluxe radio, deluxe interior, 2-tone paint, wsw tires, dlx wheel covers, clock, left o.s. mirror | Ford-O-Matic transmission, radio, fender skirts, 2-tone paint, wsw tires, wheel covers |
| Engine | 90° V-8 | 90° V-8 |
| Bore/stroke | 3.75 x 3.0 | 3.80 x 3.44 (3.75 x 3.3) |
| Displacement | 265 cubic inches | 312 (292) cubic inches |
| Compression ratio | 8.0:1 | 8.4:1 (8.0:1) |
| Hp @ rpm | 170 @ 4,400 | 225 @ 4,600 (200 @ 4,600) |
| Torque @ rpm | 257 @ 2,400 | 324 @ 2,600 (285 @ 2,600) |
| Taxable horsepower | 45.0 | 46.2 (45.0) |
| Valve configuration | ohv | ohv |
| Valve lifters | Hydraulic | Solid |
| Main bearings | 5 | 5 |
| Induction system | 1-4V carb, mech. pump | 1-4V carb, mech. pump |
| Lubrication system | Pressure | Pressure |
| Electrical system | 12-volt | 12-volt |
| Exhaust system | Dual | Dual |
| Clutch | Single dry disc | Single dry disc* |
| Diameter | 10 inches | 10 inches |
| Transmission, standard | 3-speed (plus overdrive, optional) | 3-speed (plus overdrive, optional)* |
| Ratios | 2.94/1.68/1.00 (2.94 reverse) | 2.37/1.43/1.00 (3.21 reverse) |
| Overdrive ratio | 0.70:1 | 0.70:1 |
| Transmission, automatic | Powerglide** | Ford-O-Matic |
| Ratios | 1.82/1.00 (1.82 reverse) | 2.37/1.43/1.00 (3.21 reverse) |
| Max. ratio at stall | 2.10 | 2.10 |
| Differential | Hypoid | Hypoid |
| Ratio | 4.10 w/o.d., 3.55 automatic | 3.89 w/o.d., 3.22 automatic |
| Drive axles | Semi-floating | Semi-floating |
| Steering | Semi-reversible recirculating ball, power assisted | Worm and 2-tooth roller |
| Ratios | 20.0:1 gear, 23.3:1 overall (Without power assist: 20.0:1 gear, 25.7:1 overall) | 20.1:1 gear, 25.3:1 overall (Same ratios, with or without power assist) |
| Turns, lock-to-lock | 4½ | 5¼ |
| Turn circle (curb/curb) | 41' 6" | 41' 2" |
| Brakes | 4-wheel hydraulic drum type | 4-wheel hydraulic drum type |
| Drum diameter | 11 inches | 11 inches |
| Effective area | 158 square inches | 180.2 square inches |
| Chassis & body/frame | Double-drop box girder type | Box section steel, X-member |
| Body construction | Steel | Steel |
| Body style | 2-door hardtop | Town victoria 4-door hardtop |
| Body colors | Onyx Black/Inca Silver | Raven Black/Colonial White |
| Suspension, front | Independent, coil springs | Independent, coil springs |
| Suspension, rear | Solid axle, semi-elliptic leaf springs | Solid axle, semi-elliptic leaf springs |
| Tires | 6.70/15 4-ply | 7.10/15 4-ply |
| Wheels | Pressed steel, drop-ctr rims | Pressed steel, drop-ctr rims |
| Shipping weight (std equip) | 3,200 pounds | 3,440 pounds |
| Wheelbase | 115 inches | 115.5 inches |
| Overall length | 197.5 inches | 198.5 inches |
| Overall width | 73.7 inches | 75.9 inches |
| Overall height | 60.6 inches | 62.1 inches |
| Tread, front/rear | 58"/58.9" | 58"/56" |
| Min. ground clearance | 6.5 inches | 6.5 inches |
| Front leg room | 43.7 inches | 44.3 inches |
| Front shoulder room | 56.8 inches | 57.0 inches |
| Front hip room | 62.0 inches | 60.5 inches |
| Crankcase capacity | 5 quarts | 5 quarts |
| Cooling system capacity | 17 quarts (w/heater) | 20 quarts (w/heater) |
| Fuel tank capacity | 16 gallons | 17.5 gallons |
| Horsepower/c.i.d. | .642 | .721 (.685) |
| Pounds/horsepower | 18.8 | 15.3 (17.2) |
| Pounds/c.i.d. | 12.1 | 11.0 (11.8) |
| Road tests (see note, below) Top speed (average) | 97.3 | 100.2 |
| Acceleration 0-30 0-60 ¼ mile | 4.3 seconds 12.3 seconds 19.0 seconds, 71 mph | 4.0 seconds 11.6 seconds 18.6 seconds, 75 mph |
| Braking (from 60 mph) | 146 feet | 174 feet |

\* Ford driving impressions were taken from a car with 292 c.i.d. engine, standard transmission and overdrive. Photo subject has 312 c.i.d. engine and Ford-O-Matic. Figures in parentheses refer to the former car.

\*\* Powerglide-equipped Chevrolet was not tested. Specifications are provided for information only.

Note: The Chevrolet road test was made with the corresponding 1955 model. The Ford test used a 1956 car. Both were equipped with automatic transmissions. Tests were conducted by *Motor Trend.*

*Right: Chevrolet's big, sweep-style speedo is easier for quick reading than, **below**, Ford's smaller, round instrument.*

## SIA comparisonReport

well over the years.

The two automobiles pictured here have both been California cars ever since their delivery to their original purchasers. Jim Marsden's Town Victoria, in fact, was built at Ford's Long Beach plant. Jim is only its third owner, and it

is obvious that he and his predecessors have given the car the very best of care. The second owner had overhauled the engine and transmission and reupholstered the seats. Otherwise — after more than 100,000 miles — the car is in original condition, even to the carpeting on the floor and the lining in the trunk. The condition of the Raven Black and Colonial White finish indicates that the Ford has never been involved in even a minor fender-bender. (Those of our readers who are familiar with traffic conditions on southern California freeways will appreciate the significance of that statement!)

Marsden, incidentally, is obviously partial to 1956 Fords. He owns seven of them! It's a sentimental attachment, he admits, stemming from the fact that his first brand new car was a '56 Fairlane Sunliner. He owns four such ragtops today, including one that is identical in every respect to his original car. (In addition to the Town Victoria and the fleet of convertibles, Jim's collection includes a Club Victoria and a four-door sedan.)

Don St. Ours, Sr., father of the present owner of our comparisonReport Bel Air, reports that when he purchased the car from its original owner, eight years ago, the man's wife and kids cried as he prepared to drive away. "It's part of the family," the wife explained.

The two Dons tore down the engine, although at that time the Chevy had logged only 61,000 miles. Most of the driveline was gone through, though the clutch remained untouched — a mistake, young Don now believes, for it chatters a bit now. New upholstery was professionally installed, brightwork was replated and Don Jr. repainted the car in its original Onyx Black and Inca Silver. He also added dual exhausts, in the interest of enhanced performance.

This car has taken a couple of first-place trophies at local shows, but basically it's a "driver." In fact, it has covered

## Transition Time

In some respects the mid-1950s could be thought of as a time of transition. Artist Antonia Byatt referred to the period as "the quiet, forgotten, static time...after austerity, before affluence." And so it was, though beneath the tranquil surface there were more crosscurrents than most of us realized — or cared to admit.

Take 1956, for example:

• Dwight D. Eisenhower — nearly everybody's favorite father-figure — was handily re-elected to the presidency, despite the illness that had threatened for a time to incapacitate him. But meanwhile, high among the bestsellers on the non-fiction list was *Profiles In Courage*, a book written by a political newcomer, a promising young fellow named John F. Kennedy.

• Also a best-seller that year was Edwin O'Connor's *The Last Hurrah*, a joyous novel about old-fashioned machine politics. But at the same time a deliciously naughty story called *Peyton Place* was ushering in a new era in the world of fiction.

• Nikita Khrushchev astonished the free world by condemning the isolationist policies of his predecessor, Josef Stalin, thereby opening the Soviet Union to foreign trade. Yet political demonstrations in Hungary that November were met by a crushing Russian force that annihilated an estimated 32,000 Hungarians and exiled 25,000 others to Siberia.

• Grace Kelly made "High Society," a delightful confection co-starring Bing Crosby — and then forsook her Hollywood career to marry Monaco's Prince Rainier.

• Grand-scale circus became a thing of the past when the Ringling Brothers and Barnum and Bailey organization folded its tents for the last time on July 16.

• And aviation history was made when an army helicopter flew non-stop from San Diego

to Washington, D.C. — a "first" for that type of aircraft.

Certainly it was a time of transition in the world of music. Broadway's big hit that year was Lerner and Lowe's "My Fair Lady," opening a run that would last for six long years. Yet those of us who grew up with the romantic lyrics and gentle melodies of the thirties and forties ("Please believe me, I was in heaven last night; please believe me, I caught the moon in its flight....") were jarred to find our kids listening to the likes of Elvis Presley's "You Ain't Nothin' but a Hound Dog"!

And of course it was a time of transition in Detroit, as well — especially among the cars of the low-priced field. Not yet had Chevrolet and Ford grown to the enormous — not to say excessive — size that they would achieve in the years that followed. But still, who could have predicted, just a few years earlier, that the industry's price leaders would rest on wheelbases of 115 inches or so — nearly a foot longer than that of the fabled Model A? Or that their V-8 engines would be capable of propelling them from rest to 60 miles an hour in as little as ten seconds? Or that their top speed would nudge the century mark? Or that automatic transmissions, power steering, power windows and seats and even air conditioning would appear on the option list?

So in a very real sense our comparisonReport cars represent the coming of a new generation of automobiles, a new definition of low-cost transportation, a new set of standards for the industry. True, some people groused about the prices; after all, a person could easily lay out as much as $3,200 for a well-equipped Ford or Chevrolet! But upon reflection most of us agreed that the money bought more comfort, more style, more performance, more automobile than ever before.

*Left and below: By 1956, Ford's dominance of V-8 performance in the low-price field was being quickly overshadowed by Chevrolet's small block eight introduced the year before.* **Center:** *Both cars have more than adequate trunk space for a family vacation.* **Bottom:** *Ford's dual exhausts exit through bumper tips, which can become permanently discolored very quickly. Chevy's duals expel the vapors in a more conventional manner.*

some 22,000 miles since it left its original owners, most of that distance having been logged since Don Jr. bought the car from his father. "It's a fantastic highway car," the younger St. Ours reports. And with the help of the overdrive, according to young Don, it has delivered as much as 28 miles to the gallon in moderately paced highway use.

It's interesting to note that the 1956 Bel Air hardtop, while less valuable than either its 1955 or 1957 counterpart, brings a premium price on the collector-car market. The Town Victoria is also prized by collectors, though its value doesn't match that of the Chevrolet. Both cars are appreciating steadily, indicating good investment potential.

Perhaps Tom McCahill had it right when he suggested that cars shouldn't grow any larger than the 1956 models. They did, of course, Ford ballooning in size for 1957 and Chevrolet following suit the next year. But in neither case is the enlarged version as valuable today as our two comparisonReport subjects!

Maybe this even helps explain why, back in 1956, the attractive cars from Chevrolet and Ford cut into the market previously claimed by the medium-priced marques. ☐

**Acknowledgements and Bibliography**
*Pat Chappell*, The Hot One: Chevrolet 1955-1957; *Dave Emanuel*, "1956 Chevrolet V-8," Special Interest Autos #76, August 1983; *Allan Girdler*, "Chevy 1955-1957," Automobile Quarterly, *Vol. XVII, No. 3; Beverly Rae Kimes and Robert C. Ackerson*, Chevrolet, a History from 1911; *Richard M. Langworth*, Encyclopedia of American Cars 1940-1970; *David L. Lewis, Mike McCarville and Lorin Sorensen*, Ford, 1903 to 1984; *Tom McCahill*, "The Chevrolet," Mechanix Illustrated, *June 1956; Tom McCahill*, "The '56 Ford," Mechanix Illustrated *(issue unrecorded); Don McDonald*, "The '56 Ford," Motor Trend, *November 1955;* *Ray Miller*, The Nifty Fifties Fords; *Walt Woron*, "'56 Chevrolet," Motor Trend, *November 1955; Great Cars of the Fifties (Consumer's Guide);* "'56 Chevrolet Road Test," Motor Trend, *March 1956;* "'56 Ford Road Test," Motor Trend, *January 1956.*
*Our thanks to Lynn Augustine, River-side, California; Ray Borges, Wm. F. Harrah Automobile Foundation, Reno, Nevada; Dorothy Brown, Stockton, California; Ralph Dunwoodie, Sun Valley, Nevada. Special thanks to Jim Marsden, Glendora, California; Don St. Ours, Sr. and Jr., Covina, California; Gary Richards, Riverside, California.*

# 1957 Chevrolet, Ford and Plymouth

**by Arch Brown**
photos by Vince Manocchi

IT WAS 1957, a year of shifting loyalties in the automobile business.

• Lincoln's production was down 23 percent, while Cadillac's was slightly up and Imperial sales more than trebled.

• Buick's volume dropped by more than a quarter. Chrysler, meanwhile, scored a 25 percent gain.

• Oldsmobile lost ten percent of its market, compared with the previous year; Mercury moved ahead by about the same fraction.

• Pontiac scarcely more than held its own, while rival Dodge surged ahead by 42 percent.

• And in the all-important low-priced field, which accounted for well over half of the total market, a similar shift was taking place: Chevrolet, the traditional leader, slipped by six percentage points, while Ford scored an 11 percent gain and Plymouth recaptured its traditional third place status with a spectacular 45 percent sales increase!

It's worth examining, as best we can, the reasons why.

We'll leave the medium- and high-priced fields for another time, except to note that the public obviously didn't cotton to General Motors' new B body, featured by both Buick and Olds. No surprise here; we never liked it, either! And in the luxury market, while Cadillac and — especially — Imperial wore fins that were an integral part of the design, Lincoln's were clumsily appended to what had been an exceptionally sleek profile. The effect could hardly have been worse, and the public's negative reaction should have been predictable!

But the low-priced field was another matter. There, Chevrolet stood pat on what had been, for the past two years, a winning hand. Ford came out with the biggest car in its history, up to that time. And Plymouth declared, "Suddenly it's 1960!" Differing from one another more sharply than they had done in years, all three were exceptionally attractive automobiles.

Two years earlier, Chevrolet had fielded a car that was almost totally new, both visually and mechanically; and suddenly the Chevy's image had changed — radically. Fresh new styling — just curvaceous enough to be a little suggestive without being too obvious about it — was accompanied by a new, lightweight, free-breathing V-8. Or perhaps we should say "fire-breathing," for the new engine was a great little performer! And if some of Chevy's available color schemes were a little much — coral and charcoal, for instance — there were some really

stunning alternatives.

There had been a "facelift" for 1956. The purists called it "excessive," but the public ate it up; and while everybody's sales were down that year, Chevrolet had at least managed to increase its market share — at the expense, evidently, of its two major competitors.

A second "facelift" for 1957 was, in the eyes of the critics, a good deal more effective. An attractive new grille was accompanied by a cleaned-up profile and a sleek, fin-like treatment for the rear fenders, and 14-inch wheels made possible a slightly lower profile. It obviously wasn't a fresh design; yet the result was a handsome little automobile.

The Ford, on the other hand, could hardly be described as "little." Actually, there were *two* Fords that year, and even the smaller one was nearly two inches longer than the Chevy. Known as the Custom (or in upscale trim, Custom 300) series, it was also three inches longer than the 1956 Ford. But the public, as Ford had accurately perceived, was enamored of size; and the car upon which the company really pinned its hopes was the Fairlane. This one, too, was available in two trim lines — Fairlane and Fairlane 500 — and it was a big, handsome, impressive-looking automobile. The better part of eight inches longer than the Chevrolet, it came within an inch of the overall measurement of the Buick Century, and its profile was lower than any car in

GM's barn save only the Corvette. It was more than 3½ inches lower than the Chevy, in fact, and of course that only added to the illusion of length!

Ford's styling, despite the size of the package, was neat and trim, and a pair of vestigial fins atop the rear fenders picked up the popular theme of the day in a tasteful, subdued way. This was a car with which to impress the neighbors, and the public loved it!

But if one of 1957's "low-priced three" could be described as *sensational*, clearly it was the Plymouth. For stodgy old Plymouth, the school-teacher's standby, wasn't stodgy any more! The Chrysler Corporation had invested $300 million in the development of their new cars, and they were unmistakably the block-busters of the industry that year. The Plymouth's wheelbase had been extended to 118 inches, three inches longer than the year before, and as much as five inches had been chopped from the overall height. Wider as well as lower, the Plymouth had a slinky look that made it seem much longer than it really was.

To some extent the appearance was deceiving, for although the new Plymouth was very nearly as big as Ford's Fairlane, it was actually a trifle shorter than the conservatively styled 1956 Plymouth! The broad, flat hood, the forward thrust of the headlight brows (an aerodynamic disaster, but a styling tour de force!) and the high-flying rear

## 1957 Chevrolet-Ford-Plymouth Price List
### (Federal excise tax and handling charges included)

| Base series | Chevrolet | Ford (116" WB) | Ford (118" WB) | Plymouth |
|---|---|---|---|---|
| | One-Fifty | Custom (& Ranch Wgn) | ----- | Plaza |
| Business coupe | $1,985 | $1,979 | ----- | $1,974 |
| Sedan, 2-door | $2,096 | $2,091 | ----- | $2,084 |
| Sedan, 4-door | $2,148 | $2,142 | ----- | $2,130 |
| Station wagon, 2-door | $2,407 | $2,401 | ----- | $2,405 |
| **Middle Series** | **Two-Ten** | **Custom 300/ City Sedan** | **Fairlane** | **Savoy** |
| Sedan, 2-door | $2,222 | $2,205 | $2,335 | $2,222 |
| Sedan, 2-door special trim | $2,262 | ----- | ----- | ----- |
| Sedan, 4-door | $2,274 | $2,257 | $2,386 | $2,269 |
| Hardtop, 2-door | $2,304 | ----- | $2,393 | $2,392 |
| Hardtop, 4-door | $2,370 | ----- | $2,457 | $2,304 |
| Station wagon, 2-door | $2,502 | $2,497 | ----- | $2,515 |
| Station wagon, 4-dr, 6-pass | $2,556 | $2,551 | ----- | $2,569 |
| Station wagon, 4-dr, 9 pass | $2,663 | $2,656 | ----- | $2,724 |
| **Upscale Series** | **Bel Air** | **Country Squire** | **Fairlane 500** | **Belvedere** |
| Sedan, 2-door | $2,338 | ----- | $2,381 | $2,339 |
| Sedan, 4-door | $2,390 | ----- | $2,433 | $2,385 |
| Hardtop, 2-door | $2,399 | ----- | $2,439 | $2,424 |
| Hardtop, 4-door | $2,464 | ----- | $2,504 | $2,494 |
| Convertible | $2,611 | ----- | $2,605 | $2,613 |
| Station wagon, 4-dr, 6 pass | $2,680 | ----- | ----- | $2,697 |
| Station wagon, 4-dr, 9 pass | ----- | $2,784 | ----- | $2,697 |
| **Specialty models** | **Nomad[1]** | ----- | **Skyliner[2]** | **Fury[3]** |
| | $2,857 | ----- | $2,942 | $2,900 |

[1]2-door station wagon; [2]Retractable hardtop; [3]Hardtop coupe
Note: Prices listed include base V-8 engine

## SIA comparisonReport

fender fins all contributed to the illusion of length.

The Plymouth's engine was bored for a little extra margin of power, but if one mechanical innovation were to be singled out for special mention it would have to be the suspension system. Torsion bars replaced the front coil springs of prior years, and ball joints were used for the first time in a Chrysler product. The effect upon the car's handling was a felicitous one, as we shall see presently.

All of the "low-priced three" were available with either six-cylinder or V-8 power, and in all three cases the latter was the overwhelming favorite. Ford's was the only truly modern six in the group — a short-stroke, overhead-valve unit that carried the highest horsepower rating of the three: 144, compared to 140 for the Chevrolet's familiar "stovebolt six" and 132 for Plymouth's hoary flathead.

Chevy's base V-8 measured, as it had from the time of its introduction, 265.1 cubic inches, and was conservatively rated at 162 horsepower. The figure fails to convey the spectacular difference

between Chevrolet's six-cylinder and V-8 performance. And for those who wanted still more pizzazz, there was the optional 283-c.i.d. version, available in several stages of tune.

Ford had a slightly smaller V-8 for its shorter-wheelbase Custom models, but for the Fairlane they used a 292-cubic-inch version. As fitted to cars equipped with the automatic transmission, it was rated at 212 horsepower. And a 312-c.i.d. mill — the Mercury engine, essentially — was optionally available.

Plymouth's smallest V-8, basically the 1956 engine, was available only in the base Plaza series. The more expensive Savoy and Belvedere models came with a bored version, measuring 301 cubic inches and producing a healthy 215 horsepower. The premium-priced, high-performance Fury sport coupe, however, was powered by a 318-cubic-inch V-8. Fed by twin four-barrel pots and squeezed to a compression ratio of 9.25:1, the Fury put out 290 horsepower — only ten short of the contemporary Cadillac!

All of the cars came with a "three-on-the-tree" manual transmission as standard, but very few were delivered that way. Chevrolet gave the buyer a choice of two automatics: Powerglide,

the tough old two-speed standby, and the flashy new Turboglide. Reviews in the automotive press universally praised the latter's performance, declaring it to be well worth the small premium over the Powerglide's price. But owners found it to be trouble-prone, and within a few years it was quietly dropped.

Ford, meanwhile, stayed with its familiar Fordomatic, a three-speed unit rigged to start from rest in second gear. Plymouth's bread-and-butter automatic was the two-speed Powerflite, but the newer, three-speed Torqueflite was used for the top-of-the-line models such as the hot-footed Fury.

For our comparisonReport, photographer Vince Manocchi arranged to bring together three fine two-door hardtops, representing the "Big Three" of the low-price field in 1957. And let's admit at the outset that in certain respects the cars are not really comparable. Nevertheless, they are close enough to give us some insight into these three disparate marques — the cars that dominated the market in their day.

The Chevrolet is a top-of-the-line Bel Air, powered by the optional 220-horsepower, four-barrel version of the 283-c.i.d. engine, linked to the traditional

Powerglide transmission. Fresh from a frame-up restoration, it is virtually a new automobile in every respect.

The Ford, on the other hand, is a working automobile, its owner's daily driver. Sound and solid still, and newly painted and reupholstered, it nevertheless betrays in some subtle ways its long years of regular use. It is equipped with the base 292 V-8, producing 212 horsepower, driving through the Fordomatic transmission.

The Plymouth, by way of contrast, is literally a museum piece — part of the "Yesterday Once More" collection of songwriter/pianist Richard Carpenter. It is the premium Fury model, built for high performance as well as high style. Its standard, 290-horsepower, 318-c.i.d. engine is by far the most powerful of the group, and its equipment includes the Torqueflite automatic transmission as well as power steering and power brakes.

1957 saw a neck-and-neck race between Chevrolet and Ford, with Ford well ahead in model year production but Chevrolet maintaining — by the narrowest of margins — its lead in calendar year output. But the difference between the two, which had amounted to nearly a quarter of a million cars in 1956, was whittled down to a scant 128 units in '57! Ford's policy of building a bigger car

— not to mention the advantage of its complete restyling — had paid off. For that matter, although Plymouth was a distant third in the sales race, its percentage gain over the previous year was even more impressive than Ford's!

But a funny thing happened on the way to the used car lot. Or at least, on the way to the collector-car auctions. For to today's hobbyist the 1957 Chevrolet Bel Air hardtop coupe is worth 3½ times as much as the corresponding model from either Plymouth or Ford!

## Driving Impressions

Henry Lopez's Chevy Bel Air was restored from a solid, one-owner original car. In most respects it was a sound enough unit, but at 130,000 miles its

*Facing page, left: Wheel cover design ranges from futuristic Plymouth, top, to sporty ersatz "knock-off" Chevy design, bottom. Center: Chevy's performance is fast in medium speed range; handling's hampered by slow steering. This page, top: Ford's performance was slowest of the three; handling was somewhat mushy. Above: With Fury option Plymouth is among fastest of '57 cars; handling is exemplary. Left and below: All three cars' front-end appearances have a thrusting, aggressive look.*

*This page, right and below:* Ford and Plymouth boasted all-new body styling for '57, while Chevy performed an extensive, attractive facelift to its '55 body shell. *Below center and bottom:* Plymouth put accents on top of front fenders; Chevy added a couple of bomb sights to its hood, while Ford stuck to traditional center-mounted hood ornament. *Facing page, left and top:* There's no question who wins the biggest tailfins contest here! *Bottom left to right:* All three cars had excellent visibility through wraparound rear windows.

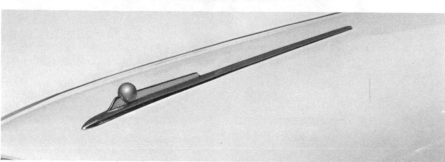

# SIA comparisonReport

engine had grown weary, the brakes were shot, and several other mechanical components needed attention. So Henry farmed it out to Bill and Gary Wingate for a thorough mechanical rejuvenation.

A bit of body work was required, as well. All of its life the Chevrolet had been housed in a narrow garage, and on a number of occasions the fenders had become altogether too intimate with the garage doorposts! Also, much of the bright trim had been damaged and had to be replaced. And in the course of the restoration, Henry refinished the Chevy in its original color, Harbor Blue, a 1956 hue that appeared on only a few 1957 cars, produced early in the model run.

This is a well-equipped car, featuring — in addition to the 230-horsepower "Power Pac" engine and Powerglide transmission — power steering, power brakes, E-Z-Eye glass, radio, deluxe heater and "flipper" hubcaps. About the only other piece of equipment that one could wish for would be air conditioning, but of course that feature was seldom seen in a low-priced car back in 1957.

Diana Geiger has a "thing" about 1957 Fords. Perhaps it's partly sentimental, for her father owned one when she was a teenager and she used to enjoy driving it. But mostly it has to do with the looks of this particular model. "It just has such beautiful lines," she explains. "It looks like it's moving when it's standing still!" That's high praise from this source, for Diana is a successful professional artist.

So when Diana married Jack Geiger 16 years ago, Jack bought her a lovely black '57 Fairlane 500 victoria. Diana drove that car for eight years, putting at least 100,000 miles on it. By that time it needed help, so when an attractive offer was made she sold it. Almost immediately she knew she had made a mistake. Jack got her a Buick, but as Diana puts it, "For the next eight years I was in mourning!"

Poor Jack! There was only one thing he could do. Last year he started combing the classified ads in the *Los Angeles Times.* Following up on various leads, he found himself inspecting some incredibly high-priced junk! But finally his persistence was rewarded when he found this fine Inca Gold over White victoria. Freshly painted and upholstered and fitted with a rebuilt engine, it needed only some front-end work before it was ready to go. And so, for several months now the Ford has been Diana's daily driver as well as her special pet.

As regular *SIA* readers know by now, high-performance cars from the Chrysler Corporation are the special feature of Richard Carpenter's collection at "Yesterday Once More." Little is known of the history of his '57 Plymouth Fury, except that it came to the collection as a decent, 70,000-mile original car. Mechanically it was sound enough that Richard has left it alone, but cosmetically it has been fully and authentically restored by Chrysler specialist Gary Goers. Like all Furys of this vintage it is finished in gold over eggshell, accented by a gold anodized aluminum spear running the length of each side — as well as by a gold anodized grille.

We were able to road-test the three cars — Chevrolet, Ford and Plymouth — over parts of the Los Angeles freeway system, as well as on some of the side streets of the owners' neighborhoods. And in this era of cookie-cutter automobiles it was refreshing to observe how different they are from one another.

Take the seating position. Driving the Chevy, one sits up fairly high. The seats are marvelously supportive, with good, firm cushions. Leg room is more than adequate, head room is generous enough to permit even the tall driver to wear a hat, and visibility is excellent. The steering wheel is positioned too high for comfort over the long haul, however, and the seats are more suitable for two

abreast than for three.

Seats in the Ford are lower and wider than those of the Chevrolet. Leg room is adequate, and front head room, while no match for the Chevrolet's, is sufficient. The driving position is fairly comfortable, but the advantage in this respect clearly goes to the Chevy — except that the Ford's steering wheel is positioned at a better angle. Rear seat passengers will find plenty of leg room but not enough head room. And the heavy windshield posts are no help at all to the driver's visibility.

The Plymouth's seats are wide, but uncomfortably low — so low, in fact, that the driver finds himself sitting on the end of his spine. There's ample leg room and sufficient head room in front, but the rear-seat passenger, unless he is a midget, will find insufficient space for either his head or his knees. In sum, the

passenger accommodations in the Plymouth are by far the poorest in our three comparisonReport cars. Visibility, however, is excellent; the windshield in this car is larger than that of any other American automobile of 1957 vintage, save only some of the larger Chrysler products.

It's not really fair to compare these three cars for performance, of course, since their powerplants range from the base V-8 in the Ford to a mild performance option in the Chevrolet and on to a real scorcher in the Plymouth. But we'll relate our driving impressions and let *SIA* readers draw their own conclusions.

The Chevrolet's 283-c.i.d. engine is simply a bored-out version of the original 265 V-8. This one, fed by a four-barrel carburetor, is both docile and responsive. (A dual four-barrel version, rated at 270 horsepower, was also avail-

*Right and below:* Windshields offer a study in design variations. Plymouth's front glass is a graceful semi-wraparound, while Ford rakes theirs back to an even greater extent than Chevy. *Below center and bottom:* Plymouth's trunk ornament is a somewhat meaningless stamping. Chevy proudly proclaims its V-8 power, while Ford's a bit more subtle about its V-shaped motivator.

## SIA comparison Report

able in 1957 — and even a fuel-injected version. Both were hotshot performers, no doubt, but even this 230-horsepower setup is no slouch!)

In a sense, it's a pity that the lively little Chevy V-8 is linked to the two-speed Powerglide automatic. For, while the transmission shifts smoothly enough — especially in the lower speed ranges — it doesn't provide a lot of punch, off-the-line. Once the car hits 25 or 30 miles an hour, however, its acceleration is downright exhilarating!

The power steering preserves a good deal of road feel. But at four turns, lock-to-lock, it is unnecessarily slow. And since the Chevy is several inches shorter than the Ford, we fail to understand why its turn circle is the larger of the two by nearly a foot and a half. The Chevrolet heels over more than we like on hard cornering, though it poses no problem to the driver in terms of maintaining control.

The brakes seem to be very good, stopping the car in a nice, straight line. We had no opportunity to test them for fade resistance, however. Floyd Clymer, reporting on a similar car for *Popular Mechanics* back in 1957, noted that some fade was experienced, "when braking constantly in descending sharp grades."

Instruments in the Chevrolet are conveniently positioned and easy to read. We'd much prefer gauges to the "idiot lights" that monitor the oil pressure and generator, but the same criticism holds true of both the Ford and Plymouth as well.

Chevrolet had a new ventilating system for 1957, one that effectively distributes fresh air (and heat, when it's needed) throughout the car. But sometimes the "fresh" air isn't quite fresh, for the intakes are positioned above the headlamps where — at least for the Los Angeles driver — fumes from other cars are picked up more easily than not. A

country boy must have designed this system; surely a city dweller would have known better!

The Chevy's ride is a good compromise, neither as soft as the Ford's nor as firm as that of the Plymouth. Road noise is moderate, and in typical Fisher Body fashion its structure is solid and tight.

The Ford, not unexpectedly, has a big, "cushy" feel to it. For many years the performance leader in its field, the Ford had metamorphosed by 1957 into the leading low-priced apostle of the "boulevard" ride.

Not that the Ford is a slug; it's not. But even in comparison with standard V-8-powered cars from the competition it carries more weight per horsepower than either Chevrolet or Plymouth —

with predictable effects upon its acceleration.

The Ford's suspension is very soft — *too* soft; at times the car seems to float. But a lot of people like a softly sprung car. The Fordomatic shifts smoothly, and in general this is the quietest of the three cars covered in this report. The brakes aren't power assisted. Probably, given the weight of this car, they should be, for they require quite a bit of pedal pressure. But basically they do their job well.

Steering is another matter. It's a little numb and much too slow for a power-assisted unit. And on hard turns the Ford leans and plows to an annoying degree.

The dash layout isn't quite as readily visible as that of the Chevrolet. The ig-

nition switch is to the left of the wheel, an inconvenience unless the driver happens to be a southpaw. But at least it's out of the reach of small fry!

One of the better features of this car, to our way of thinking, is the front-hinged hood. We understand its disadvantage from the mechanic's perspective, but from a safety standpoint it's great: No chance of the hood becoming unlatched and blowing back across the windshield, obstructing the driver's vision. Another of the Ford's advantages is its heating and ventilating system. Alone among our comparisonReport cars, it takes in its fresh air just below the windshield, away from at least the worst of the fumes.

There was some feeling of nostalgia when we slid behind the wheel of Richard

# Comparative Specifications: 1957 Chevrolet, Ford and Plymouth (Equipped as tested)

| | Chevrolet | Ford | Plymouth |
|---|---|---|---|
| Price* model tested | $2,399 | $2,439 | $2,900 |
| Engine (as tested) | Ohv V-8 | Ohv V-8 | Ohv V-8 |
| Bore and stroke | 3⅞ inches x 3 inches | 3¾ inches x 3.297 inches | 3.91 inches x 3.31 inches |
| Displacement | 283.0 cubic inches | 291.6 cubic inches | 317.6 cubic inches |
| Compression ratio | 9.5:1 | 9.1:1 | 9.25:1 |
| Horsepower/rpm | 220/4,800 | 212/4,500 | 290/5,400 |
| Torque/rpm | 300/3,000 | 297/2,700 | 325/4,000 |
| Carburetion | 1-4 bbl | 1-2 bbl | 2-4 bbl |
| Automatic transmission | Powerglide | Ford-O-Matic | Torqueflite |
| Number of speeds | 2 | 3 | 3 |
| Ratios | 1.82/1.00 | 2.40/1.47/1.00 | 2.45/1.45/1.00 |
| Differential | Hypoid | Hypoid | Hypoid |
| Drive axles | Semi-floating | Semi-floating | Semi-floating |
| Ratio | 3.36:1 | 3.10:1 | 3.36:1 |
| Front suspension | Independent, coil spring | Independent, coil spring | Independent, torsion bars |
| Power steering ratio (overall) | 23.3:1 | 27.0:1 | 19.8:1 |
| Turn circle (curb/curb) | 41 feet, 6 inches | 40 feet, 2 inches | 42 feet, 4 inches |
| Turns, lock/lock | 4 | 4.3 | 3½ |
| Brakes, type | Hydraulic, drum | Hydraulic, drum | Hydraulic, drum |
| Drum diameter | 11 inches | 11 inches | 11 inches |
| Lining type | Bonded | Riveted | Bonded |
| Effective area | 157.0 square inches | 180.2 square inches | 184.0 square inches |
| Tread, front | 58.0 inches | 59.0 inches | 60.9 inches |
| Tread, rear | 58.8 inches | 56.4 inches | 59.6 inches |
| Cooling system capacity** | 17 quarts | 20 quarts | 21 quarts |
| Fuel tank capacity | 20 gallons | 20 gallons | 20 gallons |
| Shipping weight (model tested) | 3,305 pounds | 3,442 pounds | 3,595 pounds |
| Wheelbase | 115 inches | 118 inches | 118 inches |
| Overall length | 200 inches | 207.7 inches | 206.1 inches |
| Overall width | 73.9 inches | 77.0 inches | 79.4 inches |
| Overall height | 61.5 inches | 57.9 inches | 55.3 inches |
| Minimum road clearance | 5.9 inches | 6.0 inches | 4.9 inches |
| Tire size | 7.50 x 14 | 8.00 x 14 | 8.00 x 14 |
| Front leg room | 44.7 inches | 43.2 inches | 45.7 inches |
| Front head room | 36.0 inches | 33.9 inches | 34.1 inches |
| Front hip room | 62.1 inches | 60.0 inches | 63.0 inches |
| Front shoulder room | 56.9 inches | 57.3 inches | 61.0 inches |
| Front seat adjustment | 4.4 inches | 4.0 inches | 5.0 inches |
| Front seat height | 13.1 inches | 10.7 inches | 10.5 inches |
| Registrations (calendar year) | 1,456,288 | 1,493,617 | 595,503 |
| Production (calendar year) | 1,522,536 | 1,522,408 | 655,526 |
| Production (model year) | 1,508,931 | 1,676,448 | 759,357 |
| Production (this model) | 166,426 | 183,202 | 7,438 |
| Horsepower/c.i.d. | .777 | .727 | .913 |
| Pounds per horsepower | 15.0 | 16.2 | 12.4 |
| Pounds per c.i.d. | 11.7 | 11.8 | 11.3 |
| Acceleration, 0-60*** | 11.3 seconds | 13.8 seconds | 8.5 seconds |

*Prices are f.o.b. factory with standard equipment, including excise tax and preparation charges.

**Including heater

***Chevrolet and Ford acceleration figures from *Popular Mechanics* road tests; Plymouth figures from a *Sports Car Illustrated* road test.

*Top left to right: Arch-style taillamps are unique to '57 Chevys. Ford went with traditional round taillamp design. Plymouth's flying wedge taillamp lenses helped to accent fins. **Right:** Chevy hides its gas cap above taillamp housing. Plymouth uses traditional door in fender route, while Ford sticks with its rear center location. **Below and bottom:** Plymouth produced the most "modern" instrument panel; Chevy's big, round speedo is the most readable, while Ford transmits road speed info in a sweeping arc.*

## SIA comparisonReport

Carpenter's Plymouth Fury. We owned a '58 Plymouth years ago — a car whose driving compartment and dash layout were virtually identical to this one. The sensation of *deja vu* ended when the Fury got under way, however. Our old Plymouth never performed like this! The '57 Fury engine employs special domed pistons, high-intensity cams, high-load valve springs and solid lifters, a high-performance electrical system, dual exhausts, a 9.25:1 compression ratio (compared to 8.5:1 on the Belvedere and Savoy models) and two four-barrel carburetors. Numbers on the speedometer read all the way to 150 miles an hour — a wildly optimistic figure, of course — but the Fury will readily do an honest 115.

Not only will the Fury go like blazes — zero to 60 in 8½ seconds, for instance — it will also stop in a hurry, and with a minimum of fade. The torsion-bar suspension was supposed to eliminate 65 percent of "brake dip," and the car's performance appears to bear out that claim. The Plymouth corners flat, too — again thanks to the front torsion bars. Griff Borgeson, who has never been one to go out of his way to praise American cars, was moved to write in *Sports Car Illustrated*, "Here's a big Detroit sedan that can easily out-corner many bona fide sports cars!"

The Torqueflite transmission is both smooth and efficient. It is so good, in fact (and Plymouth's three-speed manual

*Left:* Plymouth's 318 develops an awesome 290 bhp. *Below left:* Ford's 297 engine is good for 212 bhp. *Below:* Chevy's legendary small-block V-8 pumps out 220 bhp in our driveReport car. *Below center and bottom:* Back seat hip room in all three hardtops is adequate and seats are reasonably comfortable, but Ford and Plymouth lack head room for taller passengers.

gearbox is so poor) that off-the-line an automatic-equipped Fury will move out ahead of a stick-shift unit! But if the transmission is superior, the power steering is not. When Borgeson spoke of it as "dead and flaccid," he was exactly correct.

Still, it's a delightful car to drive. At moderate speeds its performance is actually quicker than the 1957 300-C — Chrysler's "Super Car" — though the latter will blow the doors off the Fury at full bore. Despite the fact that the springs and shocks are 25 percent stiffer than those of the Belvedere, there is no harshness in the ride. And although it can't match the Ford's silence, with the windows rolled up the throaty sound of the Fury's dual exhausts is almost inaudible.

Some of the Fury's attributes would be missing if we had tested one of the more plebeian Plymouths, of course: the extra-diameter torsion bars, for instance, the wide-rimmed wheels with oversize (8.00/14) tires, and of course the ultra-high-performance engine. But even the base Plaza series came with the superb torsion bar suspension, and the engine used in the Savoy and Belvedere models was the largest in Plymouth's field.

*Chevy's rear-end styling is tidy and restrained. Ford's round taillamps and small canted fins lend a strong visual focal point to rear of their '57 cars. And who can ever forget the first time they came upon a set of these fins?*

## SIA comparisonReport

And so we come to the bottom line: which of the three to choose if we were to return to 1957 and go shopping for a low-priced car? And the answer comes down to the matter of one's individual preferences.

• If a big, impressive car with a nice, soft ride is your priority—along with great, wide seats and superior sound insulation—then the Ford, in our judgment, is the clear choice for you. But don't buy it for the traditional qualities associated with earlier Ford V-8s: taut suspension and brisk performance. Ford had drastically changed its image by 1957, and the latter qualities are better represented by either Chevrolet or Plymouth.

• On the other hand, if you want to lead the fashion parade, or if you're a driver who likes to push a car hard—one who values sparkling acceleration and fast, flat cornering, one who wants to be able to hit the brakes hard without standing the car on its nose—the Plymouth is your car. But don't buy it

for the nice, chair-height seats that Plymouth used to feature; they went out when the low profile came in. And don't buy it for the built-like-a-tank constitution that used to be associated with Plymouth, either; the body structure of the '57 model leaves a lot to be desired.

• If conservative styling, trim size, and good maneuverability—together with responsive performance—are your thing, better look to the Chevrolet. You'll get the huskiest body structure in its price field as an added bonus. But be prepared for an automatic transmission that is distinctly lacking in flexibility, and don't expect the car to comfortably accommodate more than four adults.

Any way you go, you'll get a hell of a lot of car for your money. The choice is up to you. ∂⊘

### Acknowledgments and Bibliography

Automotive Industries, *March 15, 1957 and June 1, 1957; Griff Borgeson,* "Plymouth Fury Road Test," Sports Car Illustrated, *August 1957; Floyd Clymer,* "Clymer Drives 1957 Chevrolet V-8," Popular Mechanics, *January 1957; George H. Dammann,* Illustrated History of Ford; *Allan Girdler,* "Chevy, 1955-57," Automobile Quarterly, *Vol. 17, No. 3; John Gunnell (ed.),* Standard Catalog of American Cars, 1946-75; *Jerry Heasley,* The Production Figure Book for US Cars; *Richard M. Langworth,* Encyclopedia of American Cars, 1940-1970; *Ray Miller,* The Nifty Fifties Fords; Northern Automotive Journal, *December 1956;* "Chevrolet Road Test," Motor Life, *February 1957;* "Chevrolet Road Test," Motor Trend, *January 1957;* "Ford Road Test," Motor Trend, *January 1957;* "Plymouth Fury Road Test," Motor Life, *April 1957;* "Plymouth Road Test," Motor Trend, *January 1957; Chevrolet, Ford, and Plymouth factory literature.*

Our thanks to Dave Brown, Durham, California; Ralph Dunwoodie, Sun Valley, Nevada; Gene Horner, Santa Ana, California; Tom and Nancy Howard, Riverside, California; Jim and Bill Ogle, Santa Fe Springs, California; Bill and Gary Wingate, West Covina, California.

Special thanks to Richard Carpenter, Downey, California; Diana and Jack Geiger, Santa Ana, California; Henry Lopez, West Covina, California.

The Fairlane 500 Town Victoria

# Buy a FORD and bank the difference

**It's yours for half the fine-car price . . . runs for less . . . resells for more.**

When you're basking in the reflected glory of a '57 Ford, it's hard to think of your new beauty as a business investment. When you're whispering cross country on its Thunderbird V-8 wings, the thought of selling or trading this companion in pleasure is furthest from your mind. Yet in terms of cold cash-value, *this* new kind of Ford is the hottest news of the year.

It's a completely new kind of Ford from the wheels up. There's a brand-new frame, suspension and body all bolted and bonded into one solid, silent unit. Its advanced styling will set a trend for years to come. Then, under the hood there's ultramodern power from a wide choice of Thunderbird V-8 engines or the famous Mileage Maker Six. And Ford

is a car that's proved its ability to take it. It set 458 world speed and endurance records at Bonneville, Utah. No wonder Ford is called the fine car at half the fine-car price. No wonder Ford is worth more when you buy it . . . worth more when you sell it!

There's a <u>new kind</u> of value in the new kind of **FORD**

*you'll love Chevrolet's new light-touch driving!*

# Flying Off in a New Direction

**by Tim Howley**
**photos by the author**

In January 1958 Ford introduced the successor to the beloved 1955-57 two-seater Thunderbird, which never sold in very large numbers. The four-passenger 1958 Thunderbird, offered in both a hardtop and convertible, was arguably the most innovative car of the decade. Unfortunately it was born in that disastrous year of the Edsel, the chrome-dripping Buick, air-suspension, and the Eisenhower recession. (See *SIA* #138, December 1993.)

From the very beginning, the "Squarebird" was not very well received by collectors, and only in recent years has it come into its own. But make no mistake, it was a success. In this article we shall attempt of put the 1958 Thunderbird in its true historical perspective.

1. It was the most advanced and trend setting of all fifties cars, primarily because it was styled first and engineered later.

2. The Squarebird, not the Continental Mark II, filled the opening in the marketplace left by the discontinuation of the 1948 Lincoln Continental.

3. It was a radical new concept in unitized construction.

4. It was the most significant automo-

tive contribution of Robert S. McNamara, who has long been much misunderstood and maligned by collectors.

For these reasons, in this driveReport we have picked not a 1959 or 1960 model, or a convertible, but a 1958 Thunderbird coupe, which was the original concept that put the Thunderbird on the map and started the whole personal luxury car movement.

The origins of the four-passenger Thunderbird can be traced back to the experimental Continental X, later named the Ford X-100 and now on display in the Henry Ford Museum. This was Ford's answer to GM's show cars of the day, primarily the Buick LeSabre and XP-300. The Ford X-100 incorporated some then very advanced styling themes which all found their way into the 1958 Thunderbird. These themes were: a four- or five- passenger person-

al luxury car with a very low silhouette, front bucket style seats with center console, space age instrument panel and truly breakthrough styling.

Going all the way back to 1939, Ford introduced America's first personal luxury car. That was the Lincoln Continental developed out of customizing a 1938 Lincoln-Zephyr. The Lincoln Continental was first built for Edsel Ford's personal use. But the public reaction was so enthusiastic that Ford built a total of 404 for the 1940 model year, 350 cabriolets and 54 coupes which were nearly hardtops. Edsel Ford died in 1943, leaving the Lincoln Continental to flounder. Never built for any year in very large numbers, it was discontinued at the end of the 1948 model year, which turned out to be May 1948.

Immediately dealers and the public began to clamor for its return or at least something to replace it. Ford answered obliquely with the $10,000 1956-57 Continental Mark II and the 1955-57 two-passenger Thunderbird, which never sold much more than 21,000 units in 1957. What Ford buyers wanted was an affordable successor to the original Lincoln Continental, with room

*Above and below:* Dramatic new styling proclaimed that this Bird was quite unlike its two-seat predecessors in numerous ways. **Top right:** Thunderbird badge design was carried over, however. **Center:** So were turbine-style wheel covers. **Bottom:** Hood scoop also originated with two-seaters.

for at least four passengers and offered in both a convertible and an enclosed model. Nobody in Ford management seemed to grasp this simple marketing fact better than Robert S. McNamara, one of Henry Ford II's original "Whiz Kids." McNamara had strong support in Lewis D. Crusoe, whom he succeeded in 1955 as head of the Ford Division. Some say it was Crusoe who began promoting a four-seater. It was really McNamara with Crusoe's backing. Crusoe was the father of the original two-seater Thunderbird. McNamara was the father of the four-seater. (See sidebar, page 89.)

Others key to the project were: Tom Case, product planner; Joe Oros, Damon Wood, and Bill Boyer, styling; Bob Hennessey, chief engineer; and engineer John Hollowell, who had been in charge of the aborted Mark II retractable hardtop program.

As Bill Boyer told *SIA* in 1972 (see "Little Bird Meets Big Bird," *SIA* #11, July-August 1972), "Lew Crusoe had been the man behind the two-seater, of course, and it was Crusoe, too, who pretty soon insisted that we start working on a four-place Bird. But I think it

was really Bob McNamara — I would really attribute to him the fact that the 1958 Bird was ever born, because, as I said, there was a lot of controversy about the car, whether to drop the Bird altogether, and McNamara really fought for it. He thought it was a good concept. He went in and fought for it and won." One other point about McNamara. Once it was decided to build the car in the new Lincoln unitized assembly plant in Wixom, Michigan, Lincoln-Mercury wanted the car to be badged under their Division. But McNamara fought to keep it a Ford Division project all the way, and won again.

In the beginning, which would have been March 1955, the 1958 Thunderbird program was purely a styling exercise. This was why the car was so radical. Had engineering been involved at the outset, there would have been a strict package drawn up which would have inhibited "blue sky" styling. But engineering did not get intensely involved until some time later when the program was finally "validated." Then, for one of the very few times in Ford history, the engineers had to fit their pro-

gram into the styling specifications. It made for some refreshing design improvements coupled with a lot of engineering compromises.

Also in the beginning, there was a plan to build two Thunderbirds for 1958, the four-passenger, and a two-passenger with similar styling to the four-passenger, but on a 102-inch wheelbase. The four-passenger was originally on a 108-inch wheelbase, later was raised to 113 inches. The two-seater program, which got as far as the clay stage, was not abandoned until February 1957. The two-passenger T-Bird would have been built on the existing 1957 frame, while the four-passenger employed an entirely new unitized frame. Joe Oros recalls that the two-passenger program never was seriously considered. What finally killed off the two-seater program was McNamara and marketing research. Some buyers didn't like the cumbersome top, the limited luggage space and the lack of a rear seat. Production numbers that permitted high factory and dealer profit just weren't there. McNamara put profit before prestige leaders, and in the end the

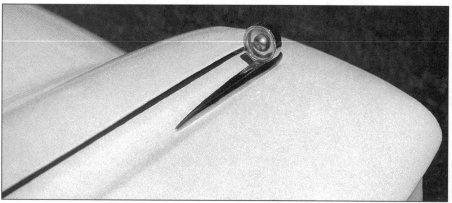

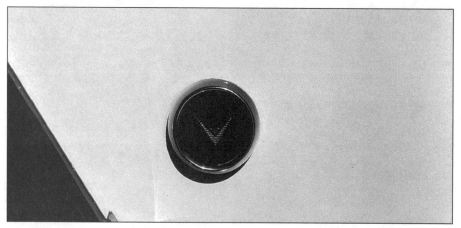

*Above: Fender "gunsights" helped relieve flat expanse of metal up front. **Below:** Decorative badges appear on roof panels. **Facing page:** Restyled Bird used unibody; was targeted toward wider market than two-seater.*

# 1958 THUNDERBIRD

two-seater version program was canceled. Of course, McNamara was correct, as always. Not always liked, but always correct.

The growth in personal luxury cars like the Thunderbird in the sixties was in the four-passenger market, not the two. A 1958 two-seater could have sold at a small profit, adding a lot of prestige to the company. But McNamara simply wanted it dead, just like he wanted the Edsel dead. McNamara nearly always got his way. End of discussion.

At this point, something called "unitized" mania fell on Ford like a plague. (See sidebar, page 91.) Ford's top man-

agement in 1955 thought that the whole world would go unitized, and they laid ground for their new Lincoln plant in Wixom, to build unitized Lincolns, the largest unitized cars ever. To take up unused production space it was decided to build unitized Thunderbirds in the same plant. Now, nobody had ever built very large unitized cars before. Production monsters never dreamed of lurked in every new corner. Building the unitized 1958 Lincoln became a production nightmare. Building the unitized 1958 Thunderbird was only a slightly bad dream. In the end it worked out quite well, producing the lowest American car to date, only 52.5 inches high (approximately 9 inches less than the standard passenger car of the day), yet allowing excellent seating and interior dimensions. Leg room and head room front and rear still measured up to other luxury cars of the day. With no frame to fight, the floor could be set low, and the doors weren't hampered with a big step sill. Ground clearance was a mere 5.8 inches. Of course, there was a problem with the huge floor tunnel. But the Ford design staff covered that up quite nicely with a sleek center console that incorporated the radio, power window buttons, and the heater/air-conditioner controls, but not the shift. This console inspired an elegant Thunderbird spread wing style instrument panel. It had a thick, molded padding at the top, recessed instruments and glove box, and swept right down into the console. Nothing like it had ever been done before.

The body hardly looked at all like the 1955-57 model. While retaining the functional air scoop, the hood had a more dominant power dome over the carburetors than previous years. The hood extended right into the new bumper grille for a forward thrust. The wide dual headlamps were framed in a gullwing design that swept way back into the doors. These wings became a concave crease swooping down over the rear section of the front doors where they met a rocket spear section that started in the front section of the doors and extended back to the rear bumpers. For 1958 only that spear carried five hashmarks. There were still fins, similar to the 1957 fins, moving so subtly into the taillamp area that you hardly noticed them. From the back, the fins became integral with two large pods sculpted into the bumper. The pods each carried two round taillamps with backup lamps on a textured chrome grid. The center of the deck was sculpted lower to accent the pods. A few years earlier this sculpture in steel was not possible. But new steel fabrication techniques first used on the 1957 Ford brought about some really daring advancements in Ford styling that made use of previously unheard of creases in steel. It is interesting to note that all of

## 1958 Thunderbird Details

Anybody with a sharp eye for early Thunderbirds will say that this 1958 has 1957 wheel covers. That is a debatable subject. 1958 and 1957 Thunderbird wheel covers look alike to the untrained eye, but, yes, these are 1957 wheel covers. Some experts believe that some or all of the earliest 1958 Birds still had 1957 wheel covers and that 1957 wheel covers continued to appear on some 1958 models throughout the year. This is probably because when it was decided to take the 1957 out of production there was still a good supply of wheel covers left over. To the best of the present owner's knowledge, these are the original wheel covers for this particular car.

Some other items on this car should be noted. This car has the rare dress-up package that was offered by both the factory and dealers from 1958 through 1960. It consists of chrome headlamp bezels, chrome front of the air scoop, chrome windshield wiper wells and chrome upper and lower rear panel trim. You could not

buy these items chromed individually. You had to buy the entire package.

This car also has the engine dress-up kit, which consists of chrome air cleaner, rocker cover, voltage regulator cover and oil filler cap. You will note that there is a wing nut on the air cleaner extension but no ducting up from the exhaust manifold. This is correct. The ducting was offered only on the 430 engine, which was not available on the Thunderbird until 1959.

At a base price of $3,640 for the hardtop, you got a very stripped Thunderbird. You paid extra for heater, radio, fender skirts, power steering, power brakes, power windows, power seat, and white sidewall tires. This car has all of these items except the power seat. It also has outside rearview mirror, floor mats, and tinted glass. The list price for this car was about $4,500, plus taxes and shipping, a lot of money for a school teacher to pay in 1958. She must have liked chrome. We rather suspect the car was originally a demo or salesman's car at the dealership.

these styling themes appeared on the slightly smaller two-seater convertible, which was aborted.

A word about the roofline, because it later swept both Ford and the industry. The roof was completely a Ford Thunderbird innovation. It didn't taper off in the rear, and it had a nearly flat backlight. The idea was to give rear passengers maximum head room. What resulted was a roof treatment so dramatically different from anything that proceeded it that it started a trend. In 1959 Ford grafted the Thunderbird roof onto the Fairlane to create the "Galaxie" look, which was retained until 1963. While competitors didn't exactly copy the look, they certainly aped it, and to this day the Thunderbird roofline still crops up in cars worldwide.

The front end was a breakthrough in its own right with a very costly *one-piece* grille/bumper with a mouthlike jet aircraft intake opening. Credit does not go to the 1956 Oldsmobile front end, which looks like one piece but is actually two. The rear bumper was also an intricate and costly affair that was very nicely integrated into the body and whose center section moved high into the deck area. Budd made the main sections for the bodies plus doors, hoods, decklids and fenders. The car was entirely assembled and appointed in the new Wixom plant in the same mix with Lincolns, which had to cause production fits and starts for both makes. The low silhouette of the 1958 Thunderbird and all of the appealing styling features that went with it were only possible through unitized construction. (During the eighties, the Lincoln people pushed the Thunderbird out of the plant, claiming they could not maintain Lincoln quality and continue producing Thunderbirds.)

MacPherson-strut front suspension was originally planned for the '58 Thunderbird as an alternative to air suspension, but eventually cost limitations forced more conventional unequal length A-arms with coil springs for the front suspension. Still the T-Bird got coil suspension in the rear, which turned out to be a mixed blessing. Originally, it was expected that all Ford products would have optional air-suspension by mid-1958; hence big towers had to be provided to accommodate the air suspension domes/bellows. When air-suspension didn't work out on 100 Fords so equipped, the program was canceled for Thunderbird, Mercury and Lincoln. What remained for all of the 1958 model year was a Thunderbird with rear coils, the trailing link type with upper links on each side running near parallel to the arms. These were the first and last rear coils that Ford used until 1965. Under hard acceleration, especially in reverse with a standard transmission, the rear arm system caused wheel hop. To compensate, Ford service engineers added

torque reacting links — short arms pivoted at both ends, running forward from the spring pockets to the body. While these links cured wheelhop during acceleration, they caused it on washboard roads. In 1959 the Thunderbird returned to parallel leaf suspension.

Another problem with the suspension was that it allowed the tires to scrape against the body sides. Hence, quite late in the program they had to add an inch to the width of the car, right down the center.

For 1958 Ford introduced a whole new generation of engines based on the Lincoln 430. The 430 engine was not available for the Thunderbird in 1958 except for NASCAR racing and export. The standard powerplant for the 1958 Thunderbird was the new 352, developing 300 horsepower. You paid extra for Cruise-O-Matic, but rarely was a Thunderbird sold with the standard manual transmission, with or without overdrive. None were equipped with Fordomatic. Early on, the 361 engine was considered, but it was finally decided to give the Edsel this advantage. Originally there would have been a choice of four 361 engines, one of them with fuel injection. One of the problems with the Thunderbird was that it had to pay its own way by borrowing features from other makes. This was particularly true for the engine and suspension. For a car that looked this radical, underneath it was about as exciting as a Saturday night with Kate Smith. But another reason for this was that the program was not approved until late November 1955. This meant there was no time left for exotic engineering ideas to match the styling.

There were, however, some interesting

## Robert S. McNamara

Robert S. McNamara tends to get overlooked in any discussion of fifties Fords. Yet he was a key player and a dramatic shaper of the cars. The greatest contribution he made to the industry was promoting the Squarebird to reality. What he did to the Little Bird is another story. Hired on as part of the original Whiz Kids team in 1945, he became head of the Ford Division in 1955, and then President of the entire Ford Motor Company in November 1960. But two months later he left to become Secretary of Defense on President John F. Kennedy's "New Frontier."

A graduate of Harvard's Business School, McNamara was specialist in statistical control. Anything that could be counted, qualified or made into a mathematical formula was his speciality. Today, McNamara not only takes the rap for this county's long involvement in Vietnam, he gets blamed by collectors for killing the two-seater Thunderbird and the Edsel. The truth is, the Edsel didn't need anybody in particular to kill it. It was a loser that was ultimately doomed. The whole Thunderbird program was something that Ford's top management wanted to kill off after the 1957 model, probably because they had such high expectations for the Edsel, and it was McNamara who kept the T-Bird alive by promoting the 1958 model.

McNamara also promoted the 1957 Ford, the 1959 Ford, and the 1960 Falcon. McNamara had a sixth sense for what would sell and what wouldn't. He correctly named all the wrong cars and all the right ones, and made so much money for the Ford Motor Company that Henry Ford II ultimately elevated him to the position of corporate President, then was devastated when McNamara resigned. Surely without McNamara, the Ford Motor Company would have survived, but there might never have been a 1958 Thunderbird, or any Thunderbird after 1957. Some people have dubbed the late fifties at Ford as the "square McNamara look." That square '59 Ford outsold Chevrolet, as had the '57. In addition, the 1958-60 Thunderbird and 1960 Falcon were resounding successes. It would seem that McNamara never made a mistake during his years with Ford, except for the '58 Ford. (See sidebar, page 92.) But he managed to bend a lot of noses out of shape along the way, especially with collectors.

# specifications

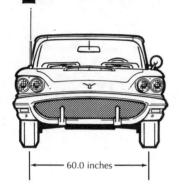

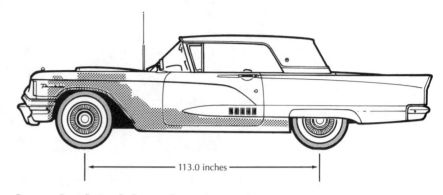

← 60.0 inches →

← 113.0 inches →

## 1958 Thunderbird hardtop coupe

| | |
|---|---|
| **Base price** | $3,630 |
| **Price as equipped** | $4,500 (approximately) |
| **Options** | Cruise-O-Matic, power steering, power brakes, power seat, power windows, white sidewall tires, fender skirts, heater/defroster, chrome dress-up groups, floor mats, tinted glass, larger tires, rear view mirror, brakes ($42); metallic linings |

### ENGINE

| | |
|---|---|
| Type | Ohv V-8 |
| Bore x stroke | 4.00 inches x 3.50 inches |
| Displacement | 352 cubic inches |
| Compression ratio | 10:1 |
| Horsepower @ rpm | 300 @ 4,600 |
| Torque @ rpm | 395 @ 2,800 |
| Main bearings | 5 |
| Induction system | 4-barrel |
| Fuel system | Vacuum pump, camshaft driven |
| Exhaust system | Dual |
| Valve lifters | Hydraulic |
| Ignition system | 12-volt battery/coil |

### TRANSMISSION

| | |
|---|---|
| Type | Cruise-O-Matic 3-speed automatic, torque converter, planetary gears |
| Ratios: 1st | 2.37:1 |
| 2nd | 1.84:1 |
| 3rd | 1.00:1 |
| Reverse | 1.84:1 |

### DIFFERENTIAL

| | |
|---|---|
| Type | Hypoid |
| Ratio | 3.10:1 |

### STEERING

| | |
|---|---|
| Type | Linkage power steering, recirculating ball and nut |
| Turns lock-to-lock | 4.1 |
| Ratio | 24.0:1 |
| Turning circle | 38.5 feet |

### BRAKES

| | |
|---|---|
| Type | 4-wheel hydraulic drums, internal expanding |
| Drum diameter | 11 inches |
| Total lining area | 175.32 square inches |

### CHASSIS & BODY

| | |
|---|---|
| Frame | Fully welded unit body/chassis |
| Body construction | Welded steel |
| Body style | 2-door, 4-passenger convertible hardtop |

### SUSPENSION

| | |
|---|---|
| Front | Independent A arms, balljoints, coil springs, hydraulic tubular shock absorbers, link stabilizer bar |
| Rear | Coil springs and control arms, hydraulic shock absorbers, rear stabilizer bar |
| Tires | 8.50/14, 4-ply tubeless white sidewalls |
| Wheels | Five lug steel disc |

### WEIGHTS AND MEASURES

| | |
|---|---|
| Wheelbase | 113 inches |
| Overall length | 205.4 inches |
| Overall width | 77 inches |
| Overall height | 52.5 inches |
| Front track | 60 inches |
| Rear track | 57 inches |
| Min. road clearance | 5.7 inches |
| Curb weight | 3,708 pounds |

### PERFORMANCE

| | |
|---|---|
| Acceleration: 0-30 mph | 4.2 seconds |
| 0-45 mph | 6.4 seconds |
| 0-60 mph | 10.9 seconds |

(Source: *Hot Rod*)

### GAS MILEAGE

| | |
|---|---|
| City | 12-13 mpg |
| Highway | 15-16 mpg |

*Right:* Lowness is no illusion. Ground clearance is less than six inches. *Facing page, top:* New Bird displayed twice as many taillamps as the previous one. *Below left:* Horizontal brightwork helped finish off roof and add to long, low look of car. *Right:* Heater/vent controls occupy upper end of center console.

# 1958 THUNDERBIRD

concepts that never made it into production. One was the clamshell retractable hardtop. Another was the T-top. In fact, the convertible hardly made it into production, and did not come out until April 15, 1958. The hardtop debuted in January. The initial convertible top was a pain to operate. First you unlocked the decklid by pushing a button; then you unlatched two windshield header clamps manually. Then you manually raised the decklid. You activated the folding mechanism by pushing a second button. Remember, the Thunderbird top folded into the trunk, the only place for it to go due to the design and size. The top did go down automatically, but you still had to close the decklid on top of it manually. Not until the 1960 model was an automatic top system installed. It operated in the same way as the Lincoln Continental convertible top system of the sixties.

The T-top was a fascinating experiment that went nowhere. One version even incorporated flippers. Another worked like a roll-top desk. In the end, all that ever appeared was a sunroof, and that did not come until 1960. This was the first sliding sunroof on any postwar American car.

In April 1957 four 1958 Thunderbird engineering prototypes were taken to Ford's western proving grounds at Kingman, Arizona. There they were subjected to a torture track designed to break a Rolls-Royce. All the prototypes developed considerable sag and showed weld separations. By comparison, a unit-bodied Hudson broke down even quicker than the Thunderbird, and the 1958 Lincoln prototypes broke in the middle like pretzels. As failures in the Thunderbird were found, extra welds and gussets were added. (Try cutting one of these cars up today and you'll find out how really strong they are in the middle.) But the bodies weren't the only problem. On the production line they had no end of difficulty dropping in the engine and transmission.

It took so long to get the 1958 Thunderbird into production that the production of the 1957 Bird had to be continued until the end of the 1957 calendar year, thus accounting for the high production of 1957 models compared to 1955 and 1956 models.

Despite the horrendous production problems, which delayed introduction by three months, 1958 Thunderbird hardtops began coming down the line at Wixom on January 13, 1958. The car was an instant hit, with 35,758 hardtops and 2,134 convertibles produced for the first model year. That was nearly twice the 1957 Thunderbird production. More could have been sold despite the

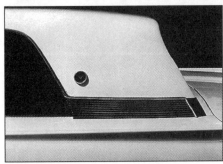

recession year, but Wixom couldn't produce them fast enough. The 1958 Thunderbird gained press attention like no other car that year. It was the final answer to "Why don't they still build the Lincoln Continental?" It hit the mark that everything else in Detroit missed. For this, *Motor Trend* named it "Car of the Year." In the year when the Edsel flopped and the whole economy floundered, the Thunderbird was a real winner. Consider the music: "The Chipmunk Song," "Yakety Yak" and "The Purple People Eater." And how about all the duds out of Hollywood: *Cat on a Hot Tin Roof, A Farewell to Arms, Peyton*

## The Unitized Body and the Thunderbird

Perhaps the 1958 Thunderbird's single most significant contribution was unitized construction. Now this was nothing new in the industry. The unit body went all the way back to the 1922 Lancia. It first appeared in the United States in the 1934 Chrysler Airflow, which flopped, and then in the 1936 Lincoln-Zephyr, which succeeded. Nash became unitized in 1941, Hudson in 1948, and Chrysler in 1960. Today nearly all smaller cars worldwide and many mid-sized cars are unitized, but not big cars. We know a lot more about unitized construction today than we did in 1958.

Unitized construction provides for savings in weight and material, provided that the stress is distributed evenly over the entire structure — the aircraft "monocoque" principal. In smaller cars, at least it helps eliminate the rattles.

You can go so far in unitized construction before you run into serious problems. The 1958-60 Lincoln demonstrated going too far with unitized cars. When you get up to that large a wheelbase, all of the advantages of unitized fall off. But the unitized body is essentially a sounding box; it picks up road sounds to a much greater degree than separate body and frame cars, especially as the size of the car approaches that of a concert hall. In smaller cars it is not costly to isolate the noise. The bigger the car, the more costly noise isolation becomes. This was the case in the 1958-60 Lincoln. It was also the case in the 1961-69 Lincoln, which remained unitized. Every year the car got heavier, to cut down on the noise. Eventually Ford simply went back to separate body and frame construction for its biggest cars. Today the Lincoln Town Car is separate body and frame. But the Lincoln Continental and Lincoln Mark VIII remain unitized. The Thunderbird was unitized through 1966, then returned to separate body and frame for all those late sixties and seventies models that shared their structure with the Lincoln Marks. Today the Thunderbird is back to unitized. Let's just say that the 1958-60 Thunderbird is about as far as you can effectively go in size with unitized before you run into some real production problems.

*Above:* 352 V-8 is rated at 300 bhp. *Below:* Two-tone upholstery treatment fits T-Bird's personality well. *Facing page:* Handling and ride were softened up on four-seat cars compared to earlier T-Birds.

# 1958 THUNDERBIRD

*Place* and *The Vikings.* And, by the way, the United States failed on four attempts to circle the moon, but did manage to get several satellites into orbit. Face it, the Thunderbird was the most memorable thing that happened in that unmemorable year; well, not counting San Francisco gaining the Giants, the Russians electing Nikita Khrushchev Premier, and the world discovering Brigitte Bardot.

## Driving Impressions

Our driveReport car is a concours restored Casino Ivory (yellow) and white 1958 Thunderbird hardtop owned by Robert L. "Lew" Brahm of El Cajon, California. This car was originally owned by a school teacher in Chula Vista, and it has only 50,000 original miles. The second owner did extensive restoration work on the car to bring it up to show condition. Brahm, who is the third owner, bought it 12 years ago. The car has Cruise-O-Matic but no factory air-conditioning.

Stepping into a 1958 Thunderbird today doesn't seem like much. But back in 1958 it was an exhilarating experience. Bucket-style seats, center console, passengers cradled between the side rails of a cavernous step-down unitized body. There simply was nothing like it. Vision is excellent except for the slightly blind rear quarters; visibility of instruments and accessibility of all controls is very good. Entry and exit for all but the fat lady who sings at the ball games is excellent, and that includes the rear seat. The reasons are the wide doors, low step rails and a front seat back that practically vanishes into the seat bottom. Ford claimed the T-Bird had the widest doors in the industry, 48.8 inches.

Now you might think that this first year unitized body would pick up a lot of road rumble. Surprisingly, it is as quiet as a '59 Cadillac. There's not a lot of wind roar around the windshield and wind wings at high speed either, some-

## Former Ford Chief Stylist, Joe Oros, on '58 Thunderbirds and '58 Fords

Joe Oros was involved with all of the Thunderbirds from the beginning, first as a consultant working for George Walker's firm, then as chief stylist of the Ford studio. Joe Oros held this position from 1956 to 1968. During 1994 this author interviewed him several times at his California home on his entire association with Ford, which went all the way from the 1949 Ford to his retirement in 1975. Specifically regarding the 1958 models, this is what Oros had to say:

"There wasn't a T-Bird designed that I wasn't connected with in some way or other in its direction and development, beginning with the 1955 model through 1968 when I was transferred to Ford of Europe Inc., as Director of Ford of Europe, Inc., Design.

"Yes, I was involved in the '58 Thunderbird, the first four-seater Thunderbird. I was the chief stylist at the time. Bob McNamara was the Vice President of the Ford Division at this time. Product Planning was also involved with the 1958 T-Bird. Bill Boyer was continuing as design manager in the T-Bird Studio. Lew Crusoe, Executive V.P., was also in favor of changing the successful [two-seat] T-Bird because it had reached a saturation point in sales. They could never get much more

than 21,000 units per year [in 1957] approximately. The big complaint from teenagers was that you couldn't double date. So that's how the product planners and Bob McNamara got involved. That was possibly Bob McNamara's first T-Bird.

"But the first car that I was involved with officially after I was hired as staff to the Vice President of Design, George Walker, could have been the '57 Ford. The '58 Ford gave me the most trouble aesthetically because we were attempting to give a sedan the same feeling that the Thunderbird had, and they were two entirely different packages.

"I can tell you what happened. First of all, to put things a little bit in perspective, it's easy to do Monday morning quarterbacking on anything. When the 1957 Ford came out we didn't know we were going to beat Chevrolet. We didn't know we were going to have such a super-duper, hot, hot car. We liked what we did and I felt it was a very handsome car. But we didn't know to start with that we were going to clean Chevrolet's clock with this car. Nobody knew that. On the '58, Product Planning people got into projections of what they thought would be good marketing-wise. That was to 'lunch' off the ['58] T-Bird. But we couldn't do it properly because the belts were so far out of line with each other. One

was a sedan, the other was a sporty car.

"We had started the '58 Ford before the '57 was introduced, and at the time there was a feeling to use the design that will give the Ford car its greatest prestige. Some of that was, let's lunch off the T-Bird. We tried to lunch off the T-Bird, and we got into a package problem. We got into weight and cost problems. We lunched off the T-Bird's front end somewhat. The package is different on the T-Bird. The cowl height for instance, was substantially different from the Ford car. Headlight location and belt heights were substantially different. We were picking up the cues of the T-Bird mildly. On the back end of the '58 Ford we couldn't possibly put the taillights down low in big pods of the bumper; we couldn't do that economically and call it a Ford car. To make things worse, the Thunderbird didn't have to worry about trunk space, and we could do all kinds of things with recessed lights and so forth that we couldn't even begin to do on the sedan because we had to consider the trunk area. Costwise and weight-wise it was an entirely different ball game. But had everybody had the advantage of hindsight that is so easy after the fact, we should have made a more evolutionary change from the 1957 Ford to the 1958 Ford."

thing you can't say for the '59 Ford Galaxie.

For a car that looked like it would go like sixty, it really didn't. The best 0-60 time was about 10 seconds. *Motor Trend* reported that a car equipped with Cruise-O-Matic and optional 3.10 rear end had a 0-60 time of 13.5 seconds, and 10.5 when shifting from D-1 to D-2 at 50 mph. They ticked off the quarter mile in a non-sizzling 16.8 seconds at 81 mph. *Motor Life* very correctly noted, "Acceleration was somewhat lacking when compared to recent hot sedans and many standard passenger cars. The blame can be traced in part to the 3,800 pounds of weight and the 3.10:1 gear ratio that is standard with the Cruise-O-Matic transmission." *Hot Rod* attained a 0-60 time of 10 seconds with Cruise-O-Matic and a 3.10 gear ratio. Their top speed was 114 mph. Tom McCahill's 0-60 time with Cruise-O-Matic was 9.9 seconds and his top speed was slightly over 110 mph. Trying to be as kind as he could about handling, he said, "Ride and stability through corners and over dipped roads is typical family-car-style, with not even a remote hint of the 'sports car feel'."

Only *Hot Rod* commented extensively on the handling, and the comments

## Bittersweet 1958 Thunderbird Memories

Few other cars run through the windmills of my mind like 1958-60 era Thunderbirds. Being a square kid from Hicksville, Minnesota, I never took much to the Early Bird. But I will never forget the first time I saw a 1958 Thunderbird. In 1957 and 1958 I had a persnickety little girlfriend named Colleen X. Anyway, in March 1958 I took her to the 1958 auto show at the Minneapolis Auditorium, now razed in the name of progress like the Marigold Ballroom nearby and the Prom Ballroom in St Paul. What a show that was, a whole hall full of glittering 1958 losers. But there was one winner. There on a turntable in the center of the hall, with beautiful fifties-style models in low-cut gowns demonstrating, was a fabulous turquoise with a white top 1958 Thunderbird hardtop. I was never so impressed, nor was Colleen who taunted, "Why don't you buy me one, Tim?" What, over $4,000 and I don't even have a job yet! "I'll find you a job, Tim," Colleen cooed. Remember, this was a recession year, and I was about to graduate from the U of M in June. Colleen did find me a job, all right, as an announcer at $75 a week at radio station KSUM in Fairmont, Minnesota. They later reduced that salary to $45 a week when they found I couldn't announce, but I could write, after a fashion. Meanwhile

Colleen found another beau and fled for California. I hope he bought her a whole dealership full of 1958 Thunderbirds. Me, I could hardly afford to buy gas for my '55 Chevy on what that cheap radio station paid me. Oh the woes of my "Summer of '58."

In the sixties I was in Chicago and doing a bit better. In 1968, I bought two really nice 1959 hardtops in Park Ridge, Illinois, a black one and a white one. That summer I drove the white one to San Franciso, all the way from Chicago on the old Lincoln Highway, and the Bird never missed a beat. Of course, it cornered about as well as a duck-billed platypus on roller skates, but what a fabulous car for the open road in the West. No wonder you still see them in movies. Later, in Marin County, California, I bought a 1960 Thunderbird hardtop, and still had it when we moved to San Diego in 1977. Those were the days when you could still buy pretty nice Squarebird hardtops for around $500. They were the slowest of all collector cars to catch on, and when I came to California in 1968, bringing one out here was like hauling the proverbial coals to Newcastle. Not anymore! Squarebird convertibles have always been rare and desirable. Squarebird hardtops now have become nearly as popular.

*Above: Speedo may read 140, but car can't get near that figure at top end. Below left: Easy-reading instrument panel is plenty flashy. Center: Console adds to sporty feel of the four-seater. Right: Trunk capacity was a definite improvement over two-seaters.*

# 1958 THUNDERBIRD

were not very good. They complained about the rear coil suspension, then said that the new Bird rode softer and could not hold a candle to its little brother when it came to cornering and handling. The problems which they correctly noted were several: engine placed too far forward, weight of the car and very conventional front suspension. Specifically, *Hot Rod* stated, "The biggest beef we had to register had to do with stability and handling, not only in the corners but also on straight stretches of road that were inclined to be the slightest bit bumpy. The trailing arms in the rear, with their rubber mounted pivots, allowed a certain amount of rear wheel steer over the bumps, causing the entire car to wallow or 'skate' over the road. This was especially prominent at speeds of 60 mph or better, and it did not disappear completely even at moderate speeds." Some of the remedies they suggested were stronger, stiffer shocks; increasing the rate of the rear springs, and a bigger stabilizer bar in front.

My own impression is that all 1958-60 Thunderbirds are just plain "wallowy," because the car was styled first and engineered later. There is not a lot you can do to improve them if you want to keep them original. You just have to live with these cars for what they are: simply beautiful, extremely spacious inside for their day, but if you're looking for a ride to match the looks, you better look elsewhere. On the plus side, the balance is nearly a perfect 50-50 weight distribution with four passengers aboard.

One of my biggest complaints is the slowness of the steering: more than four turns lock to lock. The overall ratio of 25 to one was applied to both standard transmission and Cruise-O-Matic. It's about the same as all Ford products that year, and not nearly quick enough for a pseudo sports car.

Braking is another weak point. The car was originally planned to have 3.5-inch-wide front brakes, but this didn't allow enough room in the wheel wells for the wheels to turn. They ended up with 2.5-inch brakes, which just wasn't enough. A total brake lining area of 175.32 square inches, adequate enough for a '58 Ford Fairlane, just didn't cut it

for a car that weighed 360 pounds more. In driving my '59 Bird from Chicago to San Francisco in 1968 and on many later mountain trips, I can remember the brakes being the Achilles' heel of the entire automobile. Disc brakes, originally considered, should have been mandated.

In summing up, the '58 T-Bird is a great touring car with adequate power, plenty of room for four passengers on a long trip, unheard-of luggage space for a Thunderbird, and looks that were certain to impress even a Las Vegas doorman. Easy to beat from the stoplight, but hard to beat in the status department. ✍

**Acknowledgments and Bibliography**
Motor Trend, *February and May 1958;* Motor Life, *March and July 1958;* Sports Car Illustrated, *April 1958;* Hot Rod, *June 1958;* Car Life, *October 1958;* Mechanix Illustrated, *June 1958;* "Little Bird Meets Big Bird," SIA #11, June-July 1972; The Personal Luxury Thunderbird Story, *Richard M. Langworth, Motorbooks International, 1980. Special thanks to Joe Oros, Bill Brahm and Ken Harkama.*

# THUNDERBIRD

## New Ford Thunderbird seats a <u>foursome</u> —in lap-of-luxury comfort!

Step into the new Ford Thunderbird and you're in an enchanted land! For this jewel of a car is pure Thunderbird in line and design—and it gives four fortunate people full fine-car room, comfort and luxury!

Thunderbird's new 300 horsepower, 352 Special V-8 barely whispers. A touch of your toe—and away you go into Thunderbird country. (Wherever you find people of spirit and taste—that's Thunderbird country!)

Here is the neatest, sweetest driving car that ever enlivened the Ameri-can scene. It handles, corners, climbs and parks as only a Thunderbird can. Thunderbird compactness . . . Thunderbird roadability . . . Thunderbird performance . . . now you get all this *and more*—for four! The new Thunderbird has winning ways that will be a revelation to even the most ardent T-bird enthusiasts—and they come pretty ardent!

Your Ford dealer invites you to see America's most individual, most exciting car. It is, happily, priced *far* below other luxury cars!

**Completely new** Thunderbird trunk compartment gives you over 20 cubic feet of space! It takes four full-size suit-cases, golf bags, other gear. Where does all the room come from? Thunderbird's remarkable *single unit* construction!

### AMERICA'S MOST INDIVIDUAL CAR

FORD'S NEW Falcon was unveiled to the American public on October 3, 1959. But a compact car was nothing new inside the Ford Motor Company. Ford investigated the possibility of building a small car in 1947, 1952 and 1954. However, studies showed that making such a car removed value faster than cost, as the car could not be built on a volume basis. In 1954, Ford extensively tested car size versus car value; thus the 1957 Ford was introduced on two wheelbases. (See *SIA #64*.) The larger Fairlanes increased value faster than price, outsold the regular Fords, and brought Ford into the number one sales position over Chevrolet. But at the same time that the 1957 Ford was introduced, the Ford market research wizards began to believe that a two-pronged trend was developing. Demand was growing at two extremes, the small car and the very big car.

It was at this time that the Falcon concept was born. In order to confuse competitors, Ford gave it the code name XK Thunderbird, and rumors quickly spread that Ford was going to bring back the small Thunderbird with a six-cylinder engine. Later the name was changed to Lavion, then Astrion. The name of Falcon was finally picked from some 10,000 names considered.

The car began as a paper plan in market research. The goal was to build a car that would weigh ¾-ton less than a conventional car, give 50 percent better gas mileage and sell for under $2000. It would have unitized construction, weigh 2100 pounds, carry five passengers and have a four-cylinder, in-line, cast-iron block. As discussion proceeded, opinion became divid-

ed between five passengers and six. Henry Ford II decided to resolve the problem personally. He authorized the most extensive and expensive market research to that date, actually purchasing many makes of import cars and putting them in the hands of research subjects. Reactions were sought to four, five and six passenger cars at different prices and with varying fuel economies. The research showed the optimum car from an engineering standpoint would be 2100 pounds, but from a consumer standpoint it would be 2400 pounds and would carry six passengers.

There soon developed a tug-of-war between Charles F. Baldwin, special projects manager for Product Planning, and Jack Hooven, Falcon project engineer. Baldwin had strict orders to hold to the original design and budget package. Engineers kept suggesting modifications which added to weight and cost. Their most important recommendation was proposing a six-cylinder engine, which finally won out over a four. The four, the slide-rule crowd said, would lug and would require downshifting. Ultimately, Ford's top management decided they would not want to be the first to convince the

# Full Dress Falcon

### by Tim Howley
### photos by the author

American public that four up front and four on the floor was more fun.

Hooven's task was no easy one. "We had to make the car feel like a big car," he said, "but we had to have the good handling foreign car buyers are always bragging about. The car had to avoid usual small car troubles. It had to be pussy-foot quiet on washboard roads and it couldn't have any harsh general noise."

High level meetings went on endlessly. Research continued and showed an ever-growing market for small cars. An automatic transmission was added to the plan. So was a four-door sedan. A station wagon was added, then dropped, then added again. A Ranchero was added, but would be marketed through the Ford Truck Division. A deluxe trim package was added to all passenger cars.

At the end of the research period the project was turned over to Product Planning. By this time specifications were quite tight. Length, width, height, weight, wheelbase, number of passengers, number of cylinders, horsepower and much more were all locked in. Still, nobody knew what the car would look like.

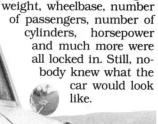

# 1963 Sprint V-8

Styling now began under Eugene Bordinat. The project was removed from the regular styling section and was housed in a special room. Special keys were issued so any leaks could be traced to those who had access. In the early stages an effort was made to keep styling in line with the Ford family designs, but later this idea was discarded in favor of a completely new design with softer, more flowing lines. Ultimately, the full-sized 1960 Ford followed somewhat the same lines as the Falcon.

Some of the first Falcons proposed had a distinct Thunderbird flavor with a front-end treatment similar to the Edsel. The next style considered was the Lavion which looked rather like a 1958 Lincoln from the rear with rear grillework, squared-off tail, tail fins and reverse slanting rear window. The Lavion ended up having more influence on the Mercury Comet and was followed by the less extreme Astrion which reached the full-scale clay model stage but was rejected for lack of rear seat head room.

At no point in the development were designs definitely frozen. Designing became a continuing process of give-and-take among the various groups to coordinate ideas and components into an integrated whole that would meet the overall concept as originally outlined by Market Research. Endless sketches were submitted. When tentative approval was made they were developed into renderings. When renderings were approved they went to ⅜-scale models. The Falcon was one of the ⅜ models, but it was one of 20 designs, all of which went to full clays. The final Falcon was one of the more conservative designs, yet it was not really a copy of any other Ford-built car. It had its own distinctive concave sweep to the side panels, a unique concave, horizontal grille and a distinctive version of the famous Ford tube-type taillamps.

Several basic considerations made the Falcon look the way it did. They were cost, weight, six-passenger size, unitized body construction and production cost. Because of the uniqueness of the car, its new production methods and plant facilities and its clean-sheet design, the cost of the Falcon program exceeded that of the Edsel program, which was approximately $150 million. The fact that the Falcon was

smaller than the Edsel and would sell for much less had little or no influence on tooling and machine costs. The company would have to recover its high development costs through greatly simplified assembly and high volume. The new facilities had to be capable of turning out at least 650,000 Falcons a year. Thus production was expanded to three plants instead of one.

Fortunately, during the period that the Falcon was under development the market for small cars grew rapidly. By the time of the Falcon's introduction, Detroit's Big Three could expect to sell 750 thousand to a million small cars annually against half a million imports and half a million more Ramblers and Larks.

Only 19 months elapsed from the time the final design was approved until "job one," when the first car rolled off the assembly line. The Thunderbird had taken 24 months. Experimenting, testing and modifying continued right up until introduction date. Jack Hooven had a team of 168 hand-picked engineers who worked around the clock and around the calendar. "They were all very bright young fellows," said Hooven, "and the majority of them didn't know all the reasons why things couldn't be done, so they just went ahead and did them."

The Falcon was the most conventional of the Big Three's small three (Falcon, Corvair and Valiant). The car had about the same interior dimen-

# 1963 Sprint V-8

sions as the 1954 Ford. It weighed some 1500 pounds less, cost $150 less and got 50 percent better gas mileage than a full-size 1959 Ford. Engineers had cut out weight in many ingenious ways such as making the floor of the luggage compartment the top of the 14-gallon gas tank. Body and door panels were thinner and lighter. The door frame, for instance, was made up of two pieces rather than the customary 21. In all, the Falcon body had 200 fewer parts than the standard Ford. Even the crisp, clean look with a minimum of trim was designed in part to keep weight and cost down.

Before the Falcon was built, engineers stripped apart such rival cars as Renault, Rambler and Lark. Much was learned from both the strengths and weaknesses of all the competitors. Actual road tests of the Falcon began by using mechanical components in Ford Taunus and British Ford bodies. Road tests were an integral part of the entire program. Much of the final road testing was done between Detroit and Cincinnati. Finally, the first Falcons off the line were sent on a trip covering every last mile of numbered Federal Highway in the country. It took 22 days of around-the-clock driving.

Much was uncovered in the road tests which greatly improved the cars, and improvements kept being made after the introduction date. Late spring 1959 road tests revealed that the engine smoked at high altitudes, so more expensive piston rings were fitted. It wasn't until July 1959 that the car's heater problems were finally solved. They had built such an efficient engine that it did not provide enough hot air to feed the heater. About this same time engineers discovered a hum in the drive shaft. It only developed at excessive speeds when the car was pushed to its limit, but Hooven's group demanded that it be corrected.

Originally the Falcon was powered by a 144 cid six-cylinder engine which developed 90 hp at 4400 rpm. This was the first totally redesigned Ford six since 1952. It contained 120 fewer parts than its predecessor. The manifold and cylinder head were cast together in one piece. The block was also cast iron, but pistons, flywheel housing and transmission extensions were all aluminum.

Carburetion was by a single-throat Holley mounted on the right side of the engine. The engine and its components were so simply designed and had so few parts that complete engine weight was a measly 345.5 pounds.

Transmission, driveshaft and axle were all of conventional design. The standard rear-end ratio of 3.10 coupled

*Above: Big, round taillamps, a Ford trademark off and on for many years in the fifties and sixties, were shared by Falcon. Right: Dash-mounted 6000 rpm tach was part of Sprint package. Opposite page: Falcon exhibits especially good riding qualities for a compact car.*

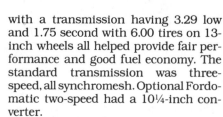

with a transmission having 3.29 low and 1.75 second with 6.00 tires on 13-inch wheels all helped provide fair performance and good fuel economy. The standard transmission was three-speed, all synchromesh. Optional Fordomatic two-speed had a 10¼-inch converter.

Front suspension was similar in construction to the full-size 1960 Ford, but with different placement of springing and shock absorbers. On the Falcon these components were mounted from the upper arm to the tower of the body structure. The lower arm and stabilizing strut formed an A-frame serving to guide the lower part of the spindle as the wheel moved. The stabilizing strut also cushioned fore and aft thrust, and an anti-dive factor was designed into the system. Rear suspension incorporated five leaf springs with a large isolating front eye bushing, angle mounted shocks and an axle insulator

to minimize road noise transfer. There was really nothing unusual about the Falcon's suspension system except the result. It soaked up road shock every bit as effectively as cars weighing 1000 pounds more.

Steering was developed expressly for the Falcon, but again was a conventional design utilizing an overall ratio of 27:1. Brakes also were conventional, but used 30 fewer parts than the big Fords.

The Falcon sat on a 109.5-inch wheelbase compared to a 118-inch wheelbase for the 1959 Ford Fairlane. Overall length was 181.1 inches compared to 208 inches. Yet interior head room and front leg room were actually greater than inside the big Ford. Rear leg room was about the same in the four-door sedan. Only hip room was less, and it was not significantly reduced. Perhaps Falcon's most remarkable feature of all was that it cut exterior size and

weight drastically without sacrificing interior room.

The Falcon interior was big enough to accommodate comfortably a driver nearly six feet tall. A minimum of door thickness helped seat three passengers front and rear. Elimination of roof supports permitted inches of extra head room, though the safety of this feature must have been questioned.

Another place where little room was sacrificed was in the trunk. It was 24.5 cubic inches, enough room for two men's suiters, a lady's ensemble, a lady's overnight case, a lady's vanity case, a man's overnight case and a set of golf clubs.

Interiors were tastefully finished in high quality vinyl, nylon and viscose yarn. Material on the door panels was electronically bonded, a Ford practice since 1956. Foam polyurethane was used in all seat cushions. Instruments and switches were all well placed and instruments were easily visible through the triangular deep-dish steering wheel. Instruments included a speedometer, temperature and fuel indicator, plus warning lights for oil and battery, all in the same cluster. Front door moldings were swept into the instrument panel for a more expensive car interior touch.

The 1960 Falcon was offered in four models, two-door and four-door sedans and two-door and four-door station wagons. All models came in standard and deluxe versions. The Ranchero is not found in the passenger car bro-

chure as it was sold through the Ford Truck Division. So confident was Ford in the Falcon Ranchero that the full-sized Ranchero was dropped altogether for 1960.

Falcon passenger car production reached 435,676 for the 1960 model year. This was several hundred thousand units less than expected, but it was more than the combined production for Corvair and Valiant. This pattern would continue for as long as the other two compacts were produced. The Corvair, in particular, was infinitely more innovative. But Ford had struck on a design that produced real sales success. The Falcon was a big American car scaled down into a small American car. That was what America wanted at that time. In fulfilling this need, the Falcon sold nearly half a million units in its introductory year.

For 1961 an optional 170 cid engine was offered. Essentially, this was a bored and stroked version of the 1960 engine. The larger engine, rated at 101 hp, was given a 3.50-inch bore and 2.94-inch stroke. Along with this, crankshaft, main bearings, connecting rods and pistons all had to be redesigned. The cylinder head was reshaped to preserve the 8.7:1 compression ratio with larger intake ports and valves. There were also distributor, carburetor, cooling system and muffler modifications. Despite these changes, the 170 cid six weighed only seven pounds more than the 1960 engine,

which was now downrated to 85 hp. One new model was added. This was the Futura with custom wheel covers, custom trim accents and high-styled all vinyl interiors with individual front bucket seats and center console. Falcons for 1961 have a subtle grille change. The 1961 grille is convex. The 1960 grille is concave. Total 1961 model year production was 474,241.

For 1962, Falcon again expanded the lineup. Now there was a Falcon Squire even offered with an optional Futura interior. The 1962 Falcons are identified primarily by sharp edges at the front of the front fenders and a newly designed grille with vertical bars. Model year passenger car production for 1962 was 396,129. Some of this production drop can be accounted for by the introduction of the intermediate size Fairlane. Nearly 300,000 Fairlanes were produced during the first model year.

The year 1963 saw more models again. A Futura hardtop and convertible were added, followed by the Sprint convertible and hardtop introduced midyear. The Sprints had a 260 cid 164 hp "Challenger V-8" engine as standard equipment. Again, there were minor trim changes including the grille which went back to a new horizontal design. There were 328,339 Falcons produced for the 1963 model year.

Falcon styling changed for 1964 and again for 1966. As a name, the Falcon finally faded away. As an idea it was the

# specifications

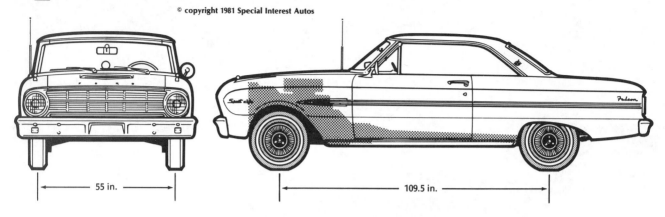

55 in.          109.5 in.

## 1963 Falcon Sprint

| | |
|---|---|
| **Base Price:** | $2320 fob Dearborn. |
| **Optional equipment:** | Back-up lights, windshield washers, Fordomatic, padded dash and visors, radio, seat belts. |

### ENGINE:
| | |
|---|---|
| Type: | Cast iron 90 degree V-8, overhead valves. |
| Bore & stroke: | 3.80 x 2.87 inches. |
| Displacement: | 260.8 cid. |
| Max. bhp @ rpm: | 164 @ 4400 rpm. |
| Max. torque @ rpm: | 258 @ 2200. |
| Compression ratio: | 8.8:1. |
| Induction system: | 2 barrel carburetor. |
| Exhaust system: | Cast iron manifolds, dual or single exhausts. |
| Electrical system: | 12-volt battery/coil |

### TRANSMISSION:
| | |
|---|---|
| Type: | Fordomatic 2-speed automatic. |

### DIFFERENTIAL:
| | |
|---|---|
| Type: | Hypoid semi-floating, standard ratio. |

### STEERING:
| | |
|---|---|
| Type: | Recirculating ball and nut. |
| Turns lock to lock: | 4.7. |
| Turning diameter: | 38.8 feet. |

### BRAKES:
| | |
|---|---|
| Type: | Hydraulic duo-servo, self adjusting. |
| Front: | 9 inch diameter x 2 1/4 inches wide. |
| Rear: | 9 inch diameter x 1 1/2 inches wide. |
| Total swept: | 114.3 square inches. |

### SUSPENSION:
| | |
|---|---|
| Front: | Independent, single lower arm; coil springs with stabilizer strut; direct-acting tubular shocks. |
| Rear: | Rigid axle; 5-leaf semi-elliptic springs; direct-acting tubular shocks. |
| Tires: | 6:50 x 13. |

### WEIGHTS AND MEASURES:
| | |
|---|---|
| Wheelbase: | 109.5 inches. |
| Overall length: | 181.1 inches. |
| Overall height: | 54.5 inches. |
| Overall width: | 70.0 inches. |
| Front tread: | 55 inches. |
| Rear tread: | 54.5 inches. |
| Ground clearance: | 5.9 inches. |
| Curb weight: | 2438 pounds. |

### CAPACITIES:
| | |
|---|---|
| Crankcase: | 5 quarts. |
| Fuel tank: | 14 gallons. |

### FUEL CONSUMPTION:
| | |
|---|---|
| Average city driving: | 17 mpg. |
| Average open road driving: | 19 mpg. |

*Cornering ability of the Falcon is impressive. You'll feel some body lean, but the chassis sticks like flypaper.*

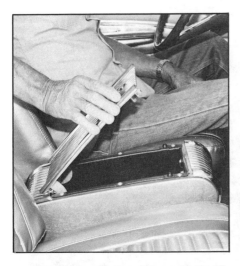

*Far left: Console between front buckets offers handy storage space. Left: Sprint emblems occupy rear roof pillars. Below: Stock Falcon instrument panel is used in the Sprint, but steering wheel design's a precursor of the Mustang.*

# 1963 Sprint V-8

most successful car ever conceived by the Ford Motor Company. Falcon and its derivations eventually accounted for 19.3 million cars produced. The derivations were Comet, Fairlane, Mustang, Cougar, Maverick, and ultimately the Granada, Monarch and Versailles. The original Falcon has been produced around the world, and it is still being produced today in Argentina, where it sells in the $25,000 to $30,000 range.

One might ask why, if Ford had a success formula in the simple, unadorned Falcon of 1960, did they gussy it up so much in later years? The reason lies with one man, Lee Iacocca, who took over as Ford's general manager in 1960. All of the 1960 Ford cars had been greatly influenced by the conservative presidency of Robert S. McNamara, who left in 1961 to become John F. Kennedy's secretary of defense. The cars done under McNamara all looked like they wore rimless glasses and parted their hair in the middle. The 1960 Falcon was a dependable but uninspired car.

Iacocca immediately added horsepower, more colors, sporty models and more options. He was convinced that the key to the Falcon's long-range success would be adding sporty flavor to the line and eventually expanding the idea into other lines. Iacocca's biggest success car, the Mustang, was enormously influenced by the Falcon, both in styling and body engineering. The 1963 Sprints, with their V-8 engines and sporty look, were essentially Iacocca's ideas. The Falcon may have started out as the ultimate "disposable" automobile. Thanks to Iacocca's ideas they and their derivatives are now the cars that every collector wants to keep forever. And thanks to the outstanding job of engineering done under Jack Hooven countless thousands of them have held up long enough to collect.

## Driving Impressions

It was Lee Iacocca who invented the Sprint by dropping a Fairlane V-8 under the hood and adding sports trim and features throughout. The Sprint came along in the spring of 1963 in both a hardtop and convertible. Before the Sprint, any 1963 Falcon could be ordered with a 260 and four-speed transmission. The Futuras came very close to the Sprints in that they had bucket seats, center console and many deluxe trim options. All of these were Iacocca's ideas.

During the 1963 season, Falcon started off with a class win in the Monte Carlo. This was followed by overall wins in the Tulip, Geneva and Mexican rallies, plus another class win in the Alpine rally. The team also finished second, third and ninth overall in the Trans-Canada rally to take both the team award and the manufacturer's award. Again, it was Iacocca who put Ford back into competition events in a big way.

Our driveReport car is a 1963 Sprint hardtop owned by Swede Anderson, a retired Navy chief shipfitter living in San Diego. The car's color is Glacier Blue with a bright metallic blue interior.

This particular car was purchased from the original owner, who had driven it about 99,000 miles in 15 years. The restoration consisted primarily of repainting, rechroming and detailing. The original engine is still running strong. Original new old stock seat upholstery was obtained from the original supplier to Ford. Standard Sprint features included front bucket seats with center console, 164 hp "Challenger" V-8 engine, a special muffler and 390 police "power hum" air cleaner, tachometer, Sprint molding and trim, simulated wire wheel covers, bright metal rocker panel molding, chrome dress up on the engine, and simulated wood grain steering wheel (same as used on the 1964½ Mustang). Options added to this car included pushbutton transistor radio, seat belts, windshield washers, backup lights,

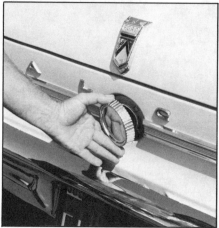

*Above:* Stock 260 V-8 carries chromed valve covers and air cleaner in Sprint version. *Right:* Another carryover to the Mustang; center fill gas cap location. *Below:* Flashy door trim was electrically bonded to door metal.

# 1963 Sprint V-8

padded instrument panel and visors.

What does it feel like to drive a Ford Falcon, especially a Sprint? A Falcon does not feel like a small car. You expect it to feel small, but it doesn't. It has neither small car ride characteristics nor the cramped feeling you got in so many imports of the sixties. The total feeling is a lot closer to that of many full-sized Fords of this same period. We also couldn't help but be impressed with the quality of the car throughout. The tightness of the unit body construction after 18 years, the quietness of the engine after over 100,000 miles and the firmness of the front end which has received little more than routine attention—all left us with one impression. This was a period when Ford quality was at an all time high, and that quality must have gone into every single car they built—big or small.

The unit body has a lot to do with the car's solidity after all these years, but that was only part of the lasting quality we found in this little Falcon. We found it in the front end, the rear end, the door handles, the tight fit of the windows, we found it everywhere. At higher speeds there was almost a complete lack of road noise and very little wind

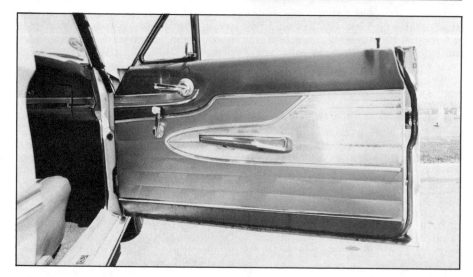

noise. On bumpy streets there was a total absence of the shakes and rattles that seem to go with so many older cars. We were especially impressed with how well the car held in corners with little body sway or tire squeal. You will eventually reach the breakaway point, but when you do the rear wheels slide nice and easy for confident control under any driving conditions.

*Motor Trend* tested the Falcon every year, though not the Sprint. This is how they described the handling of the 1960 model. "You can drive this car hard into turns—whether you mean to or unintentionally go into one too fast—and come out with no more than a bit less rubber. The car will lean quite a bit, all four wheels will slide quite a bit, but by allowing it to go and steering a new line you'll get through with no trouble. In ordinary driving you'll never need to concern yourself, for the car handles just as well as any other."

A year later *MT* commented on improved riding qualities resulting in part from slight changes in the suspension system. Said *MT* in 1961, "Like any car with a relatively short wheelbase, the Falcon tends to pitch on uneven pavement. On the open road, the car has a quiet, stable ride, disturbed by a slight sensitivity to cross winds."

In 1963, *MT* picked a Falcon Futura convertible, a six with four speed. Like us, they praised the car's quality. "In our opinion," said *MT*, "the Falcon is one of the quietest, most solid cars on the road. The suspension isn't marshmallow soft, and gives the driver a feeling of real stability on most roads at most speeds. At low speeds the front end will push in tight corners, but on the average mountain road the Falcon responds quickly to both steering wheel and throttle."

Braking was good but not exceptional. Ford's Buyer's Digest for 1963 lists power brakes available for the Fairlane but not the Falcon. Power steering did become available for the Falcon this year. We were sorry our driveReport car did not have it. Like all the earlier Falcons the steering was a

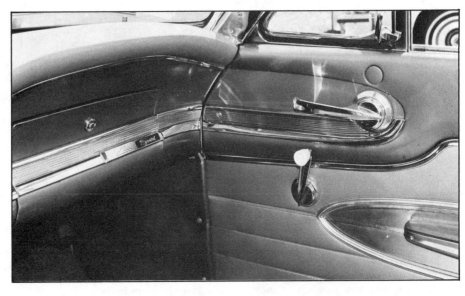

trifle heavy and stiff, even more so with the V-8 engine. It takes 4.7 turns from lock to lock, hardly what you'd call quick.

Other than the steering, one will find little to complain about in any well maintained or restored early Falcon. Unlike the 1949-51 era Fords, this was one crash program that didn't turn out like a crash program. Thousands and thousands of Falcons, now 18 to 21 years old, are still around to provide dependable and economical transportation and affordable collectability. I was never a Falcon lover when these cars were new. I was a skeptic when I first heard that Falcons were fast becoming collectables. "Why on earth would anybody want to collect such an ordinary little car?" I thought. "Fal-

cons were always so conventional." However, researching this article, doing a driveReport and meeting with the Ford Falcon Club here in San Diego has made me a Falcon believer.  □

**Acknowledgements and Bibliography**
Encyclopedia of American Cars, 1940-1970, *by Richard M. Langworth; Life magazine, September 14, 1959; Ford Buyer's Digest of New Car Facts for 1963; Speech—"The Small Car - Ford's Falcon"—by C.F. Baldwin Jr.; Motor Trend, various issues, 1959-1963.*
*Our thanks to W.R. "Mike" Davis, Ford Motor Company Public Relations, members of the Ford Falcon Club, San Diego, California. Special thanks to Everett "Swede" Anderson.* ·

**Top:** *Door moldings sweep stylishly into dash pading for an integrated look in the front compartment.* **Above:** *Sprint identification appears on front fenders; simulated wire wheel caps were also part of the package.* **Left:** *For a compact, "fun" car, trunk space is very respectable.*

# Hot and Heavy

AS FAR AS many collectors are concerned, the old Ford world still is flat as a flathead, though growing numbers concede it probably reaches to the end of the fifties. The Mustang, they say, is a phenomenon. But a few are already exploring the uncharted world of sixties Fords. It is a world of outstanding engineering, spectacular stock car performance, and durability almost beyond belief. The pinnacle year seems to be 1964, and the three year period, 1962-63-64, is beginning to show signs of a singularly exciting era of new Ford collecting.

These are not particularly significant years from a styling standpoint. You really have to drive an early sixties Ford to become a believer. And the cult of believers is now growing at such a fast rate that it is already virtually impossible to find a good original or restored Galaxie 500XL model offered for sale at anything resembling a bargain price. In fact, the demand for the XL models of the "Total Performance" Fords is already so great that it took us nearly two months to find a suitable drive-Report car on the West Coast. Most of the best ones have already been hustled eastward.

Back in Dearborn, it's hard to find anyone who admits to having been associated with early sixties models. Falcons, Comets, Mustangs, Fairlanes, yes. But not the big sleds. Joe Oros, who headed up Ford's styling studio at the time, has quietly retired to Santa Barbara, California. George Walker exited as Ford's chief stylist in 1961 to the opposite sun coast in Delray Beach, Florida. Elwood Engel went on to Chrysler and then into retirement. John Dykstra was vice president of Ford manufacturing when Ford's rigorous quality control program started in 1959-'60. As Ford president, he was Henry II's No. 2 man, 1961-63, followed by Arjay Miller, 1963-68. Had Robert S. McNamara, Ford president briefly in the fall of '60, not been called by President Kennedy to head up the Defense Department, he, too, might have dropped away like old Fords that go bump in the night. The early sixties was a period of unmemorable styling and enormous product improvement played to the tune of musical chairs at every corporate level. Who designed the '62 or '63 Ford? You might just as well ask who was responsible for the Edsel. These were years of high politics, with the full story yet to be told.

We have been given a glimpse behind the grey flannel scene of the time. When Ford Division returned to racing in 1956, they were on the threshold of a new era not predicted by marketing research. The most important contributions to Ford's new future were to come from without; not from within. Ford's better ideas were born not in the testing labs but on the stock car tracks. The new Ford heroes were the drivers, and they were beholden to no one whose name was Ford.

MEANWHILE, back in Dearborn, the award winning style of the '57 Fairlane gave way to the styled-by-committee '58. With the clouds of the Edsel still hanging heavy, nobody thought the '59 Fords would have much of a chance. Especially when Ford's Peeping Toms got some early photographs of the '59 Chevrolet Impala with its rounded body lines, extreme gull wings, and horizontal teardrop taillamps. It was too late to do anything about the soapbox '59 Galaxie design, but the '60 models were "crashed" through to follow along Impala lines. Alex Tremulis was called in to do it, but nobody seems to remember what he did. Product Planning was doing it all in those days. The stylists just did what they were told. The real kick in the spread eagle rear end came when the '59 Ford unexpectedly outsold the '59 Chevrolet. Then it was too late to change the '60. Production was already committed for three years. The best Marketing could do was order new outer panels for '61 and '62, which would return styling as near as possible to the squared-off lines of the '59. It was a see-saw situation all around.

Little wonder that the early sixties are Ford's forgotten years. But this was also a time when management's and engineering's main concentration was placed on the compact Falcon and Comet, the intermediate Fairlane, and, finally, the revolutionary Mustang. The full-sized Ford was still a bitter reminder of past mistakes. Remember, the '60 Ford shared its body with the stigmatized Edsel. Management didn't feel completely comfortable about any of their full-sized cars until they came out with the all-new quiet-riding '65. People at Ford are a little surprised that the early sixties series are beginning to catch on with collectors.

Truth is, Ford was placing its heaviest bets in lighter cars in those years, and a lot more stock in stock car racing than in styling. When Lee Iacocca became Ford Division General Manager in November 1960, he immediately got rid of the Robert McNamara look—cars that looked like they wore rimless glasses and parted their hair down the middle. Iacocca fostered Ford's new youth oriented image of "Total Performance" that took Ford racing on all fronts. "I wasn't as interested in stock cars per se as I was in a more sophisticated approach," he later told the press. The 1962-64 Fords mark an important era in that their styling did not dictate an image. There was a sharp turn from the Detroit dreamboats of the fifties to styling and engineering forged out of hard-fought racing victories. The real beauty of these cars as collectors' items now lies in their function, not their form.

THE NAME "Galaxie" was a holdover from the fifties, and it is as meaningless as "Bel Air" or "Belvedere." But the "500" stands for all the 500 mile races in which Ford was turning in distinguished performances at the time. "XL" might have meant "Experimental Limited," though Ford people contended it simply meant XL. Interestingly, in the early fifties, Ford built any number of XL experimentals and prototypes, and one of them was named the XL 500. Thus the name "Galaxie 500XL" all adds up, and seems to have evolved as logically as the car itself.

Basically, the XL model is a standard-bodied hardtop or convertible with bucket seats, center console, deluxe appointments, etc., but not necessarily with a hot engine. Ford practically invented the center console with the '37 Lincoln-Zephyr, then Bill Boyer re-invented it in doing the '58 Thunderbird. The low unit-bodied floor tunnel was so huge that he covered it with a console. This tunnel also dictated bucket seats. A practical solution to this one car's interior design problems quickly set a trend of far-reaching effects. In 1960, the Chrysler 300F came out with four buckets and a center console. Pontiac followed with a special edition of the Bonneville. The 1961 Studebaker Hawk had buckets but no console, as did sports models of all GM's new compacts. Ford's

By Tim Howley

drive report

PHOTOS BY THE AUTHOR

# 1964 Ford
# Galaxie 500XL

*Galaxie 500 XLs had interiors unlike any other Fords of the time. Big, deep-dish steering wheel, **left**, carried XL logo as did rear seat speaker, **above right.** Accelerator and brake pedals were festooned with bright metal trim, and all XL shifters stuck up from the center console.*

## 1964 Ford Galaxie 500XL

'61 Falcon Futura and Mercury Comet S-22 had buckets and center console. The stage was now set for the bucket beauties.

The first of the real bucket brigade was the Oldsmobile Starfire convertible, introduced in March 1961. It carried a standard Olds 88 body with complete sports interior treatment. Priced at $4647, it listed for $10 more than a Thunderbird. Ford considered it no serious threat. Chevrolet came out with its Super Sport convertible and hardtop package with a 409 engine in 1961, and early in the 1962 model year the Super Sport got the bucket seat and center console treatment. While this model did not affect Thunderbird marketing, it did cause concern right at the top of the full-sized Ford line.

Ford's policy all along had been to build its Galaxie models with bench seats and keep the Thunderbird distinctive and free from competition from within the Ford family. By early 1962 this was no longer possible. It was now clear that nearly every single make would have a bucket seat luxury model wedged right in between the Ford and the Thunderbird. Thus, the 500XL convertible and coupe were hastily designed. The XL models were introduced in April 1962, simultaneously with Plymouth's Sports Fury, Buick's Wildcat and a few others. Looking back at the '62 XLs now, it is hard to believe they were last minute models. They were exceedingly well-done cars.

The initial standard power train was the 292 with Cruise-O-Matic. There was an optional 352, the standard 390 which produced 300 hp, plus two high-performance 390s. Any of these engines could be

ordered with three-speed, overdrive, or a new Borg Warner four-speed. The potent 406 was made available for the XL, but was seldom opted for in this model. The 390 was essentially a bored and stroked 352, and the 406 was very little changed from the 390. There was a .080 larger bore (with the cylinder block casting recored for thicker walls), and the compression ratio was raised from 10.6:1 to 10.9:1. Pistons and connecting rods were beefed up to take some of the additional torque.

FORD HAD CERTAIN components mandatory with the 406, such as heavy-duty springs and shocks, harder, heavy-duty brake linings with three-inch wide drums on the front, a big three-inch driveshaft and a beefier rear axle gearset. It was not a comfortable package and had fairly heavy understeer, tending to nose-dive in the front and plow when the car took sharp corners. It was not offered with power steering, power brakes, air conditioning or automatic transmission, the theory being that the fan-belt driven accessories would not stand up under the high revs the engine was capable of producing. For these reasons dealers discouraged customers from ordering XLs equipped with the 406, and steered enthusiasts over to the plain brown wrapper models. This sales policy makes XLs with the 406 extremely rare today, though not necessarily desirable from a driving standpoint.

The XL, now as then, is desired for its

luxury and nimble handling qualities. The 390 with Cruise-O-Matic is still the most popular power combination.

The XL was initially offered in only two models, a two-door hardtop with the notchback Galaxie roofline and a two-door convertible. There were seven interior colors, all solids, and nearly all of Ford's exterior colors were eventually made available. The most popular XL colors in 1962 were white, black, red, fieldstone tan and silver grey. The XL had special deluxe wheel covers and exterior identification. The entire interior was unique to the model, with special door panels and bucket-styled rear seats. The shift was always in the center console, never mounted on the steering column. This console was handsomely trimmed with chrome and had a handy package compartment. Front buckets, of course, were standard. It was possible to special-order leather seats, but in a very limited choice of colors. Doors and side trim panels were accented with chrome-like mylar. Automatic courtesy and safety lights were added to the bottoms of the door panels. Extra-thick weave carpeting, full chromed instrument panel controls and deluxe instrument aluminum accents, special deluxe arm rests, padded visors, and bright metal accents on accelerator and brake pedals all added to the XL touch. Authentic wire wheels or even simulated wire wheel covers were options. Surprisingly, such features as AM radio, power steering, power brakes, remote control outside rear view mirror and foam-cushioned instrument panel were all extras, though few cars left the factory without them. The base price of the two-

*More of what makes an XL an XL. **Left:** Door panels were highlighted by chrome-like Mylar, had built-in safety and courtesy lights. Big, spinner-style caps carried the XL identification. **Right:** Front buckets were standard-issue and semi-buckets in rear gave interior continuity and harmony of design.*

door hardtop was $3268, but it would take another $400 in options to make it comparably equipped to the Thunderbird hardtop with standard equipment. Though even when fully equipped, an XL fell about $800 short of a Thunderbird in price.

The XLs carried the standard full-size '62 body. While there was virtually no change in overall size from the 1961 models, there were significant changes in outer sheet metal. There was a new "T-Bird" roof panel and roof rails, upper back panel, quarter panels, deck lid, lower back panel, rear floor area and rear cross members. The '62 Ford is the last model to show George Walker's influence, though it is debatable just how much influence he had after the '59 model. The '62 Ford can best be described as "a congenial car designed by a committee responding to the comittee who designed the '61 Chevrolet." It might also be described as "non offensive." The only individual design trademark of the '62 Ford seems to be the big, round tail-lamps. There's a simple story behind them. Bill Boyer did the original round taillamps for the '52 Ford. (He was also one of the main stylists behind the Thunderbird from the beginning through 1964.) The lamps became a major Ford theme a la the Cadillac fins. They were removed in '58, came back bigger than ever in '59, were off again in '60, returned in '61 and stayed on through '64. It seemed that management couldn't live with them—or without them.

Mechanically, the '62 Fords were refined versions of the '61 models. Ford's quality control program, initiated with the '61s, allowed for extended service intervals. Oil changes were stretched to 6000 miles. There was now a 30,000 mile coolant. Beginning with the '61 models,

Ford went to a 12,000 mile or one year warranty. For 1962, Ford made many corrections to add to car life. Special attention was given to the elimination of corrosion areas. More nylon bushings were employed to eliminate lubrication and greatly reduce wear, and more parts were plated to eliminate corrosion. All single exhaust system mufflers were aluminized. Dual exhaust mufflers combined stainless steel and aluminized steel.

Ford was seriously trying to solve the quality control problems which had dogged the industry since the beginning. John Dykstra, then Ford president, in a 1961 interview with *Machinery Magazine,* put it this way: "You must design and build quality into a product. Over the years some models have been better in some respects than others. Some engines were better, some interiors, some chrome plating, but no manufacturer ever built a car that was better than previous years' in all respects. This is what we are trying to do, get car value off the designer's drawing boards and into the customer's garage. If the design of the car is good and the production equipment is properly tooled, good parts will be produced. Good parts, properly assembled, should result in better cars."

In the past, somewhere in the scheme of things there were problems, and too many "rejects" wound up on the road. The problem of the automobile industry was not unlike that of the missile industry, which used the quality control concept to drive mechanical failures out of their products. It was called "reliability engineering," or "debugging in advance."

Many years earlier Ford had realized that it needed a standard method of measuring quality, a method which could be applied to all of its products at all of its plants. All vehicles, sub-assemblies, parts and materials had to meet engineering specifications in all respects. The system provided for identifying the defects and tracing them to their source. Behind this system was a far greater and more penetrating effort to improve component and sub-assembly quality through the company's quality control center.

As early as 1959, a pilot assembly line was made which duplicated in every essential the operations of all of Ford's assembly plants. Here hundreds of potential problems were exposed and solved before they ever got into production. All suppliers, inside and out, had to submit samples of parts to the pre-production centers. From here the thousands of details involving assembly were communicated to Ford plants. Key assemblymen were trained in new production techniques months before the cars were built and assembled.

A second phase of this quality control program was racing research. Ford had been committed to racing since the introduction of the 312 in 1956. In the late fifties they learned a lot the hard way. Their bloopers flew all over the tracks for the whole world to see. But when Lee Iacocca stepped up to General Managership, Ford began spending millions to support competition, and their racing research was directly applied to their products. The Monte Carlo and Shell 400 rallies helped give Falcon's V-8 sharper steering and stiffer front suspension. Competition showed the potential of the 352, and its principles led to the 390, 406 and finally the 427. The Indianapolis 500

Illustrations by Russ von Sauers, The Graphic Automobile Studio

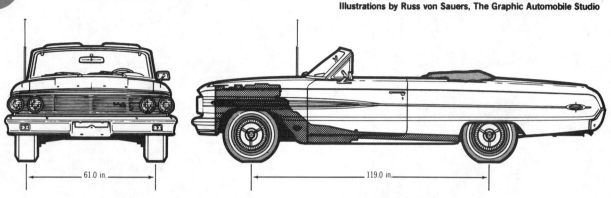

61.0 in.    119.0 in.

## 1964 Ford Galaxie 500XL Convertible

Price when new ............................. $3484.

Standard equipment ...500XL trim package incl. bucket seats. and center console.

Options ............Leather seats, wire wheels, wire wheel covers, radio, power steering, power brakes, remote control outside mirror, padded dashboard, wsw tires.

**ENGINE**
Type ...................................... Ohv V-8.
Bore & stroke ....................... 4.05 x 3.78 in.
Displacement ........................... 390.0 cid.
Max. bhp @ rpm ..................... 300 @ 4600.
Max. torque @ rpm ................. 427 @ 2800.
Compression ratio ..................... 10.8:1.
Induction system ........ 4-bbl. downdraft carburetor.
Exhaust system ......Cast-iron manifolds, dual mufflers.
Electrical system ..................... 12-volt coil.

**TRANSMISSION**
Type: ...................... Cruise-o-matic, 3-speed.

**DIFFERENTIAL**
Type ......................... Hypoid, semi-floating.
Ratio ............................. 3.00:1 standard.

**STEERING**
Type ..................... Recirculating ball-and-nut.
Turns lock to lock ............................. 3.9.
Ratio .................................... 23.0:1.
Turn circle ............................. 41.0 ft.

**BRAKES**
Type ............. Hydraulic, dual-servo; vacuum assisted; cast-iron drums.
Drum diameter ...... front: 11 in. x 3 in.; rear: 11 in. x 2.5 in.
Total swept area ....................... 212 sq. in.

**CHASSIS & BODY**
Frame ............. Ladder type, full length boxed side rails, four crossmembers.
Body construction ......................... All steel.
Body style ........ 2-door, 5-passenger convertible, pillarless side windows.

**SUSPENSION**
Front ............ Independent coil spring with upper and lower A-arms, direct-acting tubular shocks, anti-roll bar.
Rear ............. Rigid axle, with 5-leaf semi-elliptic springs, direct-acting tubular shocks.
Tires ................. 7.50 x 14 tubeless whitewalls.
Wheels ..................... 5-lug pressed steel disc.

**WEIGHTS & MEASURES**
Wheelbase ........................... 119.0 in.
Overall length ........................ 209.8 in.
Overall width .......................... 78.6 in.
Front tread ............................ 61.0 in.
Rear tread ............................ 60.0 in.
Curb weight ......................... 4080 lbs.

**CAPACITIES**
Crankcase ................................. 6 qts.
Cooling system ........................... 20 qts.
Fuel tank ............................... 20 gals.

## 1964 Ford Galaxie 500XL

proved the tremendous potential of the Fairlane V-8 design and sparked immediate development of overhead cams and fuel injection. From stock car competition the big Fords extracted a new freedom from air drag and a fabulous level of engine performance and durability. Ford-powered Cobras cast new lights on cams and carburetion.

During the 1962 season, Ford and Pontiac slugged it out on NASCAR's Grand National circuit with Ford winding up with a slight edge in the eight major races at Daytona, Darlington, Charlotte and Atlanta. It was four wins for Ford, three for Pontiac and one for Chevrolet. But the big Pontiac 421 set the fast times,

the surest indication of superior machinery.

While the Ford 406 in a lighter body was a match for the 421, Ford's 1962 body design was an aerodynamic drawback. Ford had been Pontiac's biggest NASCAR challenger for '61 with its 390 engine and streamlined "fastback" Starliner coupe body. But it presented a paradox for 1962 with more power, more durability, but new wind resistance from a return to the squared-off Galaxie roofline which produced 14% more drag at high speed. Race drivers tried to improve their advantage by adding fiberglass fastbacks, but NASCAR quickly ruled them non-stock. Ford was particularly hampered in high-speed races like Daytona where Pontiac was untouchable.

FORD'S SUCCESS in 1962 came by virtue of its improved connecting rod design, better power-to-weight ratio, some new gear ratio variances and a four-speed

gearbox. The standard Galaxie was the most popular model on the track. The 500XL had a weight disadvantage. Top drivers Nelson Stacy, Fred Lorenzen, Marvin Panch and Ned Jarret may have sent their wives to the store in factory supplied XLs, but they never put one on the track. Nor did Holman & Moody, who had been building up all the performance Fords since 1957, do their number on the XL. The car was the result of Ford's NASCAR reputation, not the reason for it.

The new 1963 Ford body strongly reflected Ford's racing bent, but it was designed more to help hold Ford in second place in industry sales. The outer panels of a now four-year-old body were reworked for the fourth time. There was a new roof, hood, deck lid, more angular side and door panels, a new grille and new rear end treatment. The instrument panel was completely redesigned for greater safety and better visibility. At new model

*Above: Low hoodline and big engines meant something had to give. In this case it was the radiator expansion tank. 500XL shows its tail to other traffic, something these cars could always do with ease. **Right:** Husky Ford is nose-heavy but can corner flat and fast thanks to excellent suspension.*

introduction time, the sporty 500XL models were offered in a convertible, two-door hardtop with Galaxie rear window treatment, and a four-door hardtop. The last is exceedingly rare today with only 12,596 originally produced. The interiors were not greatly changed from 1962. Then, in the spring of 1963, Ford announced new "63½" Galaxie 500 and 500XL two-door fastback models. The fastbacks were designed to give race drivers a slightly better edge. They were designed overnight and were highly touted to the public. This writer vividly recalls a parade of them down Michigan Avenue in Chicago. The fastback turned out to be more than a fad, however. It has dominated Ford two-door hardtop styling ever since.

The XL series sold much better in '63 than in '62. There was a better selection, increased availability, and the car was offered for the entire model year. But there was also now a trend back to the loaded up luxury car. The Edsel had failed in '58 partly because the public didn't want big, overloaded cars. Now Ford was offering Falcons, Comets, Fairlanes and Meteors, but the public was going back to full-sized models. During the 1962 model year, when there was a minor recession, the Galaxie line accounted for 46% of Ford Division sales, and the latecomer XL accounted for one Galaxie sale in every eight. In 1963 both the standard Galaxie and the XL took an even bigger slice.

*Motor Trend* was duly impressed with a 1963 Galaxie 500/XL convertible with a 390 engine and Cruise-O-Matic. Writing in the April issue, Technical Editor Jim Wright clocked a 4150 lb. XL convertible from 0 to 60 mph in 9.8 seconds and was pleased with the low noise level for a convertible. This was due as much to overall quality construction as to liberal use of sound deadening materials. Gas

consumption was about what *MT* expected, 11.8 mpg for 800 miles of mixed driving, 14 to 16 mpg at best.

There was a strong crosswind blowing when *MT* made the test runs, but the XL was extremely steady and only minor steering wheel corrections were necessary to keep the car straight. "Ford still favors suspension that's a bit on the firm side," said *MT*. "As a result, the Galaxie's handling qualities are good."

Ford's suspension system was somewhat antiquated by this time. It went all the way back to the '49 model, was improved greatly by the MacPherson strut and ball joints in '54, and had minor improvements just about every year thereafter. But GM was way ahead of Ford in front suspension in the early sixties. Ford did not catch up until the '65 models. For 1963, Ford had developed a "compliance link" as a suspension aid to eliminate harshness. Conventional suspensions absorbed road shock vertically, so a disturbance was felt and heard when the car went over minor bumps. The compliance link was designed to permit shock absorption in the horizontal as well as vertical planes. The lower arm front anchor was suspended on a crank which was centered by the weight of the vehicle. Road disturbances were then fed into the suspension members at a more acceptable angle, thus giving a cushioning effect. There were also several rear suspension improvements, plus a hefty anti-roll bar that kept the Galaxie quite flat during cornering. Although the

Galaxie was the heaviest car in its class for '63, the combination of front- and rear-suspension geometry was such that the car felt light and compact on most roads. Most of the suspension improvements came directly out of racing experience.

THE OVERALL quality of the '63 Ford was excellent. Even the smallest trim pieces seemed to fit just right. Major lubrication intervals were raised from 30,000 to 36,000 miles. Buyers were encouraged to drive up to 6000 miles without oil change. But any car so driven presents a sorry mess for the collector to restore now. There were six optional V-8 engines for '63 including two versions of the new 427. The standard 500XL engine was a 292 at model introduction time and a 289 when it was introduced in the spring. The optional 406 was replaced by the new 427. An optional 410 hp version of this monster with a four-barrel carburetor was offered with an optional transistorized ignition. An even bigger 425 hp version had matched four-barrel carburetors and much special equipment. Both could be ordered with Cruise-O-Matic, four-speed Warner gearbox, or a new three-speed manual gearshift transmission with full synchronization which made low range a performance gear. The three-speed was offered with optional overdrive. Rare, indeed, is a '63 XL with any engine bigger than the 390. The 427 is far more powerful than any collector could possible want, and at today's gas prices it's even less desirable than when the cars were new.

Not surprisingly, 1963 was one of Ford's best years in NASCAR racing. Dan Gurney won the inaugural event in January at Riverside in a '63 Ford. During

"Harry, how can you say I'm forgetful?
After all, I remember everything you told me about
our solid, silent SuperTorque FORD...how it's
stronger, smoother, steadier than any other car in its
field, and how its total performance
was refined in open competition.
Isn't that so, Harry? Harry? Oh, dear,
I've left him at the gas station again!"

TRY TOTAL PERFORMANCE
FOR A CHANGE!

**FORD**
Falcon·Fairlane·Ford·Thunderbird

the year, Ford captured every 500 mile NASCAR race: the Daytona 500 with Tiny Lund, the Atlanta 500 and the Charlotte World 600 with Fred Lorenzen, Darlington's Southern 500 with Fireball Roberts, and almost every other event over 100 miles as well. With more than $113,000 in winnings, Fred Lorenzen became the most monied race driver to that date. Understandably, the mid-model fastback was the most raced of all the '63 Fords, but only in the Galaxie 500 version. The 500XL was still too heavy to appeal to serious drivers. If there was one big disadvantage to all full-sized Fords prior to 1965, it was their weight. Insiders called the '63 fastback the "Freddy" after Fred Lorenzen. All of these cars were bred by John Holman of Holman & Moody in Charlotte, North Carolina.

From a collector standpoint, the 1964 model is the most desirable of all the Galaxie 500XLs. But as far as Ford Motor Company is concerned today, it was not a particularly significant car. Ford's landmark for 1964 was the introduction of the 1965 Mustang. Then, in the fall of that year, the 1965 models made their debut. These are not particularly collectable cars now, but they represented the biggest change in full-sized Fords since the landmark '49s. The collectability of the '64 is almost accidental. Ford was putting so much concentration into racing and into smaller models that they simply took the basic 1960 Ford wheelbase, chassis and inner body and kept improving it for five years. this has been the standard practice in Europe since the beginning of automaking there, but it is not the way Detroit likes to do things. Thus, without intending to at all, Henry Ford II offered the American public one of the very best cars he ever built with the 1964 model, and not a badly styled one either. For all the politics, the '64 Ford stands quite alone as the ultimate Total Performance Ford.

For the fifth straight year all the outer body panels were changed again. Ford was fighting hard to remain in second place in sales. They expected the industry to sell over seven million cars in 1964. In unveiling the new 1964 line to newsmen at Colorado Springs, Lee Iacocca said, "We have invested hundreds of millions of dollars in completely new styling this year. Sales this year could wind up as high as 7.5 million cars, and I am confident we will have our share. Our quality program is paying dividends. Warranty costs are down significantly. In the last 18 months I have seen warranty costs drop 27 percent." Iacocca also told the press of the company's continued determination to spend monstrous sums of money in competitive events.

A S MUCH AS the '64 Fords looked like all-new cars, they were evolutionary rather than revolutionary. Mechanically, there was nothing new. Styling had been carefully dictated by the aerodynamics of racing. Even the body panels were designed to be lighter than the '63s. All the closed models had fastback styling. There was a strong influence of the Torino, an experimental four-passenger luxury car, which finally was introduced as a new name for the Fairlane in 1968. Equally strong in influence was the new 1964 Thunderbird, the fourth change in the Thunderbird series. Recent show cars like the Allegro, Cougar II and the Mustang II, all aerodynamically styled, played their part in influencing 1964 Ford styling. Granted, it is not a memorably styled car. But it's not bad. As one collector put it, "The '64 is the kind of a Ford that grows on you until it fits you so well you don't want another year."

The entire 1964 Ford line was named *Motor Trend*'s Car of the Year. Said *MT*, "The basis of this year's award is engineering advancement in the concept of Total Performance based on high-performance testing in open competition." This wasn't the first time that Ford-built cars won the award, nor was it the first time the award was given for a concept rather than a machine. Ford won in 1956 for safety and in 1958 for their four-seater Thunderbird. Both times the concept was the deciding factor. *MT*'s editors said that the '64 Ford-built cars represented the best possible use of high performance testing in bringing to the motoring public a product that lives up to the claims of the maker: "Total Performance."

Ford offered three Galaxie 500XL models for 1964, a fastback coupe, a convertible, and a fastback four-door hardtop. All had the most highly styled and rugged vinyl interiors to date. Door panels had a safety foam backing with deep dish brushed aluminum inserts for the arm rests. Deep dish bucket seats might just as well have been done for Star Trek. These seats were so durable that the driver's seat on a 150,000 mile car will show no more wear than you would expect in 40,000 or 50,000 miles. Therein lies the danger of buying a '64 XL model now. The car was so well constructed that the factory did not hesitate to extend the original warranty to 2 years or 24,000 miles. With that kind of quality built into the car, all too many of them were driven for 10 years or 200,000 miles, and they just don't show their age. Rare is the low mileage '64 XL, as this was not the kind of car you bought to put away in your garage.

*Motor Trend* tested two 1964 Galaxie 500XLs, a four-door hardtop with a 390 and a two-door hardtop with a 427. *MT* could find only two faults: the cars had considerable nose dive on quick stops, and the power brakes were a bit touchy. Testers found that Ford offered one of the best driving positions they'd ever discovered, a combination of good bucket seat design and good wheel positioning. Ride was comfortable, and the car was solid and always controllable. The four-door hardtop clung to the road, storming over tight, twisting mountain routes at high speed. Never once did the four-barrel carb cough or flood, even during maximum effort cornering. Acceleration was strong all the way up to a 108 mph top speed, with no flat spots along the way. 0 to 60 took 9.3 seconds. Economy suffered from the fact that these new cars were 200 to 300 pounds heavier than the previous year's models, despite lighter weight body panels. In over 1500 miles of driving, the four-door sedan averaged 11.4 mpg on premium fuel with a hard-driving low of 9.8 mpg and a highway cruising average of 13 mpg.

The 427 two-door hardtop had no power options. Performance in every respect was noticeably better than the sedan. 0 to 60 took 7.4 seconds, and top speed of 95 mph was reached with two people aboard plus all the test gear. They didn't make a highway run, but Dan Gurney had clocked nearly 150 mph in his single-carb stocker at Riverside the previous year.

WHEN RACE DRIVERS first tried out the '64s they were a little concerned about the extra weight and 1 inch greater height. The increased performance of the 427 might not be enough to compensate for it. But Dan Gurney started off right away winning *Motor Trend's* second annual Riverside 500, taking the checkered flag on the 185th lap, aboard a 1964 Galaxie 500 hardtop. He wasn't challenged after the 59th lap and won in the record time of 94.154 mph, wiping out his previous year's record of 84.965 mph. Dan was followed across the line by Marvin Panch in a Ford, second, and other Fords placing fourth and fifth. That same race was marred by the death of Joe Weatherly on the 87th lap, when he crashed into a wall and then into a 1964 Mercury.

At Daytona the '64 Fords ran into real trouble, losing equipment left and right and plagued by bad luck. Fireball Roberts blew a transmission, Fred Lorenzen split a tire and A.J. Foyt blew an engine, as Plymouth swept the event 1-2-3. The previous year it had been Ford's race, 1-2-3-4. No explanation was ever offered for the failures. Henry Ford II was at the event and told the racing team that Ford wouldn't be unseated that easily. Ford officials petitioned Bill France to okay an $ohc engine immediately so they could have it ready for Atlanta on April 5. France mulled it over for a couple of days and said no.

For a while it looked like the end of Ford's three-year-long total performance campaign. Then the big one bounced back at Atlanta with an engine kit and chassis alterations that completely revised the trend. Fred Lorenzen whipped a Ford home first for the third year in a row at an average speed of 133.879 mph, a new record. But he was only two laps ahead of Bobby Isaac's Dodge. Ned Jarret's Ford was third. Every other car in the top eight was Chrysler-built. Ford won the Rebel 300 at Darlington, 1-2-3, but Plymouth took the World 600 at Charlotte, 1-2, a triumph that was marred by another Ford wreck which critically burned Fireball Roberts. This was a three-Ford crash. Ford still dominated the season and drew every race over 100 miles. It was the same Ford running first, Lorenzen's pearly white, blue-numbered 28, pride of the win-happy Holman and Moody stable. At Darlington, it was Chrysler, 1-2-3, with Ned Jarret's Ford taking fourth. Fred Lorenzen won three of eight super-speedway classics for Ford in 1964.

OUR DRIVEREPORT CAR was a high-mileage 1964 Galaxie 500XL convertible with 390 and Cruise-O-Matic. It was given a complete body and trim restoration by fifties and sixties Ford enthusiast, John Thayer of Carlsbad, California. But little mechanical work has ever been done on the car. We were fortunate to find any '64 Ford Galaxie 500/XL to photograph. Two years ago they were fairly plentiful on the West Coast. Today, most of them have either been driven into the ground, are undergoing restoration, or have been sold to Eastern collectors. Two 1964 Galaxie 500/XL converts were offered for sale at Harrah's 1978 Reno Swap. We tried chasing several advertised in major metropolitan papers. They were sold long before we ever got to see them. A Ford dealer in San Diego's Mission Valley quickly retailed a hardtop at $1200, and the car wasn't sharp enough to photograph. Another dealer here has a convertible sitting in his showroom at $6000. At that price it may sit there for some time. $3500 is about the current West Coast price for one in top condition. The car we finally found was in Carlsbad, about 30 miles north of San Diego, and we stumbled on it almost by accident.

This car was formerly owned by a couple of marines at Camp Pendleton. When Thayer got hold of it, it looked like it had been to Vietnam and back. But it was still running strong with who knows how many miles. There's blowby through the breather cap, steam coming out of the radiator, lifter noise, transmission clunks, et al. But after 14 years, Ford's Total Performance quality still comes through. The engine is still basically quiet and strong. The aging

suspension leaves a lot of lean in the turns, but it's still a long way from being over the hill. Considering its mileage, the car handled remarkably well on twisting mountain roads. Acceleration was still strong. though not quite up to the standards of *MT's* original report. We did not experience the nose dive or power brake touchiness for which *MT* criticized the car. A transmission job, some work on the front end and a new set of shocks would go a long way towards curing most of what ails this XL. It's still a pleasure to drive, and a few minutes behind the wheel is enough to convince any doubter of the collectability of Ford Galaxie 500XLs.

The Total Performance era is a very specific period in recent Ford history. It begins with the 1961 and 1962 models, but does not quite end with the '64s. Ford continued to offer its 2-year or 24,000-mile warranty through 1967, then followed Chrysler briefly on the 5/50 route. There is already considerable collector interest in all Mustangs through 1968, and Lincoln four-door convertibles through their last year of production, 1967. Ask any collector why he favors any Ford product of this era, and you always seem to come up with the same answer: The oustanding quality Ford was building into its cars at this time.

When we approached the Ford Motor Company in researching this project, they seemed to be a little surprised that collectors would be interested in such recent cars. This was not the exciting period of Ford in the fifties when the dreamboats got off the drawing boards. It was a period when the entire industry reached production and performance standards which we are not likely to see again. 1966 marked the beginning of government intervention in safety standards. These standards have become more constraining every year since. Today, labor problems, lawsuits and legislative dicta dog the industry like never before. Which is not to say that good cars can no longer be built. But it is making cars of relatively recent vintage more appealing to collectors than ever before. And when collectors start looking back to the recent years, Galaxie 500XLs are sure to shine among the brightest of stars. □

*Our special thanks to Bill Boyer, Mike Davis and Tom Shearer of the Ford Motor Company, Dearborn, Mich.; Jim Bradley, National Automotive History Collection, Detroit, Mich.; Gordon Buehrig, Grosse Pointe, Mich.; Alex Tremulis, Ventura, Calif.; Bob Thomas, San Diego, Calif.; and members of the Fabulous Fifties Ford Club.*

**About the author:** Tim Howley's name is a familiar one to readers of *Automobile Quarterly, Car Classics, Coast Car Collector, Autoweek,* and *Old Cars,* where his articles and columns have appeared for a number of years. By day, he's creative director in a San Diego advertising agency, but his first love is writing about, collecting, and restoring cars. Tim's an acknowledged expert on Jordan cars and their creator, Ned Jordan, and is extremely well-versed on special-interest FoMoCo products. This is his first contribution to SIA.

# 1966 FORD FAIRLANE 427

# INCREDIBLE INTERMEDIATE

O F all the great American seven-liter V-8s of the sixties, perhaps none has had more varied application than the Ford 427 wedge. It won LeMans in the Ford Mark II, it thundered under the hoods of dozens of Ford stock cars (and earned the nickname "NASCAR 427" as a result), and it transformed the obsolescent AC Ace into the firebreathing Cobra 427. Because this was the sixties, it did yeoman service in drag racing.

And because this was the sixties, you could drive a 427 on the street.

In fact, you had to. At least you had to be able to. In those innocent days before air pollution controls and space frame race cars, stock meant stock, and homologation meant that the factories had better have that minimum number produced or sanctioning bodies

### by John Matras
### photos by Russell von Sauers

wouldn't permit those models in competition. Not that they didn't look the other way sometimes. But for the most part, there were genuine production versions of the special race models, even if in limited numbers.

Thus in 1966, when the National Hot Rod Association dropped the minimum qualifying production number for super stock to 50, Ford responded by creating the Fairlane 427.

Not that there hadn't been big blocks in Fairlanes before. In 1965, there was the Thunderbolt. Produced in a grand total of 54 copies, the Thunderbolt was

an extremely specialized vehicle. The big-block Ford engine wouldn't normally fit between the shock towers of the first series Fairlanes, which had of course been designed around Ford's revolutionary thin-wall-casting small-block V-8.

To make the engine fit the Thunderbolt, the front suspension had to be redesigned, although to stay legal the basic layout had to remain, and special inner fender panels made. Exhaust headers still had to be wrapped around the suspension, however. Springs were biased to load the rear suspension for traction, with the left front and right rear being stiffer. More obvious were the fiberglass hood, front fenders, door skins, and — on early Thunderbolts — front bumper and splash pan. Because the high riser intake manifold would

# Driving Impressions

The engine rumbles under the hood with that muffled, metallic sound like horsepower rattling around inside cast iron. We're on a deserted side street, and I'm behind the hard plastic steering wheel, sitting on a cloth bench seat that looks like something out of your grandmother's car, if your grandmother's the type that believes a penny saved is a penny earned.

The whole car looks like that — almost. Black sidewall tires on steel wheels with little dog-dish hub caps, baby blue paint on a two-door sedan. There's no radio, and trim is minimal though not totally nonexistent. There aren't even any backup lights. But there's something that very few little old ladies — except maybe one from Pasadena — had. On the front fender is a badge that reads "427." And that's making the rumble under the hood.

I'd driven the car to this side street. It had been easy but certainly not effortless. Power steering was an option but not fitted, nor were power brakes. Real men don't need power accessories. And the clutch, well, there are cars that don't make as much power as that pedal required to push down. The shifter didn't help matters either, and although the Hurst unit that replaced the Ford mechanism long ago worked well enough, there's still a lot of metal for the driver to slide around down there. All in all, one would get almost as much exercise driving this car to a health spa as at the destination.

Turning was a chore with the Fairlane, not only because of the unassisted steering and the big block lump right above it, but also because of the Detroit locker rear end. This differential, made by Detroit Automotive and installed sometimes at the factory and sometimes as a dealer option, was used because Ford's Equa-lok limited slip rear end was not up to the torque of the 427. Although a system of cams was supposed to allow the outside wheel to turn faster in a turn than the inside wheel, it would be hard to prove this in practice. At least it doesn't do so willingly, audibly protesting changes in direction with loud clunks and by trying to push the car straight ahead even at speeds too slow for understeer to be a factor. This isn't understeer, it's overpush.

Drum brakes are on all around, and they're marginal at best. But they're lighter than disc brakes, and that's apparently what mattered most to the guy who filled out the order blank on this car. No radio, bench seats, not even backup lights which would have been in the center of the taillamps. On the other hand, there was bright metal trim around the wheel wells.... Still, there's no doubt that this car was built for going fast in a straight line, and most drag strips have a lot of run-off room on them anyway.

Of course, that doesn't matter at the moment. A large aftermarket 90-degree-sweep Sun tach (replacing a smaller one mounted by Ford) blocks most of the speedometer, and as I sit anticipating the moment, the engine rocks the car at idle to the sounds of mechanical lifters clicking and exhaust pushing its way through the mufflers.

Let's do it.

Feed some throttle, unleash the clutch, stomp on the right side pedal and the hood rises and the tach hits 6,000. Shift (I should have been faster into second) and on it again, and the rear hooks up, and the front end lifts, and we accelerate like a croquet ball with a death wish on the far wicket. Bang, we're at 6,000 and I shift and coast down in third, the engine burbling against the compression.

I try twice more without really banging through the gears the way it's supposed to be done. The heavy clutch and shift mechanism are much harder than anything on the market now, and I suppose with enough practice I could be a regular Dyno Don Nicholson. But the coordination required eludes me for the moment, and rather than trash the clutch, engine and/or transmission on somebody else's car, I decide discretion is the better part of testing. I am nonetheless impressed. Despite relatively narrow Firestone F70-14 Sup-R-Belt tires, the Fairlane hooks solidly, runs straight as a drag strip, and accelerates fast enough to take you all the way back to 1966.

And getting there, despite what they say, is *all* the fun.

*Above and below: It looks like a garden variety plain-jane Fairlane when it's parked, but under the hood is a different story.*

# 1966 FORD

not fit under the standard hood profile, the hood got a distinctive reverse teardrop blister. The inner pair of the quad headlamps became cold air ducts for the carburetor and were covered by hardware cloth. Side and rear glass were replaced by plexiglass, the battery moved to the rear, and the interior made as simple and light as possible. All this came for only $3,900, amazing even at 1964 prices for a factory-delivered race-ready car.

In 1964 stick-shift Thunderbolts were virtually unbeatable in drag race competition, but in 1965 the NHRA changed the rules for the S/S class: The homologating number was raised to 100, and worse, lightweight panels became illegal. The Fairlane, with a surface-deep restyling for '65, could be

had with no more than a 271-horse 289, a far cry from the Thunderbolt of the previous year. It was the Mustang's year anyway, both in sales and drag racing, where Ford's new pony, race-equipped with the single-overhead-cam 427, carried the flag in factory experimental competition.

The Fairlane, largely unchanged since its introduction in 1962, was due for the revision that came in 1966. Lower, longer and wider, the '66 Fairlane was restyled to match the styling theme set by the 1965 revisions to the Galaxie, though with the more rounded lines of the full-size '66 Ford. Quad headlamps were now in a vertical pod and taillamps became vertical rectangles. The chassis was still unitized, and the suspension remained basically the same, with leaf springs at the rear and double A-arms up front with the coils over the upper arm. This time, however, Ford engineers left enough room between the inner fenders for the big-block V-8 and wasted no time in creating a special model to celebrate it, the Fairlane GT — or, as it was known with an automatic transmission, the GTA.

The GT and GTA, available in either hardtop or convertible form ('66 was the first year for Fairlane ragtops), had Ford's venerable 390-cubic-inch engine as standard, along with creature comforts including bucket seats, a console, and other high-line items. With 315 horsepower it certainly was no slug-

gard, but was more than outmatched against a 360-horse Tri-power GTO. This didn't matter all that much, except in bragging rights, C/stock drag racing and certain traffic lights, however, because the standard was carried for Ford intermediate enthusiasts by the Fairlane 427.

New for 1966, the Fairlane 427 was not part of the normal production run and, in fact, wasn't in "general interest" Ford literature. It wasn't in sales brochures, and even the owner's manual was oblivious to the option. That's not surprising, as only a relative handful of the model would be made. Homologation for super stock was dropped to 50 again for 1966, and Ford didn't plan to build many more than that. According to plan, all of them would be white (easier to repaint for racing?), and every one would be the hardtop body style. The 427 was not available in the GT, and the only special marking on the Fairlane 427 was a small "427" badge on the front fenders.

That should have been warning enough. The "427" in the Fairlane 427 was the legendary "sideoiler" engine (see sidebar, below) introduced in 1965. As a part of the same series of engines as the 390, the 427 fit — just —but it wasn't nearly the problem it was in the Thunderbolt. The chassis and suspension could be used without major revision and, in fact, only two

*Hurst shifter has replaced Ford unit in driveReport car. It still requires plenty of rowing to get through the gears.*

## "Sideoiler"

It's hard to describe Ford's 427 wedge in anything but superlatives. It has the urgency of an avalanche and is just about as unstoppable.

Based on Ford's big block series that included the 352, 390, 406 and 428, the 427 first appeared in 1963 and was available in every full-size Galaxie except the station wagon. Power, with a single four-barrel carburetor, was rated at 410 horses (at 5,600 rpm), and a dual-quad setup boosted output to an advertised 425 at 6,000. Torque was 470 and 480 pounds-feet respectively. Remember those numbers.

In 1965, Ford took the lessons learned from competition and built a special version of the 427, the most notable feature of which was a small bulge running down the left side of the block. That small bulge was the external evidence of a new oil gallery for the main bearings that replaced the gallery located in the tappet valley. It had fed the cam bearings first, from which the oil was delivered to the main bearings via grooves passing around the cam bearings. But should the cam bearings not be seated properly, oil pressure to the main bearings would be lost — along with the engine and the race. The gallery in the side of the block served each main. It was this feature that gave the competition 427 the nickname "sideoiler."

Lubrication was a major emphasis in making the engine stay alive in competition. Details included a deep sump oil pickup with a fixed location. This eliminated any problem of air leaks from a swivel joint, and its depth kept it below any foam. Even the tip of the oil pickup pipe was bevel cut so that suction wouldn't pull the screen against the pipe and thereby reduce oil delivery. There are also two oil pressure relief valves, one ahead of the filter and a second that opens only when pressure downstream from the bearings is excessive.

The main bearings were cross-drilled as were the connecting rod journals, providing full oil delivery to each rod bearing during 360 degrees of crank rotation. The crankshaft was a steel forging good for far more than its official 7,000 rpm limitation. Connecting rods were unique in that hollow dowels fastened with steel cap screws replaced the conventional bolt and nuts holding the cap on. The threads on the screws were unique as well, having a triple lobe contour, all in the name of better stress management. The main bearings are held in place by regular vertical bolts and by cross bolts, the heads of which can be seen outside the block.

In 1965, NASCAR made high riser intake manifolds illegal, so Ford engineers simply developed a lower-rise manifold that flowed as much as the old high riser but encroached on hood space. Lightweight sodium-filled valves also carried

heat away from the valve head for longer life. The valve stems had only a .030-inch wall, and the hollow was filled with sodium which transfers heat much more efficiently than steel.

The 427 engines also got special streamlined cast iron exhaust manifolds that, judging from looks alone, must have been almost as good as tube headers.

A 90-psi Holley fuel pump fed a ⅜-inch i.d. fuel line that hooked up to a log resting on the right side of the pair of Holley 650-cfm, four-barrel carburetors that came on most 427s. The 427 could have been had with a single four barrel, but most were delivered with dual quads. Horsepower was rated at 410 (@ 5,600 rpm) and 425 (@ 6,000 rpm) respectively. Take those numbers for what they're worth, as they're exactly the same as when the engine was introduced and never changed.

Although an extremely limited number of 1966 Fairlane 427s were built, the 427 was a regular production engine, even if not the most common engine in the Ford lineup. Very different was the 428, the new-for-'66 Thunderbird engine having hydraulic lifters, a single carb only, and a different bore and stroke. The "only 345 horsepower" top T-Bird mill was a better engine for most folks: smoother, quieter and easier to care for. But for all-out, drop-dead, follow-my-tailpipes performance, there was nothing out of Dearborn like the 427.

# specifications

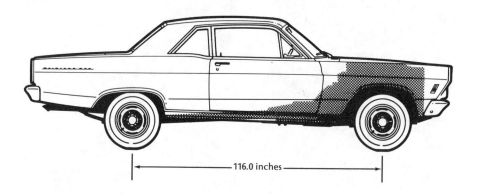

116.0 inches

58.0 inches

## 1966 Ford Fairlane 427

**Price** $2,423
**Options** 4-speed transmission, 427 engine, Detroit "locker" differential

### ENGINE
**Type** 8-cylinder 90° vee, ohv
**Bore x stroke** 4.2346 x 3.784 inches
**Displacement** 427 cubic inches
**Max bhp @ rpm** 4V: 410 @ 5,600; 8V: 425 @ 6,000
**Max torque @ rpm** 480 lb./ft. @ 3,700
**Compression ratio** 12.0:1
**Exhaust system** Dual

### CLUTCH
**Type** Single dry plate
**Diameter** 11.5 inches

### TRANSMISSION
**Type** 4-speed, floor mounted
**Ratios: 1st** 2.32:1
**2nd** 1.69:1
**3rd** 1.29:1
**4th** 1.00:1
**Reverse** 2.32:1

### DIFFERENTIAL
**Type** Detroit "locker"
**Ratio** 3.89:1

### STEERING
**Type** Recirculating ball
**Power assist** No

### BRAKES
**Type** 4-wheel hydraulic drum
**Power assist** No

### CHASSIS & BODY
**Body construction** Unit body, steel

### SUSPENSION
**Front** Independent A-arm, high coil, anti-roll bar, tube shocks
**Rear** Live axle on semi-elliptic leaf springs, tube shocks
**Wheels** Steel
**Tires** 7.75x14

### WEIGHTS AND MEASURES
**Wheelbase** 116 inches
**Overall length** 197 inches
**Overall width** 74 inches
**Front track** 58 inches
**Rear track** 58 inches
**Height** 55 inches (sedan); 54.3 (hardtop)
**Shipping weight** 2,923 (Fairlane 500 V-8 series)

*In profile the Fairlane looks like a ¾-scale version of full-size '66 Ford.*

# 1966 FORD

*Above left and above: Taillamp treatment is also stock Fairlane, as are the cheapie small wheel covers. Below: The one giveaway to this car's power potential is the small badges on the front fenders.*

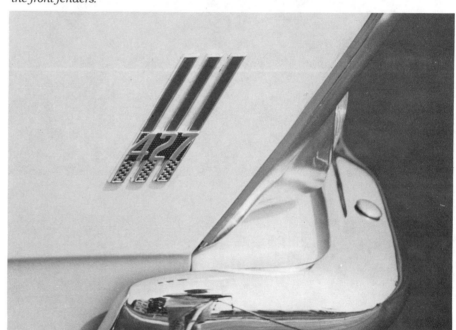

modifications had to be made for the engine to fit. One was the drilling of the inner fenders in strategic locations to allow the exhaust manifold bolts to be fully withdrawn to remove the manifold. The other was a fiberglass hood with small scoops along the leading edge. The hood was not on the normal hinges, but instead was held down by pins at all four corners, and the hood was simply lifted off for service. The scoops were there not so much for ventilation but to provide a bit more clearance over the air cleaner. The standard transmission, in fact the only one available, was the four-speed manual "top loader" — so named for the inspection plate that was on the top rather than on the side of the gearbox.

Although the Fairlane 427 may not have required the major surgery that the Thunderbolt did, there were significant differences from lesser Fairlanes. Suspension was beefed up front and rear, a heavy-duty transmission output shaft and universal joints were substituted for standard, and a driveshaft that looks like something from a battleship carried torque back to a "Detroit locker" differential and thence to large 31-spline axle shafts. Standard tires were 7.75 x 14, but Ford performance literature unabashedly recommended seven-inch slicks for drag racing. Otherwise one was free to specify any number of options on the Fairlane 427, although any racer worth his powershift likely ordered it stripped of everything that didn't make it accelerate faster.

Serious racers, however, ran into another problem, namely the MoPar Hemi 426, against which it was matched in A/Stock competition. If that wasn't bad enough, the NHRA ruled that fiberglass panels and hoods couldn't be used in stock classes unless they were made in quantities of 500 or more. Because only about 70 1966 427 Fairlanes were made, this bumped it up into A/FX to run against the top "factory experimental" cars such as the SOHC Mustangs, where it was thoroughly outclassed.

## General Specifications:
### Ford 427 High-Performance Engine

| | |
|---|---|
| Type . . . . . . . . . . . 8-cyl. 90-degree vee, ohv | Pistons . . . . . . Extruded aluminum cam ground; 23.31 oz. |
| Displacement . . . . . . . . . . . . . . . 427 cu. in. | Piston pins . . . . . . Alloy steel, full floating tubular |
| Bore & stroke . . . . 4.2346 x 3.784 inches | |
| Max. torque . . . . . 480 lb./ft. @ 3,700 rpm | Connecting rods . . . . . . . . . . Forged steel |
| Compression ratio . . . . . . . . . . . . . . 12.0:1 | **Cam timing** |
| | Operating tappet clearance . . . . 0.027″ |
| Brake hp . . . . . . . . . 4V: 410 @ 5,600 rpm | Intake valve opens . . . . . . . . . . 8 degree 30 sec. ATC |
| 8V: 425 @ 6,000 rpm | Intake valve closes . . . . . . . . . 36 degree 30 sec. ABC |
| Valve lifters . . . . . . . . . . . . . . . . . . . Solid | |
| Fuel . . . . . . . . . . . . . . . . . Super premium | Duration . . . . . . 324 degree theoretical |
| Exhaust . . . . . . . . . . . . . . . . . . . . . . Dual | Exhaust valve opens . . . . . . . 39 degree 30 sec. BBC |
| Cylinder block . . . . . . . Precision cast iron | Exhaust valve closes . . . . . . . 11 degree 30 sec. BTC |
| Cylinder head . . . . . . . Precision cast iron | Duration . . . . . . 324 degree theoretical |
| Crankshaft . . . . . . . . . . . . . . . Forged steel | Valve opening . . . . . . . . . . . . 96 degree theoretical |
| Camshaft . . . . . . . . . . . Precision molded special alloy iron | Valve lift, int. and exh. @ zero lash . . . . |
| | . . . . . . . . . . . . . . . . . . . . . . . . . . . . . . 524″ |
| Intake valves . . . . . . . . Special alloy valve steel-chrome plated stem | |
| Exhaust valves . . . . . 21-4N forged steel chrome plated stem | |

# 1966 FORD

*Above and below: This is most definitely not the kind of motive power needed to pick up the kids from Cub Scouts and go grocery shopping. **Bottom:** Detroit locker rearend causes noticeable understeer in the twisty bits of the road.*

Relief came in 1967 when the NHRA expanded Super Stock from a single class (with A/S, B/S, and down for lesser cars) to five levels from SS/A to SS/E depending on power and weight combinations. The Fairlane 427, basically unchanged for '67 except that all body styles and factory colors were available, fell into SS/B, where it proved to be much more competitive.

The '66 Fairlane 427's greatest mark in racing history came serendipitously not in drag racing but in stock car competition, though it was actually pioneered by Bud Moore's efforts with a Mercury Comet driven by Darel Dierenger. The Ford effort had been with its big Galaxie, with an eye to marketing as much as to speed. However, increasing competition forced a reevaluation of this policy, and the five-inches-narrower Fairlane was too good an opportunity to pass up. On September 25, 1966, Fred Lorenzen took the checker on the Martinsville, Virginia, half-mile paved oval for the first Fairlane NASCAR victory, which he followed up with a season-closing win at Rockingham in October. From then on, as

long as there were Fairlanes it was the racer of choice for those who ran in NASCAR under the Ford banner. The 427 had found a new home and another venue to demonstrate its prowess. □

**Acknowledgements and Bibliography**
*Special thanks to John Vermersh of Ford SVO for his recollections and information on the Fairlane 427.*
*Major references included* Fearsome Fords 1959-1963 *by Phil Hall, 1982;* The Book of Ford-Powered Performance Cars, *produced by Lyle Kenyon Engel, 1966;* Ford High Performance, *by Ak Miller for Ford Motor Company, 1966, and others. Thanks also to Mel Wheeler, and to the Boulevard Cruisers of Hasbrouck Heights, New Jersey; Vinny Knapp, Raceway Park, Englishtown, New Jersey.*

*Left: Aftermarket gauges help protect against premature demise of 427.* **Above:** *Eight barrels gulping fuel and air churn out 425 bhp.* **Below:** *Trunk area, too, is as stock as your Aunt Minnie's Fairlane Six.*

## Is It Real?

Those who have read the story and looked at the photos should have noticed that the car in the photos isn't a white hardtop, like all 1966 Fairlane 427s were supposed to be, but a baby blue sedan. Nor does it have a fiberglass hood with hood pins and scoops. Nor does it have the reinforcements cut out of the bottom side of the hood the way the '67 Comet 427s did for air cleaner clearance. (There were from "zero" to "six or seven" '66 Comet 427s made, depending on whom one asks.) And the air cleaner has a 427 logo on it, which it wasn't supposed to have in 1966.

What goes on here? Is this a real Fairlane 427 — or just a Fairlane with a 427?

Well, the VIN number looks right and includes the "R" code that indicates a 427. But, according to one expert, the rivets holding the plate in place are not original. But then again, the number matches the other visible serial numbers. And if one were going to build a bogus Fairlane 427, why not build a hardtop in the first place?

The car's build plate indicates that it was put together in August 1966 at Ford's Kansas City plant (the Fairlane 427 was a production line item and not assembled by a sub-contractor) and, as says John Vermersh, now at Ford SVO but in '66 responsible for putting together the homologation papers for the race sanctioning organizations, "Anything was possible back then." That there are no records now doesn't prove that the car couldn't have been made then. Dealer special orders were very possible.

As for checking with the dealer, well, the car was originally sold, according to the owner's manual that came with the car, by California Motors in Glendale, California. Unfortunately, they went out of business in the late sixties, and we were unable to locate any "old timers" from that company. On the other hand, the owner's manual lists the same serial number as the car.

Does anybody out there know anything more about this car?

# 1966 THUNDERBIRD

**by Arch Brown**
**photos by Bud Juneau**

I t isn't often that one runs across a virtually "new" 21-year-old car, but this one surely qualifies. With 28,213 miles on its clock, our driveReport Thunderbird Town Hardtop literally hasn't a scratch on its original Honeydew Yellow finish; and the car performs as though it had just left the showroom!

The 'Bird was sold originally by University Motors, of San Diego. The buyers, William and Bessie Sladeck, paid $4,748.04 for it, cash, including $179.96 sales tax and $69.00 license fee. Since the sticker price, which took account of neither tax nor license, came to $5,536.09, one has to conclude that the Sladecks drove a very hard bargain!

They didn't drive that bargain very much, however. For four years, in fact, it lay in storage, and in 1977 the Sladecks sold the Thunderbird to a San Diego neighbor, Donald Borgen. Borgen then re-sold it, a year later, to Robert Toeffer, of Sunnyvale, 400 miles to the north. At that point the car had been driven just 17,776 miles.

Toeffer didn't use the 'Bird very much, either, and in 1984 he sold it to Stanley Phillips, of Livermore. Phillips was more inclined to drive his purchase and enjoy it, and by the time he sold the Thunderbird to Dr. Elwood Griest, a local surgeon, in 1987, he had run the mileage up to 27,900.

And by the way, all of these owners, from the Sladecks up to and including Dr. Griest, are members of the Vintage Thunderbird Club of America — an unusual circum-stance, we think.

As we have noted, this is an automobile built for comfort, not for performance, though its off-the-line acceleration (zero to sixty in 11.4 seconds) and top speed (somewhere around the century mark) aren't bad for so heavy a machine. But it's softly sprung, providing a sort of "floating" ride, and although it handles sharp dips better than one might expect, in hard cornering the T-Bird leans and plows and scrubs hell out of the front tires.

All of which really doesn't matter a bit. The chap who wanted to hot-dog his car, back in 1966, wouldn't have bought this one in the first place. He'd have gone for something smaller, lighter and faster — a GTO, maybe, or a Fairlane GT, or a Charger with a 426 Hemi under the hood. The Thunderbird, in contrast, is a freeway cruiser, a boulevardier, at its best on the long, straight stretches. In all justice, the suspension is not as mushy as that of some 1966 models, but it is clearly set up for cushy comfort, rather than high performance. Passengers are effectively insulated from road noise, and with this kind of speed at his command the driver can cruise as fast as he cares to, at least until the law catches up with him.

Crosswinds, as *Motor Trend* has noted, don't bother these cars. Directional stability is good; there's no tendency to wander. Some earlier Thunderbirds drew criticism for fading brakes following a few hard stops. But commencing in 1965 Ford cured that problem with an excellent disc/drum setup — power-assisted, of course. These binders are somewhat touchy; they take some getting used to. But according to *Motor Trend's* test crew, they cut 17 feet off the stopping distance from 60 miles an hour, as compared to the 1964 model. And we found the "nosedive" to be minimal.

The seats are quite low, yet they're exceptionally comfortable. There's little lateral support, but that's a matter of small consequence since this car was clearly not meant for "slalom" duty. Front leg room is adequate, even for the tall driver, and it's not too bad in the rear. The dash panel, with its full complement of gauges, is both handsome and legible, and the "swing-away" steering wheel facilitates the boarding process, especially for the stout driver. The contoured rear seat, which Ford referred to as a "lounge" is very inviting, though knee room is less than generous.

I've always looked upon the Town Hard-top as the handsomest of this generation of Thunderbirds, but it seemed to me — never having driven one — that the blind quarter panel would be a serious handicap to the driver's visibility. In this, I received a pleasant surprise. In part because of the wide rear window, vision is less obstructed than I expected, though I would still be grateful for a right outside mirror. All-in-all, though, this is really a very pleasant, easy car to drive.

# "BIG BIRD"

## Driving Impressions

Given its 10.5:1 compression ratio, it's hardly surprising that Dr. Griest's Thunderbird registers the occasional protest against the low-octane gas that we're getting nowadays. But that's a criticism of the fuel, not the car.

The overhead "safety" panel is an interesting gimmick — really not a bad feature.

Warning lights serve notice if seat belts aren't fastened (a much gentler reminder than the "squawker" provided by my own car), or if there's a door ajar, or if the flasher lights are in operation. Or when fuel is running low, which it will do pretty rapidly at about 11 miles to the gallon.

There's a hideaway compartment in the center armrest, big enough for a pair of gloves but not much else. The trunk, however, is commodious, thanks to its deep well.

Other interesting devices include sequential turn signals, presaging those of the 1967 Mercury Cougar, and an automatic parking brake release, activated the moment the transmission is shifted to "Drive." Ventilation is exceptionally good, thanks to a full-width air vent under the rear window. When the vent is opened (by means of a control lever on the console), a suction effect is created, drawing stale air out of the car while pulling in fresh air at the cowl. The air conditioner is an excellent unit, supplying plenty of cool air and circulating it gently throughout the car.

From time to time my work takes me to the Los Angeles area, a 350-mile drive down Interstate 5. I can't imagine a more pleasant, comfortable car for such a journey than this smooth, silent Thunderbird. On the other hand, I also make occasional trips to Reno, in order to do research at the Harrah library. For that trip I often take State Route 50 in lieu of Interstate 80, simply because 50 — though it is slow, narrow and winding — is one of the most beautiful drives known to man. For that kind of travel the Thunderbird would be a miserable choice! Much more appropriate for that purpose is the precise control of a car with taut suspension and minimal avoirdupois.

But then, no car can have everything!

*Above: Town Hardtop's blind rear quarters give 'Bird more formal appearance. Right: False airscoop was a Thunderbird styling fillip which began with the original edition back in '55. Below: Lamps as wide as car out back also house unique sequential turn signals.*

## Price List: 1966 Thunderbird

| | |
|---|---|
| Hardtop | $4,426 |
| Town Hardtop | $4,483 |
| Town Landau | $4,584 |
| Convertible | $4,879 |

## Price List: 1966 Thunderbird Options

| | |
|---|---|
| 428-c.i.d. 345-horsepower engine | $64.30 |
| SelectAire Conditioner | $412.90 |
| 6-way power seat, driver and passenger | $193.33 |
| 6-way power seat, driver only | $96.62 |
| Power windows | $103.20 |
| Limited-slip differential | $46.35 |
| Tinted glass (windshield and all windows) | $41.79 |
| Highway pilot control/unique steering wheel | $128.72 |
| Safety/convenience control panel (standard, Town models) | $56.36 |
| AM/FM pushbutton radio and antenna | $81.55 |
| AM radio with stereo-sonic tape system | $127.56 |
| Reclining passenger seat and headrest | $43.83 |
| Leather seat upholstery with reclining passenger seat and headrest | $147.03 |
| Two-tone paint | $25.07 |
| White sidewall tires with red band | $42.93 |

FORD did indeed have a "Better Idea." A series of them, in fact, as the Thunderbird has evolved over the years.

In 1955 there was the "Little Bird," the diminutive two-seater that has become the darling of collectors everywhere. Unlike Chevrolet's Corvette, it was no sports car, nor did it pretend to be. Powered by a 193-horsepower, 292-c.i.d. V-8, it was fast enough. But the chassis was set up for comfort, not for performance.

Sales, which totaled 16,155 that first year, were better than expected, and many times higher than those of the Corvette. But the little T-Bird wasn't a money-maker for the company, nor was there any realistic prospect that it ever would be. So, since division manager Robert McNamara was a man with his eye on the bottom line, the two-seater had to go.

Its replacement, popularly known as the "Square Bird," was introduced on February 13, 1958. Styled under the direction of Bill Boyer, this one was a roomy four-passenger car, two feet longer and nearly 600 pounds heavier than its predecessor. And unlike the earlier car, which had been built only as a convertible (though with an optional removable hard top), this second-generation car was available as either a hardtop or a ragtop. Built side-by-side with the Lincoln and the Continental at Ford's new Wixom, Michigan, plant, the new Thunderbird was constructed on the monocoque principle. That is to say, body and frame were unitized, the first use of this technique by a Ford car.

The extra weight of the enlarged Thunderbird called for additional power under the hood. Happily, there was a new family of Ford engines that year, derived from the 1954 "Y" block and developed by a team headed by chief engineer Robert Stevenson. Featuring larger valves and huskier bearings than the 292 and 312-c.i.d. V-8s, these were excellent engines, some versions of which would remain in production into the 1970s. As fitted to the 1958 Thunderbird, the new mill — known as the "Interceptor 352" — displaced 352 cubic inches and was rated at 300 horsepower, up from 212 bhp in the 292-c.i.d. engine employed for the 1957 model.

Also new for 1958 was the Cruise-O-Matic transmission. Derived from the earlier Ford-O-Matic, it was a three-speed unit, permitting the driver to choose between first- and second-gear starts.

One of the most remarkable aspects of the Square Bird project was the fact that only $50 million — pocket change, by Ford standards — was allocated to cover research and development, as well as tooling. Yet the finished product was good enough to win *Motor Trend's*

coveted "Car of the Year" designation. In making the award the editors cited the Thunderbird's "totally new concept in interior packaging." And indeed, the new 'Bird's interior measurements were surprisingly generous, especially with regard to head room. Compared to the Chrysler 300-D, for instance, the T-Bird stood nearly five inches lower, yet managed to preserve virtually the same head room.

Some readers will recall that 1958 was the year of the so-called "Eisenhower recession." Overall, the automobile industry took a bath that season. Buick's production, for instance, was down by 37 percent, Mercury's by 53 percent. There were, however, two bright spots in the picture: AMC's Rambler, which scored a 90 percent sales increase over 1957; and the new Thunderbird, whose production exceeded the combined totals of 1956 and '57. The Wixom plant was actually put on overtime for a while, in order to keep up with the demand, and profits from the enterprise exceeded predictions.

*Above: Formal, squared off look is carried through to back window. Left: Front directional indicator rides atop fenders. Below: Factory mirror carries Thunderbird emblem.*

Clearly, Ford was on the right track with the four-passenger Thunderbird. Electing to stand pat on a winning hand, the company made few changes for 1959, though the 430-c.i.d. Lincoln engine became available at extra cost. It had been planned to offer Ford-Aire suspension as an option, but problems with the system became altogether too apparent, even before the '59 T-Bird was introduced, and the idea was fortunately cashiered.

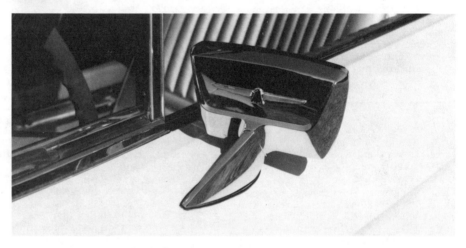

Once again, Thunderbird production nearly doubled. And the 1960 version, again with no major changes, saw another sharp sales increase.

Industry-wide, styling tended to run in three-year cycles in those days, and the T-Bird was no exception. For 1961 a very different 'Bird made its appearance. More slippery than its predecessors, it featured a low cowl, sharply sloping windshield and slightly convex sides, all of which contributed to a significantly lower coefficient of drag. Once again the design was developed under the supervision of Bill Boyer, though it is said that the inspiration came from Alex Tremulis, then a member of Ford's styling team.

Unfortunately, this model — colloquially known as the "Banana-nose Bird" — never achieved the popularity of its predecessor, and over its three-year lifespan (1961-63) sales fell far short of the 1960 figure. This, despite the fact that overall the Ford Division was doing very well.

Nevertheless, it was a better car than the Square Birds had been. Steering was quicker, handling was improved, brakes were enlarged, and this time a 390-cubic-inch engine was supplied as standard issue. Rated horsepower re-

| Thunderbird Production, 1955-1966 | | | | | | |
|---|---|---|---|---|---|---|
| | Hardtop | Convertible | Landau | Roadster | Town Hardtop | Total |
| **The "Little Birds"** | | | | | | |
| 1955 | | 16,155 | | | | 16,155 |
| 1956 | | 15,631 | | | | 15,631 |
| 1957 | | 21,280 | | | | 21,280 |
| **The "Square Birds"** | | | | | | |
| 1958 | 35,758 | 2,134 | | | | 37,892 |
| 1959 | 57,195 | 10,261 | | | | 67,456 |
| 1960 | 80,938 | 11,860 | | | | 92,798 |
| **The "Banana-Nose Birds"** | | | | | | |
| 1961 | 62,535 | 10,516 | | | | 73,051 |
| 1962 | 68,127 | 8,417 | * | 1,427 | | 77,971 |
| 1963 | 42,806 | 5,913 | 14,139 | 455 | | 63,313 |
| **The "Big Birds"** | | | | | | |
| 1964 | 60,552 | 9,198 | 22,715 | | | 92,465 |
| 1965 | 42,652 | 6,846 | 25,474 | | | 74,972 |
| 1966 | 13,389 | 5,049 | 35,105 | | 15,633 | 69,176 |
| * Included in hardtop total | | | | | | |
| Source: Heasley, Jerry, *The Production Figure Book for US Cars* | | | | | | |

*This page, above: Wheel cover makes sure you know what kind of car it's attached to. **Right:** Big backup lamp follows contours of taillamps. **Facing page, left and right:** Swing-away steering wheel made exit and entry easy for driver in low-slung 'Bird.*

mained at 300, but the torque was substantially increased, and according to Alex Tremulis the car was about six miles an hour faster than its predecessor. New features included a "swing-away" steering wheel that moved, with the transmission in "Park," ten inches to the right, for easy entry and egress.

Two new models were added to the Thunderbird line for 1962. The first of these was the Landau, a vinyl-topped version of the hardtop, featuring ersatz landau irons on the rear roof panels. The other was the Sports Roadster (see *SIA #44*), a clever modification of the standard T-Bird convertible. A fiberglass tonneau hid the latter car's rear seat, giving it the appearance of a two-passenger machine. Created thus was a rear deck the length of which, some have suggested, would have done credit to an aircraft carrier. The cover, which supplied padded headrests for both driver and passenger, was so-designed as to permit raising and lowering the top whether or not the tonneau was in place. And the cover could be removed, when desired, to expose the rear seat. Kelsey-Hayes wire wheels were supplied

## The Competition Cometh — At Last!

The surprising thing is that it took so long for the competition to wake up to the lucrative potential of the "luxury personal car" market.

Tooling costs were enormous, to be sure. Enough to make even an organization the size of General Motors think twice. Evidently GM thought three or four times, for it wasn't until 1963 that the Buick Division introduced Bill Mitchell's stunning Riviera to challenge the Thunderbird. And three more years went by before Oldsmobile entered the fray.

Originally, the Riviera had been intended as a Cadillac. At one point in its development, in fact, it was referred to as a LaSalle, representing a possible revival of Cadillac's never-to-be-forgotten "companion" car. (The reader will recall that the leading edge of the 1963-65 Riviera's fenders bore a distinct resemblance to the tall, narrow grille of the 1934-40 LaSalles. The likeness was no coincidence.)

But Buick had fallen upon hard times, plummeting from third place in 1956 to ninth rank, just four years later. A shot in the arm was needed, something flashy, eye-catching, interesting enough to attract potential buyers to Buick's showrooms. So Cadillac's LaSalle became Buick's Riviera.

In the beginning the Riviera was a little bigger (though a couple of hundred pounds lighter), a bit more powerful and

about a hundred dollars cheaper than the Thunderbird. Its lines were crisp, clean, almost classic. And fresh, whereas the 'Bird's "banana-nose" design was in its third year. Reviews were universally favorable.

Yet the T-Bird outsold the "Riv," three-to-two. Perhaps that was partly due to the fact that there were four Thunderbird variations to choose from, compared to the Riviera's single model. But far more important, we suspect, was the matter of image — and name. Buick had used the Riviera designation for a variety of hardtops, and even on sedans, as far back as 1949. The name, though a good one, had no clear connotation. The Thunderbird, on the other hand, had an established image. Everybody knew what the moniker stood for!

Three years later, in 1966, the second-generation Riviera appeared. Once again a freshly styled Buick was competing against a T-Bird whose body shell was entering its third season. Once again the Riviera was more powerful than its competitor from Dearborn, only the margin was greater this time. And now there was a new competitor, the front-wheel-drive Toronado, from Oldsmobile. At 385 horsepower, the newcomer was by far the most powerful machine of the three. *Car and Driver*, reflecting the unanimous verdict of the automotive press, noted that the Toro would "corner faster...than any American

car of similar size," adding that "It's a rare bird: a driver's car that doesn't detract from the comfort of passengers."

Meanwhile, Buick offered an optional Gran Sport package for the Riviera. Heavy-duty suspension, quicker steering and a 3.23 axle with positive traction combined to make the GS, in *Motor Trend's* view, "one of the most exciting new cars for 1966. It's a driver's car that handles, stops and goes like it seated two in the open rather than six in relaxing, closed comfort." (There's some hyperbole here, of course. With bucket seats up front, it's not easy to see where the sixth passenger would fit in, unless space was found for him in the trunk.)

But still, the softly suspended Thunderbird was by far the best-seller of the three, outstripping both the Riviera and the Toronado by margins of more than three-to-two.

Times have changed since our driveReport car was built, and the Thunderbird competes now in a different market. Downsized in 1977 and again in 1980, and featuring since 1983 a sleek, aerodynamic shape, the 'Bird is still distinctly a "personal" car, enhanced by a number of luxury touches. Yet it is offered at a much more affordable price than its erstwhile rivals from General Motors.

And once again the Thunderbird appears to be spot-on, in terms of what the market demands!

as part of the Roadster package, which fetched an extra $651 over the price of the Thunderbird convertible.

Of all the "Banana Nose" 'Birds, the Roadsters are by far the most desirable from the collector's standpoint. And the hardest to find, for only 1,427 were built during the 1962 model year, a figure which dropped to 455 for 1963. Rarest of all is the 1963 Roadster equipped with the "M" series engine. Fed by three two-barrel carburetors, this one was rated at 340 horsepower. Production totaled just 37 units.

The fourth generation Thunderbird made its debut for 1964. We refer to it here as the "Big Bird" because, although it was only marginally longer and wider than the 1963 model, it was 244 pounds heavier and much more massive in appearance. Performance suffered somewhat, for despite the additional weight, horsepower remained at 300 — and the M series engine was no longer available. Even so, *Car Life* clocked a '64 T-Bird at 115 miles an hour.

Sheet metal was completely new that year, and while the car retained the sloping prow that had characterized the 1961-63 models, most observers found it much improved in appearance, compared to the "Banana Nose." But if the exterior styling was somewhat subdued, the aircraft-inspired dash panel was not. Some called it garish; *Motor Trend* found it confusing, at least at first acquaintance. Nevertheless, the overall effect of this fourth-edition Thunderbird was one of elegance and refinement.

Evidently it was just what the public wanted. The T-Bird's popularity increased by nearly half over the 1963 figure, although industry-wide auto sales — including those of the Buick Riviera (see *SIA* #33) — were off a little for the year.

*Motor Trend* characterized the 1964 Thunderbird as "a heavy, luxurious prestige four-seater that gives its owner a soft, smooth ride and every imaginable creature comfort." Reviewer Bob McVay added that it "doesn't lend itself to fast driving," a pretty accurate appraisal, although *M/T*'s test crew recorded a top speed of 105 miles an hour. (It's interesting to note, by the way, the ten mph spread between *Motor Trend*'s test results and those of *Car Life*, using a supposedly identical car.) Acceleration — zero to 60 in 11.2 seconds, according to *Motor Trend*, was slower by three full seconds than the Lincoln-powered 1959 "Square Bird" tested by *Road & Track*.

Changes for 1965 were more real than apparent, at least to the extent that front disc brakes were adopted — a badly needed modification. There were minor differences in trim, presumably for identification purposes, but the styling theme remained unchanged.

Sales of the 1965 version were off sharply, however, although the industry as a whole (including the Ford Division) was enjoying an excellent season. One has to suspect that the record-shattering popularity of the jaunty, bargain-priced Mustang may have cut somewhat into the Thunderbird's market!

A welcome change for 1966 was an increase in the Thunderbird's horsepower, to 315 with the standard engine. And for those who wanted a little more punch, an extra $64.30 bought the optional 345-horsepower, 428-c.i.d. V-8. As *Motor Trend* noted, "The new 428 will give added snap, and the discs will be able to cope with it, too."

Joining the line for 1966 were two new body styles. Replacing the previous Landau was the new Town Landau, characterized by blind quarter panels but retaining the earlier model's vinyl roof and simulated landau irons. Its companion, the Town Hardtop — displayed on these pages — featured the same blind quarter panels, but without the added trim. Both Town models presented a more formal appearance than any previous Thunderbird. Perhaps unexpectedly, the Landau version proved to be by far the best-seller among the four T-Bird styles.

There was a further decline in Thunderbird sales for 1966, though the drop was not as sharp as that experienced the previous season. Still, sales remained comfortably ahead of those of Buick's Riviera, as well as the "new kid on the block," Oldsmobile's sensational front-wheel-drive Toronado (see sidebar, page 124).

The fifth-generation T-Bird, intro-

## Thunderbird Versus The Competition
### A Statistical Comparison

| | Thunderbird | Riviera | Toronado |
|---|---|---|---|
| Price (base hdtp, f.o.b. factory) | $4,426 | $4,424 | $4,617 |
| Engine c.i.d. | 390 | 425 | 425 |
| Stroke/bore ratio | 1.07:1 | 1.18:1 | 1.04:1 |
| Horsepower @ rpm | 315 @ 4,600 | 340 @ 4,400 | 385 @ 4,800 |
| Torque @ rpm | 427 @ 2,800 | 465 @ 2,800 | 475 @ 3,200 |
| Compression ratio | 10.50:1 | 10.25:1 | 10.50:1 |
| Carburetor | 1-4V | 1-4V | 1-4V |
| Transmission | Cruise-O-Matic | Super Turbine | Turbo-HydraMatic |
| Drive wheels | Rear | Rear | Front |
| Final drive ratio | 3.02:1 | 3.07:1 | 3.21:1 |
| Brakes | Disc/drum | Drum | Drum |
| Steering ratio (gear/overall) | 17.0/20.4 | 17.5/19.4 | 17.5/17.8 |
| Turn circle (curb/curb) | 42'8" | 44'0" | 43'0" |
| Tires | 8.15/15 | 8.45/15 | 8.85/15 |
| Wheelbase | 113" | 119" | 119" |
| Overall length | 205.4" | 211.2" | 211.0" |
| Overall width | 77.3" | 79.3" | 78.5" |
| Overall height | 52.5" | 54.5" | 52.8" |
| Track, front/rear | 61.0"/60.0" | 63.4"/63.0" | 63.5"/63.0" |
| Shipping weight (lbs.) | 4,359 | 4,424 | 4,617 |
| HP/c.i.d. | .808 | .800 | .906 |
| Lbs/HP | 13.8 | 13.0 | 12.0 |
| Production (all body styles) | 69,176 | 42,799 | 40,963 |
| Primary source: *Automotive Industries*, March 15, 1966 | | | |

# specifications

Illustrations by Russell von Sauers, The Graphic Automobile Studio

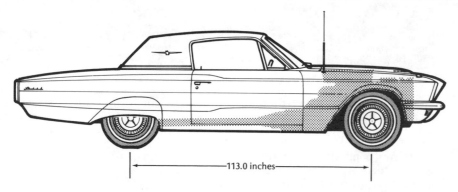

—113.0 inches—     —61.0 inches—

## 1966 Ford Thunderbird

**Price** $4,483 f.o.b. factory with standard equipment, federal excise tax and preparation charges included

**Standard equipment** Cruise-O-Matic transmission, power steering, power disc/drum brakes, AM radio, over-head safety panel (Town models only), remote control outside rearview mirror, electric clock, windshield washers, under-body soundcoating, MagicAire heater/defroster, full wheel covers, backup lights, retractable seat belts with warning light, Silent-Flo ventilation system, courtesy light, map light, glove box light, automatic parking brake release, electric clock, swing-away steering wheel

**Options on dR car** SelectAire conditioner, tinted glass (all windows), power windows, power driver's seat, power antenna, rear speaker, white sidewall tires, special wheel covers with simulated knock-off hubs

### ENGINE
| | |
|---|---|
| Type | 90-degree V-8 |
| Bore x stroke | 4.05 inches by 3.78 inches |
| Displacement | 390 cubic inches |
| Compression ratio | 10.5:1 |
| HP @ rpm | 315 @ 4,600 |
| Torque @ rpm | 427 @ 2,800 |
| Taxable HP | 52.49 |
| Valve config. | OHV |
| Valve lifters | Hydraulic |
| Main bearings | 5 |
| Induction system | 1 4-bbl carburetor, mechanical pump |

| | |
|---|---|
| Lubrication system | Pressure |
| Exhaust system | Dual |
| Electrical system | 12-volt |

### TRANSMISSION
| | |
|---|---|
| Type | Cruise-O-Matic 3-speed automatic planetary gearset with torque converter |
| Ratios: 1st | 2.40:1 |
| 2nd | 1.47:1 |
| 3rd | Direct |
| Reverse | 2.00:1 |
| Max. ratio at stall (torque converter) | 2.10 |

### DIFFERENTIAL
| | |
|---|---|
| Type | Hypoid |
| Ratio | 3.02:1 |
| Drive axles | Semi-floating |

### STEERING
| | |
|---|---|
| Type | Recirculating ball nut, power assisted |
| Ratios | 17.0:1 gear; 20.4:1 overall |
| Turns, lock to lock | 3½ |
| Turn circle | 42 feet 8 inches curb to curb |

### BRAKES
| | |
|---|---|
| Front | Disc |
| Rear | Drum, power assisted |
| Front rotor diam. | 11⅞ inches |
| Rear drum diam. | 11 3/32 inches |
| Total swept area | 408.0 square inches |

### CHASSIS & BODY
| | |
|---|---|
| Frame | All-steel unitized construction |
| Body style | Town hardtop |

### SUSPENSION
| | |
|---|---|
| Front | Independent with ball joints, coil springs, stabilizer |
| Rear | Conventional, 60-inch by 2½-inch 5-leaf springs; Hotchkiss drive |
| Shock absorbers | 1 9/16-inch Gabriel direct-acting telescopic |
| Tires | 8.15/15 4-ply |
| Wheels | Pressed steel, drop-center rims |

### WEIGHTS AND MEASURES
| | |
|---|---|
| Wheelbase | 113 inches |
| Overall length | 205.4 inches |
| Overall width | 77.3 inches |
| Overall height | 52.5 inches |
| Front track | 61.0 inches |
| Rear track | 60.0 inches |
| Ground clearance | 6½ inches (minimum) |
| Shipping weight | 4,359 pounds |

### CAPACITIES
| | |
|---|---|
| Crankcase | 4 quarts (less filter) |
| Automatic trans. | 23 pints |
| Cooling system | 20.5 quarts |
| Fuel tank | 22 gallons |

### CALCULATED DATA
| | |
|---|---|
| HP/c.i.d. | .808 |
| Pounds/HP | 13.8 |
| Pounds/c.i.d. | 11.2 |

### ROAD TESTS
| | |
|---|---|
| Top speed | 100 mph |
| Acceleration: 0-30 | 4.1 seconds |
| 0-45 | 7.2 seconds |
| 0-60 | 11.4 seconds |
| 40-60 | 6.4 seconds |
| 50-70 | 7.0 seconds |
| Standing ¼ mile | 18.3 seconds/77 mph |
| Stopping distances | 39 feet from 30 mph; 157 feet from 60 mph |

(Source: *Motor Trend*, March 1966)

*Center armrest has a small glove compartment hidden underneath.*

# 1966 THUNDERBIRD

duced on September 30, 1966, as a 1967 model, is beyond the scope of this report, as are succeeding generations down to the present day. Permit, however, a few observations:

First, the handsome Town Hardtop was gone, after only the one season. Sales evidently failed to live up to expectations. Also scratched from the 1967 roster was the convertible, reflecting the diminishing ragtop market in the late sixties. A four-door Landau was added to the line, and both wheelbase and overall length were extended slightly. (Perhaps we should call this one the "REALLY Big Bird.")

The 1967-69 Thunderbirds were rather a different breed than their predecessors. Headlamps were hidden, creating a grille that resembled an enormous open mouth. Body sides were more massive, and the 'Bird began to look more like a family sedan than a means of personal transport. And most significantly, 1967 saw the T-Bird's return to body-on-frame construction.

Now, here's a puzzle: The idea that unitized construction saves weight has been widely advertised and generally accepted, as far back as the Nash 600 of 1941. Yet the conventional, body-on-frame Thunderbird of 1967, though it was slightly bigger than its predecessor,

actually weighed 138 pounds *less* than its unitized 1966 counterpart.

How do you explain that? □

**Acknowledgements and Bibliography**
Automotive Industries, *March 15, 1966;* R.M. Clark (ed.), Thunderbird, 1958-1963; John Ethridge, "Thunderbird Road Test," Motor Trend, *March 1966;* Ford Motor Company factory literature; John Gunnell (ed.), Standard Catalog of American Cars, 1946-1975; *Jerry Heas-ley,* The Production Figure Book for US Cars; *David L. Lewis, Mike McCarville and Lorin Sorensen,* Ford, 1903 to 1984; Bob McVay, "1964 Thunderbird Road Test," Motor Trend, *February 1964;* "Olds Toronado," Car and Driver, *November 1965;* "Riviera Gran Sport," Road & Track, *February 1966.*
Our thanks to Ray Borges, William F. Harrah Automobile Foundation, Reno, Nevada. Special thanks to Elwood Griest, MD, Livermore, California.

## It's Good, Yes. But It Could Be Better!

H aving come this far with us, the reader will know that we like the Thunderbird, at least up to a point. It's a well-built, durable, beautifully finished automobile. Every consideration has been made in the interest of passenger comfort: Seating, ventilation, suspension and sound insulation were all designed with this objective in mind. Performance, while not really outstanding, is more than adequate. And styling, particularly of this Town Hardtop model, is very attractive.

But there are a couple of areas where the T-Bird seems to us to be wide of the mark:

First, there's the engine. At 390 cubes, 315 horsepower, it's no slouch. But neither was it, in its own time, any match for the competition. Just as easily as not, Ford could have supplied as standard equipment the 345-horsepower, 428-c.i.d. V-8, raising the 'Bird's output to a rating

comparable to that of the Riviera. That engine was available to T-Bird buyers, to be sure, a $64.30 option. And perhaps that was the idea: to extract a little extra money from the customer. Practically pure gravy, of course, for the 428 used the same block as the 390, with only minor differences in bore and stroke.

And then there's the suspension. Granted, the Thunderbird was built for luxury and comfort, not for performance. But an option comparable to the Riviera's GS package would have been easy enough to develop and inexpensive to produce. It might well have produced a little extra revenue for the company; Buick's version fetched a premium of $176.82. And it certainly would have had an enormous appeal for the motorist who really enjoys driving!

But then, T-Bird sales were ahead of the Riv's by a country mile, and who are we to argue with success?

# Postwar Ford Clubs and Parts Suppliers

These clubs and resources listings were compiled in July 2000. For the most up-to-date information, consult the latest issue of *Hemmings' Vintage Auto Almanac* and the Hemmings web site at www.hemmings.com.

## CLUBS

**The 54 Ford Club of America**
1517 N Wilmot #144
Tucson, AZ 85712
520-886-1184
*Dues: $15/year*
*Membership: 1,000*

**Crown Victoria Association**
P.O. Box 6
Bryan OH 43506
419-636-2475
*Dues: $29/year*
*Membership 1,650*

**Early Ford V-8 Club of America**
P.O. Box 2122
San Leandro, CA 94577
925-606-1925
*Dues: $30*
*Membership: 9,000*

**Falcon Club of America**
**Northeast Chapter**
73 Francis Rd.
Glocester, RI 02857
401-934-2105
*Dues: $8/year*
*Membership: 120*

**Ford Galaxie Club of America**
P.O. Box 178
Hollister, MO 65672
870-429-8264
*Dues: $25/year*
*Canada and Mexico: $50/year*
*Membership: 1,400*

**International Ford**
**Retractable Club**
P.O. Box 389
Marlboro, MA 01752
500-359-5857
*Dues: 32/year; Canada: $34/year;*
*Foreign: $43/year*
*Membership: 1,200*

**Classic Thunderbird Club**
**International**
1308 E. 29th St. Dept. HV
Signal Hill, CA 90806
562-426-2709
*Dues: $25/year; $15 initiation fee*
*Membership: 8,000*

**Vintage Thunderbird Club**
**International**
P.O. Box 2250
Dearborn, MI 48123-2250
316-794-8061
*Dues: $26/year (includes*
*Canada); Foreign $45/year*
*Membership: 1,400*

## PARTS SUPPLIERS

**Auto Krafters Inc.**
P.O. Box 8
522 South Main St.
Broadway, VA 22815
540-896-5910
*Extensive supply of weatherstrip-*
*ping, interior parts and wiring*
*harnesses for Falcons, Fairlanes,*
*Torinos, T-Birds, Galaxies, and*
*Rancheros.*

**Autowire Division**
9109 (rear) E. Garvey Ave.
Rosemead, CA 91770
626-572-0938
*Large selection of electrical parts*
*for 1949-1968 Fords.*

**Bob Burgess 1955-1956 Ford Parts**
793 Alpha-Bellbrook Rd.
Bellbrook, OH 45305
937-426-8041
*Wide range of NOS and reproduc-*
*tion body, interior, and mechani-*
*cal parts for 1955-1956 Fords.*

**Dennis Carpenter Ford**
**Reproductions**
P.O. Box 26398
Charlotte, NC 28221
704-786-8139
*Sizable variety of weatherstrip-*
*ping and reproduction trim parts*
*for 1947-2000 Fords*

**Dearborn Classics**
P.O. Box 7649
Bend, OR 97708-7649
800-252-7427
*Enormous array of reproduction,*
*suspension and mechanical parts*
*for Rancheros, Falcons, Fairlanes*
*and Torinos.*

**Ford Parts Store**
110 Ford Rd. Box 226
Bryan, OH 43506
419-636-2475
*Substantial variety of new and*
*reproduction body, trim and*
*weatherstripping parts for 1952-*
*1970 Ford passenger cars.*

**Northwest Classic Falcons**
1715 NW Pettygrove
Dept. VAA
Portland, OR 97209
503-241-9454
*Large selection of NOS, reproduc-*
*tion, and used parts for 1960-*
*1970 Falcons*

**Obsolete Ford Parts**
311 E. Washington Ave.
Nashville, GA 31639
912-686-2470
*Full line of reproduction and NOS*
*parts for 1949-1979 Ford cars and*
*trucks*